MW01236030

Keep On Keeping On

*Two Parents and Their Son's
Journey Through Addiction
& Parent's Journey to Justice*

Jean Davis
with
Ed Robertson

Keep On Keeping On
by Jean Davis with Ed Robertson

Printed in the United States of America

ISBN 978-1-60647-061-9

Unless otherwise indicated, Bible quotations are taken from the New King James Version of the Holy Bible.

www.xulonpress.com

In Memory of Ron

Dedicated to my husband, Brooks, who has been my rock
and encourager to write this book. Without his help,
this would not have been possible.

ACKNOWLEDGMENTS

I want to thank my husband, Brooks, my best friend, for his love and support while writing this book and for the many times he proofread and gave me suggestions.

To our son, Rick, for his love and support, who carried the responsibility of our family business.

Diane Grooms, my sister, who deserves our sincere appreciation for all her love, support and for the many weeks, days and hours she stayed with us in Atlanta at court proceedings, two jury selections and two trials.

Thank you to my mother, Ruth Stilwell, for her understanding of the many hours that this book has required.

To our family and friends, Carolyn Wilkes, Nonia Polk, Ketta Guy, Don and Doris Cunningham, Cliff and Dot Davis for their support and trips to court proceedings.

I want to thank my Prayer Partners, family and friends that are too numerous to list, who have prayed for us and Ron over these many years.

To Becky Yates of Caring Services, Inc., who continues to inspire us and honors Ron with the Ronnie Davis Memorial Scholarship Fund.

Larry Owens, Ron's mentor, friend and honors the memory of Ron by naming Bethel Christian Homes, The Davis House.

John Dodd, President of The Jesse Helms Center, for his interest and assistance.

A special acknowledgement to our high school English teacher, Miriam Hood, who had a strong influence in our lives. She was so proud of this project and did not live to see it completed.

Most of all, to God, for his grace and strength
to carry us through this journey.

ENDORSEMENTS

When you read the Davis' story--Because my office was fighting for this family every minute of those eight years, I can tell you the account you will read is true and represents a genuine American tragedy.

Paul Howard, District Attorney
Atlanta, Georgia

This book is an inspiring story with a priceless message for every person searching for help, hope, reassurance and healing.

Jesse Helms
U.S. Senator

The Davis family has shown incredible strength as they have dealt with the addiction of a loved one, the murder of a son and a legal system which seemed to favor the guilty.

Dr. Jerry McGee, President
Wingate University

FOREWORD

We, in this country, are engaged in a battle of epic proportions. The battle to which I refer is not the war we are waging in Afghanistan and Iraq, but the one which takes place in the courthouses all around our nation. It is the battle to secure equal justice for the victims of crimes who are too often ignored, patronized or otherwise mistreated and for whom justice is often delayed.

What the Davis family has gone through--waiting eight long years for justice for their son is something no American family should have to endure. The tragedy of losing their loved one in a gruesome murder was horribly compounded by a flawed criminal justice system that elevates defendants' rights over victims' rights. Their fight for justice gradually encompassed the struggle just to have the defendant brought to trial.

When 39 year old Ronnie Davis was shot, dismembered and his remains casually discarded, the horror of the murder shocked and sickened the entire Atlanta community. By the time the case was set for trial eight years later, the brutality of the murder had become a distant memory for many of the citizens; the horror lessened with the passage of time.

When you read the Davis' story--repeated appearances in court without any resolution, aggravated by continuous verbal attacks upon their son's character and not one kind word from the Court---you would not believe this could occur in America. Because my office was fighting for this family every minute of those eight years, I can tell you the account you will read is true and represents a genuine American tragedy.

It is my hope that everyone who reads this book will feel

compelled not just to support the Davis family, but will actively work to create an American criminal justice system that does not permit such travesties to take place. We owe that to the Davis family; to all our families. We owe it to ourselves and our nation to restore the meaning of swift and fair justice for all --including the victims.

Paul Howard, Jr.
District Attorney
Atlanta Judicial Circuit

CONTENTS

Prologue

W e had just sat down for a bite to eat when suddenly I heard my cell phone. I'd just that moment turned it on to check messages. I'd gotten into the habit of turning it off every morning once we got to the courthouse, and sometimes I would be so caught up in the events of the trial, I'd forget to turn it back on until very late in the day. But fortunately I remembered this time, and it's a blessing that I did. This was one phone call I did not want to miss.

It was a few minutes past eleven o'clock on the morning of Tuesday, November 8, 2005. My husband, Brooks, and I, along with my sister Diane Grooms, were in a cafeteria located in the building next to the Fulton County Superior Court house in Atlanta, Georgia. We had traveled from our home in Charlotte, North Carolina to witness the trial of Michael Benjamin LeJeune, the man accused of murdering our son Ronnie Allen Davis and mutilating his body on December 27, 1997. It was a savage, brutal killing, described by the crime scene investigator who examined our son's body-a man who had investigated over 1,000 crime scenes, including close to 400 homicides, in the course of his 16-year career-as the most heinous crime scene he had ever seen.

We were seven days into the trial, and by all accounts, things were going well. Despite some deft maneuvers on the part of LeJeune's lawyer, the prosecution continued to back the defense into a corner, thanks to a parade of strong witnesses, including one whose testimony was later described as "cross-proof." Though we missed Ron dearly, and continued to grieve over how viciously his life had been taken, with each day we could sense how close we were to seeing justice brought to his killer.

Yet at the same time, we had learned not to take anything for granted. You see, even though LeJeune had been arrested and charged with Ron's murder in January 1998-and all the evidence in the case pointed to him, and he alone, as the one who murdered our son-it would be nearly *eight years* before the case ever went to trial. Eight years of delays, eight years of false starts and dashed hopes, eight years of seeing the legal system constantly manipulated by LeJeune's attorney, an ambitious young man who sought to use the case to make a name for himself at the expense of everyone concerned: our family, the LeJeune family, and the taxpayers of the state of Georgia. Brooks and I had been through so many ups and downs and twists and turns, we never knew what to expect. It was a roller coaster ride that never seemed to end.

It was also a little like the movie *Groundhog Day*, where the man played by Bill Murray relives the same day over and over again. That's because this was actually our second attempt at a trial (the first attempt having occurred about eight months earlier, in March 2005). The first trial had also started well for our side, when suddenly tragedy erupted. On March 11, 2005, four days into our trial, a Fulton County Superior Court judge was shot and killed by a deranged inmate named Brian Nichols in the same building where our case was being heard. It was a horrible, frightening event that traumatized everyone in our courtroom, especially members of the District Attorney's Office who knew the judge and his family. Nichols went on a shooting spree, and later held a young woman hostage, before finally surrendering to authorities the next day. It was a story that made national news-but it would also impact our case in a way no one could have imagined. When the dust settled, and the trial resumed three days later, LeJeune's lawyer convinced the court to declare a mistrial, claiming that it would have been impossible for LeJeune to get a fair trial with emotions running so high in Atlanta.

Once again, our case was thrown into turmoil. Once again, our lives were put on hold, for reasons beyond our control. It was another obstacle to overcome in the most nerve-wracking experience of our lives.

That's why we've learned to brace ourselves. In the past two days alone, in fact, Brooks and I have seen more drama, and more swings of momentum in the second trial, than we could ever believe possible.

* * *

A hearing had been called for ten o'clock on Tuesday, November 8. A lot of buzzing about went on-LeJeune and his attorneys were shuttled in and out of the courtroom, as were the jurors-but nothing substantive occurred. There was speculation that a significant development was about to happen, but again that was speculation. Just before 11:00 a.m., the presiding judge, the Honorable Constance Russell of the Fulton County Superior Court, called a recess and ordered all parties to return to the courtroom by noon. That was when Brooks, Diane, and I walked over to the cafeteria. We originally went for just a cup of coffee, but with court resuming at noon, it occurred to us that lunch might be later than usual that day. So we decided to order something light to tide us over.

We had just taken a few bites when my cell phone rang. It was Theresa Strozier from the Fulton County Victim Witness Assistance Program. District Attorney Paul Howard launched this program in 1984 to help survivors of homicide, domestic violence, child abuse, and other serious crimes. The Victims Witness Assistance Program provides a wide range of counseling, support, and other services for victims, witnesses, family members, and others whose lives have been thrown into turmoil by traumatic events. As Brooks and I are from out of town (we traveled to Atlanta over 30 times during the eight years our case was on the books), we especially appreciated this program, and cannot say enough about Mr. Howard and all the other wonderful people behind it. They helped see to our needs, and more importantly, provided a source of much needed strength throughout our long legal ordeal.

Theresa Strozier had been our constant companion in the courthouse over the years, and she was especially close over the past several weeks, from the time we arrived for jury selection and continuing throughout the trial. We could always count on Theresa to be calm, even when we weren't. But this time, there was panic in her voice. "Jean, thank goodness," she said. "We've been looking all over for you."

"Is anything wrong, Theresa?" I asked.

"Jean, there's no time to explain," she said. "Just hurry back to the courtroom."

I relayed the message to Brooks and Diane. All kinds of emotions whirled in my head, but there wasn't time to sort through them. All I could say was, "They need us there *now*."

The cafeteria building was adjoined to the courthouse by a covered walkway. The three of us practically ran all the way back, yet in my mind it was like slow motion. As frantic as we were, I sensed a calmness in me that could only come from above. It was a feeling I'd experienced many times before, the strength that comes from knowing that God provides us with whatever we need, precisely when we need it. *It's going to be all right*, I thought. *We'll get there, even if He has to carry us.*

We raced through the walkway, past security, and into the courthouse elevator. Judge Russell's courtroom was five floors up. As we made our way back to the courtroom, all I could do was think of Ron

* * *

Ron was the youngest of our two sons. He was a strapping young man, 39 years old, blond, blue-eyed, earnest, hard-working, with an athletic build and the kind of sparkle in his personality that always drew people to him. It was a quality he'd shared with my father, Barney. Ron was very close to Brooks and me, yet his bond with his "Paw-Paw," as he liked to call Barney, was tighter than anyone else in our family.

But as confident as he looked on the outside, Ron had his demons on the inside. He had a drug problem, a serious addiction to cocaine that he struggled to conquer for the last 12 years of his life. Yet at the same time, he was unusual in that he was open and honest about his condition. He often spoke of how "grateful" he was for his addiction; because he knew it had brought him to his knees. After nearly throwing his life away on cocaine, he'd been given a shot at redemption, and was determined to make the most of it. He taught Sunday school at the same church he attended as a child, hoping that the youth in his community might learn from his mistakes and avoid the temptation of drugs. Equally important, he provided help, support, and encouragement to others who struggled with addiction. He shared with them his own story, how he once had "a big ego, and a self esteem you could not see," and how he had to let go of that pride and learn to trust others before he could ever be helped himself. He told them about the changes he made in his life, and how none of them would have been possible were it not for the lessons he learned from his addiction.

Ron stumbled many times throughout his own battle with addiction, but he always kept trying, never once doubting that victory in the form of sobriety was possible. He knew this, because he had achieved it before.

I thought of how close the three of us had grown, Brooks, Ron, and me: a closeness brought on by all the years he struggled with addiction. Each stumble along his path was a stepping stone of growth in spirituality and maturity-for Ron, as well as for us.

Then I thought about everything Brooks and I went through as we struggled with Ron's addiction, how we had to learn to let go of our own pride before we could learn to help our son. That wasn't easy, and it was often painful. And while we would never want to go through that pain again, we also know there's no way we could have learned the things we did-things such as unconditional love, acceptance, compassion, letting go of anger and feelings of pre-judgment, and most important of all, forgiveness-had we not gone through that experience together as a family.

I also thought of the many ways in which God sustained us over the past 20 years-first, our 12-year journey through Ron's addiction, then our eight-year journey to justice. I thought of the remarkable string of occurrences that we came to know as "nuggets of gold," an incredible series of events in the months following Ron's death that graced our lives, providing us with a lift that kept us going, even at our lowest ebb. Ron's murder left a void that can never be filled, but, through God, his legacy gave Brooks and me the strength we needed to handle our emotional roller coaster ride through the legal system.

Then I thought about the final weeks of Ron's life. He had moved to Atlanta in early 1997, and had been through just about every conceivable form of treatment, when a friend introduced him to an addiction specialist who immediately put Ron on Zoloft and one other medication. Amazingly, this was the first time anyone had ever prescribed anything to treat his condition. Ron not only responded to the medication, but took well to his new environment. He landed a job selling cars for a Cadillac dealership, became active in his church, and found help and support through other recovering addicts in a local group in Atlanta sponsored by Alcoholics Anonymous.

He also got engaged to a young lady. Ron loved this woman and her children. But when the relationship suddenly unraveled, unfortunately, so did Ron. He went off his medication and, as he had done many times before, tried to hide his pain through the use of cocaine. By November 1997, he was back in the hospital, again under his doctor's care. Though still devastated over the breakup, Ron was encouraged by his doctor to make the five-hour drive to North Carolina and spend Thanksgiving weekend with us. Ron had a chance to see the new home Brooks and I had just finished building on a lot not far from the house where Ron had grown up as a child. It was a good visit. Ron's spirits were rejuvenated, and he was eager to resume his treatment upon his return to Atlanta. It was as though he had turned an important corner.

Then I thought back to the morning of Saturday, December 27, 1997-the last time Brooks and I ever spoke to Ron. As upbeat as he was when we saw him at Thanksgiving, he was down when he called that morning-really down, a despondency the likes of which we hadn't heard in a long, long while. And it just broke my heart to hear him that way.

Hard as it was, though, Brooks and I at first believed there was nothing we could do but let his depression run its course. Ron had relapsed many times over things such as stress, loneliness, fear, and self-doubt, but he was never one to give in to his despair. Having traveled this road many times before, we believed it was just a matter of time before he picked himself up and pulled himself back together.

But something was different this time. There was a sound of urgency that Brooks and I had never heard before. Ron spoke slowly, and tried to speak calmly, but from the tone of his voice it was as if he was scared for his life.

Ron was following up on a conversation he had with Brooks a few days earlier, on Christmas Eve. His car was missing, and he said it had been towed from an illegal parking space after somehow sustaining a flat tire.

"Mom, Dad, this has been the worst Christmas of my entire life," he said. "But I found my car. It's at A-1 Tow here in Atlanta-you can call to confirm it. But I need money for the towing bill, and to buy a tire. Plus, I owe Mike $50.00. I need to pick up the car while Mike can take me. He has to return his mother's car."

"Ron, how much money do you need?" asked Brooks.

We heard him count it up before he finally said, "I need $228.00."

"I'll send you $250.00," said Brooks. "I'll call Western Union. You should have it within an hour."

We found out later that the money was picked up at an A & P grocery store.

"Dad, there's one more thing," said Ron. "There's something not right. These people stick together."

I have to admit, Ron used to con and manipulate us all the time whenever he was using, so we'd gotten used to that kind of talk. But this time, Brooks and I were so alarmed that we decided to go down to Atlanta. Little did we know, Ron had more reason to be concerned than either of us could imagine.

"Your mom and I will be down there late this afternoon," said Brooks. "Call us on her mobile phone, and let us know where to meet you."

"I really appreciate this," said Ron. "Love you, Dad."

"I love you, too, Ron."

Brooks and I were able to wire the money right away, but driving down to Atlanta right away was unfortunately not an option. The weather that day called for snowfall in the afternoon, so the earliest we could possibly leave was the following morning.

Unfortunately, we had no way of reaching Ron. He did not have a cell phone at that time, and there was no number for this guy named "Mike." In fact, we had never heard of anyone named Mike that Ron could have known in Atlanta.

We would soon discover that the "Mike" in question was none other than Michael LeJeune.

* * *

Brooks, Diane, and I got off the elevator and headed straight for Judge Russell's courtroom. As we walked through the doors, I suddenly thought back to how far we'd come, and to how it all began.

Part One:

Journey Through Addiction

CHAPTER ONE

Hard Work and Great Pride

S tatistics show that most alcoholics or drug abusers are the products of broken homes, dysfunctional families, or parents who are addicts themselves.

Ron, however, was not your usual addict. Not only was he completely open and honest about his drug problem, he also came from a strong, loving, family background with a strong work ethic and Christian values.

Brooks and I have been married for over 57 years. We raised Ron and his older brother, Rick, in a small, idyllic farming community near the town of Matthews, just outside of Charlotte, North Carolina. Our community was the kind of place where life revolved around the church, or some other spot where people tended to gather. In our case, the social hub was Mount Harmony Baptist Church, where Brooks and I were baptized, and where we would continue to worship for over 60 years.

Our neighborhood, which we called the Mount Harmony community, was also the kind of place where just about everyone who lives there was also born and raised there. Brooks and I were no exception. Childhood sweethearts, we grew up together, married young (Brooks was 18, I was 17), and raised our boys in a house on a corner of the farm property where I grew up. Both of our families lived nearby, along with many aunts, uncles, and cousins. In fact, most of our relatives lived close to each other, as did our friends and our children's friends.

My parents gave my two sisters and I each an acre of land. My sister Nancy and her husband, Don, built their home on the opposite corner of the property and raised their sons, Tim and Keenan, there also. Nancy and I were especially tight; we were more than just sisters, we were also each other's best friend. For many years, she also worked at Davis Steel, the family-owned steel fabrication business that I'll tell you about in just a second. Nancy and Don were close to our boys, and we were close to theirs. Our families did many things together, creating memories and sharing many happy moments until that sad day when Nancy died of breast cancer at the age of 42. Her death left a huge void in our lives that has never been filled, and we still miss her dearly to this day.

My other sister, Diane, is 12 years younger than me. After marrying someone from out of the area, she lived away from the family for many years. Diane and her husband, Tommy, have two sons, Corey and Collin-which means that we three daughters had two sons each. It would be many years later, after Ron's death, before Diane moved back home. We could see the hand of God moving to bring her closer, providing extra support for me, as well as for our mother.

My father, Barney Stilwell, was one of the most respected members in the community, the kind of man whom people naturally gravitated. One of his favorite pastimes was stopping by the neighborhood store, where people congregated just to sit for a spell. Whenever people saw his truck parked in front of the store, they'd pop inside themselves, hoping to catch Barney in the middle of one of his stories. Dad had a real knack for telling stories. He was the kind of man who truly enjoyed life and was a pleasure to be around.

My dad was a hard worker. So was my mom and Brooks' parents as well. My mom was orphaned when she was a young child. That made her especially determined to give her daughters the kind of home life she never had-cooking, sewing, making pretty clothes for us to wear to school, farming and growing our food, and taking us all to church every Sunday.

Brooks was the eighth of twelve children. His dad, a carpenter by trade who also ran a dairy farm, died in a farming accident in

1944, when Brooks was just 13. With his older brothers overseas serving their country in World War II and several sisters already married, it was up to Brooks, his brothers Cliff, Vann, and Beck, and younger sisters Carolyn and Doris to help their mom keep up the home place, as well as tend to the day-to-day responsibilities of running the family dairy. The farm included nearly 50 cows, and all of them had to be milked twice a day. It took a lot of sacrifice (Brooks finally had to quit school when he was 16 in order to work full time on the farm), but they dug in their heels and somehow made it work. That's what families did in the years following the Depression, as well as during and after the War. It was a time when such time-honored standards as honesty, integrity, and hard work were perhaps more important than ever. Those were the values we learned as children, and which we tried to pass on to our children.

There was a small wooden shed out back of my Dad's house. We used to call it the "chicken shed." Brooks used that shed as a iron workshop for making ornamental handrails and columns. He also spent many hours there welding and repairing equipment for friends in the community. One of our son, Rick's favorite tools was this little steel grinder. One summer, when Rick was in the Cub Scouts, he had to build a wooden race car for a racing competition called the Pinewood Derby. Rick was given a block and four wheels and had to whittle the block into the shape of a vehicle. With the help of his dad, Rick took that steel grinder, and next thing you knew, he had a really slick looking car. When the day of the race came, Brooks took him aside and said, "Rick, the important thing to remember is to do your best, and to rest in the rest."

That, of course, is one of those lessons that we all hope to live by. Whether it's sports, or any walk in life, it's how you play the game that counts.

Having married very young, we raised our boys the very best we knew how. Like many parents, I suppose, we wanted them to have more in life than we were able to have. Working hard was not an option, but rather an example that had been set before us in order to succeed. Brooks took a job in the steel industry when he was 18, and soon worked his way up to foreman. I worked for the telephone company, while also raising our sons.

27

That was pretty much the way it was throughout the first 16 years of our marriage. Then, in 1967, Brooks and I went into business for us, starting our own steel fabrication company from a concrete and steel building Brooks built at the back of our property. Like a lot of companies, we started slowly the first few years, gradually earning our wings before finally taking flight. Today, Davis Steel & Iron Company, Inc. still thrives as a successful steel fabricator for commercial buildings throughout the greater Charlotte area.

One other thing I learned from my growing up years was the value of a good reputation. In a tight-knit community such as ours, where pretty much everyone knew each other, it didn't take long for rumors to spread. If something brought shame or criticism to your family, sooner or later the rest of the community was bound to find out about it.

Brooks and I were raised to believe that what others thought of you was important. I'm not exactly proud to say that, but that's just the way it was. It was a matter of pride, pure and simple. And as we can all attest, letting go of that pride is one of the hardest things anyone of us can ever do.

That was the case for Brooks and me, and that was certainly the case for Ron.

* * *

Ron was born in 1958, six years after Rick. We always attended church together as a family Sunday morning, Sunday night, and Wednesday night. Besides going to church, Ron was active in a boy's mission group called RA's and always attended Vacation Bible School. Church was a big part of our lives, as it was for most families who lived in our community. Rick and Ron were baptized at Mount Harmony Baptist Church, the same church where Brooks and I were raised. Ron accepted Christ at a church camp and was baptized at the age of 11. Except for the times when he drifted away from family values and activities, he maintained a strong prayer life until the day he died.

Ron's childhood years consisted of many family outings with relatives and friends, such as picnics, movies, sports, county fairs, and various church activities. We spent many Sunday afternoons after church having lunch with either my family or Brooks' family, as well as with friends. We'd spend the afternoon together while he and Rick played with their cousins or with the children of our friends. A family favorite was making homemade ice cream every summer. Ron played little league baseball and Pop Warner football, and also earned a black belt in *aikido* (a form of martial arts) when he was 17.

Ron loved and emulated my dad. As a small boy, he spent many hours with his "Paw-Paw," and he loved listening to his stories. "I felt good being with my grandfather," wrote Ron in a journal entry from 1987:

> *My most exciting memories were every summer when my whole family on my mother's side would go to the east coast on vacation. It was then I felt loved and whole, because when we were together as a whole, my grandfather pulled us together with his love. He had a happy and loving lifestyle that was simply contagious.*

Though Ron was closer to me as a boy, he admired and respected his dad, with good reason. He knew that Brooks was one of the first members of our community to launch his own business and achieve the great American dream. That made Ron proud of Brooks, but sometimes it also made him feel inadequate by comparison, and it took a while before Ron learned to feel comfortable with his dad when they were alone together. Brooks made him feel "nervous," wrote Ron in his journal, "like I had some huge shoes to fill, and an impossible goal to live up to."

Looking back, we can see that part of this had to do with size and stature. Brooks is a big man, over six feet tall, and he has always carried himself with a quiet confidence. That's quite an imposing figure, especially from the perspective of a small boy, and it seemed like his dad never made very many mistakes or wrong decisions.

Eventually, Ron came to joke about it. In fact, one Saturday, after Ron had grown some hay for his horses, he and Brooks were out by the barn baling and hauling hay, along with an employee of Brooks' named Jeff. Jeff was the husband of Donna, Ron's first cousin on Brooks' side of the family. At some point, Brooks walked over to them and gave some instructions. I don't remember all the details, but basically Jeff disagreed with Brooks over how something should be done. Brooks said his piece, then turned and walked away. It took a while for Jeff to calm down, and he vented to Ron for the longest time about what had transpired. Ron just listened, never once reminding Jeff that he was talking about his father.

Finally, Jeff cooled down. Ron looked at him and said, "You know, I realize, Jeff, that my dad can make you mad." Then he paused for effect, as a grin slowly formed across his face. "But, you know what I've found out over the years?"

"What's that?" asked Jeff. "Nine times out of ten, he's usually right."

With that said, they shared a good laugh and did it the way Brooks had instructed them. Ron could not have handled the situation any better, and his respect for his dad clearly showed.

* * *

We felt that we were a normal everyday family. We worked hard to provide for the needs of our sons, and made every effort to be there for them in their formative years. Some families may have hugged more, or been more outwardly affectionate than ours, but we loved each other, and always did our best to show it. We practiced the Christian faith together, and believed firmly in the power of prayer.

Still, I guess some things can elude even the strongest of families. You might think everything is very normal, but sometimes you just don't know what is going through your child's mind, like misconception, or feelings of inadequacy-let alone, understand what causes them.

We wouldn't know it at the time, but Ron's struggles with self-esteem would worsen as time went on and would eventually pull him away from us and our family and into the world of drugs.

CHAPTER TWO

The Family Business

W hen I was a child, the Matthews area was almost entirely farm land. For most people in our community, working the land was a way of life, which meant that almost everyone in the community was on the same level, socially as well as economically. No one worried about "keeping up with the Joneses," so to speak, because the Joneses were about as busy keeping up their land as we were ours.

Families were content. We accepted our lot in life and made the most of it. That mindset prevailed when Brooks and I were young, and pretty much stayed that way once we were married and began raising our own children.

That said, one thing I've always admired about Brooks is his ambition-not necessarily in terms of money (though he doesn't mind making a dollar now and then), but simply the fact that he has always tried to make the most of his abilities. He literally grew up working hard, so he's never been one to dread work. He inherited a great deal of wisdom and common sense from his mom and dad, as well as a strong, lasting work ethic. Without a college degree or high school diploma, Brooks truly is a self-educated man, and I'll always be proud of him for that.

One day in 1967, Brooks started thinking about how he might be able to go into business for himself and work closer to home and his family, while also contributing something back to the community. He had been driving across town (Charlotte) twice a day, sometimes six days a week. He was 35 at the time, and we had been married for 16 years. He had already put in over 20 years in the work force, and was employed as a shop foreman for Southern Engineering Company in Charlotte, North Carolina. He had come to know pretty much all the ins and outs of the steel industry, and thought, "Jean, maybe it's time we start our own business."

I know it sounds funny, but the idea of starting your own company was simply unheard of in our community-not then, anyway. Most families in our neighborhood worked in the factories, or on the farm, or held down some other public job for one of the companies in town. That was the order of things, pure and simple.

For years, Brooks was the only member of our neighborhood to go into business for himself. That made us something of a curiosity, especially in those early days when we tried to get off the ground. Folks would sort of peer in from the sidelines and wonder just how on earth a little backyard startup like ours could possibly compete against the larger, more established steel contractors in town. Brooks' boss at Southern Engineering, for example, once asked, "What are you going to do after you build hand rails for all your neighbors and friends?" These kind of remarks were also made to me from a couple of people that I worked with at the telephone company.

Truth be told, sometimes we wondered about that ourselves. Like a lot of small businesses, we had to learn to crawl before we could walk. Brooks worked from the shop he had built in our back yard, which we named Davis Steel & Iron Company, while I helped supplement our income through my job at the phone company. Even the boys were asked to pitch in. Ron and Rick were expected to do chores around the house or help their dad. Rick worked in the afternoon sometimes, between sports activities and all day during the summer.

Then, slowly, we became successful and the company started to expand. We built a new shop and office building approximately three miles from our home. With growth came success, and with success came opportunity. Davis Steel gave us the opportunity to travel, sometimes for business, sometimes for pleasure. We had a chance to go overseas and also see other parts of the United States, probably before most people in the Mount Harmony community had an opportunity to.

Brooks and I have always been grateful for our success, and we have always tried to keep it in perspective. We enjoy it, and appreciate it, but have always kept a low profile about it, never flaunting it before others. As Brooks likes to say, "When you get down to it, it all belongs to the Lord. He's just letting us use it."

Still, people can be funny sometimes, especially in a small, tight-knit community such as ours. Little by little, things start to happen. Remarks are made-not necessarily out of spite, mind you, but they're made just the same. You find that even though success hasn't changed who you are or how you live your life, it can change the way you're perceived by the rest of the community. Suddenly, people you've grown up with, and have gone to church with, start to look at you differently. Sometimes they even look at you with resentment, for reasons you don't always understand.

That's a hard thing for anyone to deal with, because it's so utterly beyond your control. It can be particularly hard for young children, especially at school or playing in the neighborhood. Youngsters pick up on the things their parents say, and their remarks can often be cruel: *"Oh, you'll never have to work-your dad can keep you up."* Many times, these things are said simply to make themselves look better.

Unfortunately, kids aren't the only ones that harbor resentment toward other children. Sometimes, it's adults-even those in positions of authorities, who should know better-who are behind the disparaging remarks. Ron wrote about this in a journal he kept in 1987:

My memories of grade school were very struggling years. I was a year younger than everyone in my class and this made me always feel like I was playing catch-up or inadequate. I had a fourth grade teacher that picked constantly at me to the point of torture. It took me a lot of time to get over her. This made me feel [even] less and gave me a complex. I was pretty good at sports, especially football, and that seemed to release some stress. This was an area I could feel better about myself.

My school friends were fun and nice to me, but some friends around the neighborhood were always throwing low blows at me. Looking back, it was because of my family, who they were in the community and what we had. I felt betrayed by them and took it personal. I did not make the connection and took it as if it was my problem and not theirs. The friends that were truly my friends, I would push aside to be with the plastic friends, who I thought were the "in" crowd. I did this as a fear of not being accepted.

These experiences, as you can probably imagine, further impaired Ron's already shaky self-confidence. They would also make him that much more susceptible to peer pressure, which, as Brooks and I would learn later on, is often the single most important factor that can lead a child to drugs. Children such as Ron with low self-esteem often find themselves wanting to be liked, looking up to others and following their lead instead of finding a path of their own. Though Ron would eventually find his own path, it took many years, and many stumbles along the way, before that day finally came. He would fall into drugs many times before working his way out of the crowd and becoming a leader in his own right.

Unfortunately, Ron never said a word about this-not to Brooks and me, not to his brother, not to anyone. That was his way as a child. By his own admission, he was a strong-willed, stubborn boy who could be dying on the inside, but would never show it. Instead, he'd try to bluff his way through and act as though everything was fine. No matter how great the problem was, or how difficult the task, he'd act like he knew exactly what he was doing, when perhaps he really didn't.

You can never know exactly what's on your child's mind unless you have good communication. While Brooks and I would never want to go through the awful pain of Ron's addiction, in many ways, we, too, find ourselves as "grateful" for that experience as he was. Not only did it help us all grow spiritually, it drew us closer together than we had ever been before. Adversity often does that. As a result of Ron's struggle, Brooks and I developed a bond with our son that we never had when he was a child. The three of us remained close to each other until the day he died.

* * *

Rick was 14 when we started Davis Steel, and was nearly out of high school by the time the company started to grow. He was also six years older than Ron, which gave him that much more experience to handle whatever slings and arrows kids may have thrown at him. Plus, for whatever reason, Rick was never quite as thin-skinned as Ron was, especially as a child. Rick has always been like Brooks, in that he's the type of person where you can say just about anything to him, and he'll more or less let it slide.

Ron, on the other hand, was a "dweller." He was always sharp, but emotionally, he never quite let go of things, no matter how innocuous, the way his dad or brother could. Rather, he'd let them set there and fester, like a thorn in his side-which is funny, because in many ways, he was just like Brooks. When it came to making decisions, for example, he was always, boom, "Let's do it," without hesitation. He did that all the time. If he discovered later on that he'd made a bad decision, he'd make another one on the spot. But when it came to hurt feelings, Ron could dwell on those like nobody else. And because of that, he probably had more pressures on him as a child than Rick ever did.

Unfortunately, because Ron kept everything to himself, his attempts to tough it out served only to fester his feelings of inadequacy. This, in turn, left him all the more susceptible to peer pressure, and inevitably the lure of drugs.

CHAPTER THREE

Peer Pressure

R on was always an active child who made friends easily. As hard as he tried, though, he did struggle with other issues that made his experience at school difficult, along with the added pressure of being a year younger than some of his classmates. His teachers would tell us that he was restless and anxious, and could never quite follow through or stay focused enough to finish his assignments. Before long, however, these fears and anxieties began spilling out into his home life. Unfortunately, our efforts to help Ron overcome these traumas were handicapped by a number of factors-some of which, much to our frustration, were beyond our control.

When Ron was in third grade, for example, he suddenly had problems swallowing meat. As inexplicable as this was in the first place, there was one incident in particular that I remember finding particularly baffling. We were about to take the boys on a picnic with some neighbor friends and their children, when at the last minute Ron cried and begged not to go. Brooks and I were dumbfounded, especially since Ron had known the family for years and had always enjoyed playing with their kids before. When this problem continued, we finally took Ron to a throat specialist. After initially examining Ron, the doctor had us admit him to the hospital so that he could run additional tests on him to make sure the problem wasn't physical. When the results came back negative, the doctor concluded that whatever caused the anxiety was probably emotional and that it would go away with time.

But Ron's anxieties didn't go away, and the more they persisted, the more Brooks and I believed the cause was more than just emotional. Sure enough, it was.

Turned out there was a boy in Ron's third-grade class whom the teacher simply could not control. He was a mentally impaired child who often became easily upset. Whenever that happened, the boy would stand up and disrupt the class by doing things such as erasing the assignment from the chalkboard, or trying to stab some of the other children with a pencil or scissors. Unfortunately for Ron, this boy sat right behind him, which meant that Ron often bore the brunt of his problems. His teacher would call me at work saying, "Ron says he has a headache. Would you take him home?"

Compounding the problem, this was about the time when racial integration and forced busing started. The schools were particularly sensitive about this, which made complaining about a child-*any* child-a particularly touchy issue. Simply put, it was a hot potato none of the administrators wanted to touch.

Brooks will always regret the fact that he did not go to the principal and insist that the boy be removed from the school. I don't mean this as an excuse, but we were young, and we just weren't "demanding" in the way some parents can be. We were both taught as children not to make waves. That's just how we were raised.

Looking back, though, if we had the opportunity to do it again, there are definitely steps we would have taken. Brooks, for one, was involved with Cub Scouts at the time. He knew the principal very well as a result of their work together, and to this day wishes that he would have used that relationship to make a difference. As it happened, the next year the child was finally placed in a home for mentally handicapped children. By that time, however, the damage had already been done. Although we have since learned from other parents in the community that other children in the same third-grade class were also affected at the time, Ron was the one who had clearly been hurt the most. Suddenly, his report card remarks indicated that he "always did a good job," but never seemed to complete his work.

Brooks and I took Ron in for testing and for summer reading programs, only to find that the symptoms persisted. We then tried to get help for him, but unfortunately no one seemed to share our concern.

Of all people, even Ron's pediatrician brushed us off. "He'll get over it," he said, as though our son's increasingly short attention span was just another childhood phase that would eventually go away.

Nothing is more helpless than knowing there is a problem with your child, but you can't get anyone to listen.

Today, of course, most medical experts would have immediately recognized that Ron had been exhibiting the classic symptoms of attention deficit disorder, and would have treated Ron accordingly. But ADD, as such, didn't exist back in the '60s, because the studies and research that would bring this condition to light had yet to be uncovered. As a result, it was not uncommon for doctors to push through cases such as Ron's, if only as a matter of expediency.

Brooks and I found ourselves similarly frustrated a few years later, when Ron struggled as a seventh grader and desperately wanted to be held back. Ron's teacher, however, adamantly refused, insisting that his grades didn't warrant repeating seventh grade and that his feelings of inadequacy and low self-esteem would eventually go away. This time, however, we did appeal to the principal, only he, too, insisted that Ron be pushed ahead to the eighth grade.

In a way, these encounters were a form of "peer pressure," not unlike the kind that Ron himself was feeling from kids his own age-only this time, the pressure came from within the leadership of our own community. Once again, it seemed none of the school administrators wanted to admit there may in fact have been a problem with Ron, if only because no one wanted to admit that they didn't quite know what to do.

Peer pressure, of course, can often be a major factor leading to drug addiction. Teenage children can especially be vulnerable to peer- pressure as they enter into high school-a time when many young people, like Ron, often struggle with issues of inadequacy and low self-esteem. Hoping to be liked and searching for acceptance, they may find themselves sometimes turning to drugs to ease the pressures of school or erase the pain of loneliness.

Brooks and I didn't know it at the time, but peer pressure was also a major contributing factor behind Ron's decision to switch high schools just prior to entering the tenth grade. Though assigned to another school by the Charlotte school district, Ron adamantly insisted that we have him transferred to a different school beyond our jurisdiction. As it happened, the high school he chose, and to which he was ultimately accepted at the last minute, was the same school where his brother Rick graduated a few years before. For a long time, we thought this was the reason why he wanted the change, until we came across Ron's journal writings nearly 30 years later. That's when we realized it was more a matter of peer pressure:

My circle of friends did change. I was originally supposed to go to another high school, but transferred before the year started. I was burned out on some of my old friends. I felt used and betrayed by them. Most of my school friends did smoke pot and drink a little. My high school was an experimental school run much like a college with a lot of freedom. My use of pot was not very frequent and I didn't drink at all. I just wanted to be a part of the crowd.

Fortunately, despite his occasional dabbling with marijuana throughout high school, Ron managed to stay on track with the help of *aikido*, an ancient form of martial arts that taught him discipline in mind and body. *Aikido* provided Ron with structure and, for the first time in his life, a sense of self-esteem.

CHAPTER FOUR

Thrown for a Loss

Though Ron continued to struggle with feelings of inadequacy, things started to change a little as he entered high school. The family business began to prosper, which seemed to have a calming effect on him. Though money did not change who we were on the inside, the success of Davis Steel did seem to make Ron feel more secure. By the time he was 16, he had a steady girlfriend, a driver's license, and a new best friend, all of which gave him confidence. But the thing that really made the difference for Ron was learning *aikido*, a unique form of martial arts that centers around coordinating mind and body. Suddenly, for the first time in his life, he had structure, pride in himself and what he was about to learn and accomplish (physically, mentally, and spiritually), and a feeling of self-fulfillment.

For those who may not be familiar with it, aikido is the so-called "gentleman's fighting art" that differs from other, more traditional methods of self defense in two important respects: its sophisticated style and its essential motivations. The goal of aikido is not to attack, but rather merely to neutralize aggression in an opponent while rendering him as little injury as possible.

Some people liken aikido to the old proverb "Give a man a fish, and he has food for a day; teach a man to fish, and he has food for the rest of his life." Those who learn aikido learn a variety of moves that not only teach them how to defend themselves in the event of attack, but also provide them with a wide range of responses to any given situation. In this respect, aikido gives them valuable tools of survival that will last a lifetime.

Ron was fortunate to learn aikido from a man named Jack Mumpower, a martial arts expert who himself studied under famed master Kenjii Tomiki, a genius in the martial arts who revolutionized the sport. Jack was a longtime Matthews resident who started teaching classes in the neighborhood around 1970, when Ron was about 11 years old. Jack was a charismatic individual who infused eastern philosophy with his own Christian lifestyle. His classes proved very popular, and were attended by many families throughout the community, including ours.

Brooks, Rick, and Ron all took up aikido at the same time, so it became a sort of a family hobby. They attended classes for several months, but Ron was the only one who stayed with it. Brooks was almost 40 at the time, and while he enjoyed learning the sport together with the boys, it wasn't long before his age started working against him. Though the techniques in aikido require minimal exertion, it often takes a few tumbles on the mat before they're finally mastered. Rick and Ron, of course, were younger and much more limber, which made that sort of punishment easier for their bodies to take. Unfortunately, as we all know, it often takes longer to recover from those kinds of blows as we continue to grow older. We may not feel it right away, but we certainly feel it the next morning, as Brooks can certainly attest. He hung on long enough to earn his first belt before finally dropping out.

Ron, on the other hand, quickly became one of Jack's star pupils. Though Jack was small in stature, he was powerfully built for his size, and it was no trouble at all for him to take a man down. One day, when Ron was 14 or 15, he finally managed to flip Jack in class. From that point on, his confidence soared. He quickly moved up the ranks, earning his white belt, then his brown belt, and finally, his black belt.

Speaking from a parent's standpoint, aikido was truly a blessing-not only because it made Ron happy and was something in which he thrived, but also because it kept him away from the sort of activities that may have gotten him into trouble had he not otherwise been involved. Unbeknownst to us, Ron did dabble a little in marijuana while in high school, but as he would later write:

I didn't let it get out of hand because I was heavily into the martial arts. For a long time, martial arts kept me from falling into the drug world. It boosted my confidence and self esteem. I felt like somebody.

In fact, while Ron had his share of milestones during high school, his happiest memory was clearly the moment he received his black belt during his senior year. He wrote about this in 1987:

I was 17 years old at the time, and had trained hard for six years. It was a talent I naturally had and a big desire. I remember my instructor would often work with me one on one after class, as well as many times on Sunday afternoons. He took a personal interest in me. This really made me feel special. Receiving shotokan (first degree) black belt was a life long goal. There were times I thought I would never make it. It was the most rewarding day of my life-something that would be with me forever and could be one of my professions. My family was surprised and very happy for me. This was something I accomplished on my own, a day at a time, with a lot of sweat and determination.

Ron continued to thrive in aikido after high school. He went on to be featured once on local television, profiled in the local paper, and eventually run his own academy, Tomiki Aikido of America, where he would teach martial arts to youngsters in the Matthews community in the years to come.

Looking back, Brooks and I also realize that we were fortunate in another respect. Ron's experience with aikido truly was one that would last the rest of his life. Having earned his black belt on his own, at a young age, "one day at a time, with a lot of sweat and determination," Ron had the confidence he would need later on, when he hit bottom and had to take control of his addiction. He could now draw on the one important lesson he learned from this accomplishment: that if he worked hard and applied himself, he was capable of meeting any goal he set, no matter how out of reach it seemed.

* * *

Unfortunately, the confidence and stability that aikido gave Ron was not enough to shield him from two devastating losses (or "crushed hurts," as Ron called them) that also happened when he was 17. The first was the death of his cousin Doug (Carolyn's son), who died of cystic fibrosis during Ron's senior year. Doug and Ron were absolute best buddies, and his death would have a major impact on Ron.

A short time after Doug's death, Ron found himself thrown for another loss just before his high school graduation. The mother of his girlfriend-a woman he had grown to love as though she were his own mom-died of cancer. Ron was at her bedside when the woman died, and though he promised to take care of her daughter, it wasn't long before his relationship with the girl began to unravel.

Unfortunately, so would his relationship with his own family.

Devastated and distraught, Ron's spiritual life also fell by the wayside. Before long, he would fall in with a gang of motorcycle-riding renegades whose lives consisted of Harley Davidson's, Southern rock 'n' roll, loose women, and the high that comes from alcohol and various drugs. While some of these bikers were outcasts from society, other members, like Ron, came from Christian families and were likewise lured into this destructive lifestyle.

Ron didn't know it at the time, but by casting his lot with this gang, he was sowing the seeds of his own ruin.

CHAPTER FIVE

Black Leather and White Powder

After working as a welder for Davis Steel throughout high school, Ron decided not to go to college as Rick had done, choosing instead to stay on board with the family business by working as a draftsman. Brooks and I weren't entirely sure at first whether this was the best fit. More to the point, this was a desk job, and Ron, even at a young age, was always more of a hyper, outgoing person. We were concerned that he might find it too restrictive.

Working in the drafting department in the steel fabrication industry is a very complex, challenging job that involved taking the architectural and structural drawings of a building and making blueprints for the anchor bolts for the foundation in the building, so that the contractor could have the bolts spaced exactly right for the building that would fit on top of them. Once the blueprints are complete, the draftsman details the columns to make sure they fit on the anchor bolts, then details the beams or girders that went between the columns for each floor and the roof, as well as the beams that fit between the girders.

Drafting a building is highly technical work, especially at the time Ron graduated in 1976. Back then, there wasn't any of the automated computerized drafting software that has become standard in the industry today. You need good math skills to do this job, because on any given building there are a lot of connections for bolts from the columns to the girders and for the floor beams between the girders. You have to take into account the different elevations for the floor heights and for the thickness of the decking and concrete for each particular floor and roof. Considerations also have to be given to ensure correct openings in the floors for elevators and stairs. As important as it is, most of this work is never seen by the time you go into a finished building.

To our pleasant surprise, though, Ron initially took to the challenge very well. With the help of our chief draftsman, Larry, he detailed a four-story building when he was just 18. Larry played a big part in the early success of our company. He not only had a knack for training young draftsmen, but was also very innovative in working out problems with contractors, engineers, and architects to get the drawing finished on time and within budget. Larry and Ron worked very well together.

Drafting a building was a significant accomplishment for someone Ron's age, and one in which he took great pride. At the same time, though, it's not the most glamorous job in the world, especially when you're only 18 years old. Every building may be different, but the measurements in each building still have to be precise. Despite his aptitude for the work, Ron soon found sitting behind a drafting table and making all these calculations and drawings to be just a little too confining. Before long, his job only served to add more pressure and increase his already high level of anxiety. The more he dwelled on it, the more the monotony of being behind a desk all day drove him "nuts" (as he would later put it), which only further fueled his restlessness and feelings of inadequacy.

It was around this time that Ron endured the three crushing blows that I talked about before: the death of his cousin Doug from cystic fibrosis, the loss of his girlfriend's mother to cancer, and then finally the breakup with his girlfriend. That made the pressures he felt from his work all the more difficult to take. Unfortunately, as I also mentioned before, it was not Ron's way to talk about his problems-at least, not to us. The more he kept things bottled inside, the more sullen and inward he became, his anger channeling latent feelings of resentment and hostility toward Brooks and me that, frankly, took us both by surprise.

At first, it seemed typical, the kind of adolescent (or, in Ron's case, late adolescent) rebellion that some parents endure. Like it or not, many teenagers do tend to act out, especially as they near the end of high school. Suddenly, they begrudge us for things that may seem innocuous as far as we're concerned, but which are of utmost importance to them. In Ron's case, it was a resentment for "making us wear crew cuts when we were little," "making us go to church when we didn't want to," "making us work sometimes, when our friends and those in the neighborhood were playing," or for "all that nagging about how we dressed, how we acted, and worrying about what the neighbors thought." As painful as this is for any of us to go through, that, unfortunately, often comes with the territory of being a parent.

Brooks and I didn't know it at the time, but the rebellion in Ron's case would prove to be anything but typical. With the world as he once knew it completely ruptured, Ron's spiritual life began to go by the wayside, and in this vulnerable state he was beginning to turn more and more to drugs in order to find escape.

I was having an identity crisis. I didn't know who I was other than a Davis and martial artist. I wasn't quite sure of my direction in life and I would suppress it with pot from time to time to escape.

[Suddenly] I resented being isolated from the real world, then finding out what the real world was like and it being a slap in the face and wanting to slap them back for it. Also, the inadequate feeling of not being able to fill either my father's, my grandfather's, or my brother's shoes.

It was a sick way of telling my parents that if I couldn't be a good, good person, I would try to be a good bad person. [Everything] they told me [before] and instilled in me [the idea] that they were right and I was wrong. My radical, scandalous, trashy living was a sick way of acting this out-a form of rebellion.

Ron wrote this in 1987, several years after his rebellion, in a journal he kept during a 60-day drug treatment rehabilitation facility at Rancho L'Abri, near San Diego, California. As part of the exercise, he and the other addicts were required to take a long, hard look at their past, to examine their actions honestly, not blaming others as they may have before, but holding themselves accountable for their past actions, as well as their future ones. If he sounded a little hard on himself, that was exactly the point:

I do not blame [my parents] any longer for my misconceptions of life, but made a decision to make a complete and total change in me, about the way I handle things, view things and try to work with them as a family and not against them.

To his credit, Ron began to change. Instead of keeping everything inside, he learned to be open about his problem with drugs-and he learned once again to confide in us.

One of the first, and most dramatic, examples of that growth was the day he stood before the congregation at Mount Harmony Baptist Church and spoke frankly about his condition. That was also in 1987. Brooks and I will never forget how proud we were of our son that day as he rededicated himself to the Lord. It was as if Ron had finally turned a corner.

Unfortunately, such growth doesn't happen overnight. Ron still had to fall-and fall hard-many, many times before he could get to that point.

Not long after he first began to rebel, Ron fell in with a local gang of young bikers-social misfits whose views on life were radical and abstract. As it happened, some of these youths came from families within our community who begrudged Brooks and me because of the success of our company. Unfortunately, because Ron had his own issues as far as we were concerned, he was too blind to see just what kind of trouble he was about to walk into.

These people were jealous of my family, and they wanted me in the gutter along with them. This was a weak point in my life spiritually, and I fell for it, hook, line and sinker.

All I cared about was Harley Davidson motorcycles, black leather, and southern rock 'n' roll. Nice cars, nice clothes, nice girls were thrown out the window. This was a new identity and a good mask to hide behind. I felt wild and free.

* * *

As much as it broke my heart to see Ron act this way, that pain became even greater when my sister Nancy died of breast cancer. Nancy always cared for Ron. She worried about him so much and wrote him a long letter just before she died. Even in his rebellion, he loved his aunt Nancy so much that he always kept that letter.

For me, I was fortunate that I had others who were there to help me in my grief. I had the love of my husband, and the support of a prayer group I joined in 1983 along with four other friends shortly after Nancy's death.

For years, I was never comfortable praying in front of another person. That just wasn't for me. All my prayers were silent prayers, except for a blessing at the table before a meal. Then one day, I decided I wanted to learn more about prayer. I turned to my close friend Nonia Polk, who was involved in intercessory prayer and had organized a couple of other groups. Nonia and I discussed and prayed about who we would ask to join us. We both agreed to approach Glenda Furr and Margie Price, both of whom immediately consented. A short while later, another friend, Jackie Brown, joined us. Together we called ourselves "Sisters in Christ."

Up to that point in time, Nancy's death was the most devastating thing I had ever gone through. As I mentioned before, we were more than just sisters. We were truly best friends. Nancy was gone, but in her place God gave me four other "sisters" to help me through some of the darkest times of my life. We met monthly and in between communicated by phone. In an emergency, we could count on at least one of us to come and pray with one another at a moment's notice.

Brooks and I would have never made it through the turbulent years of Ron's addiction-not to mention, the stress and strain of waiting eight years to see his killer brought to trial-without the help of prayer. There were times when I was so weak with emotion that I could not utter a prayer, but my prayer partners "stood in the gap for me." I could always count on these four dear ladies to keep my prayer needs in the strictest of confidence.

It was during these times that I really first began to witness the power of prayer, seeing many prayers answered in the lives of those that we interceded for. God's promises became more alive for me as a result. *"I can do all things through Christ who strengthens me. The joy of the Lord is my strength."*

Somewhere along the line I began reading *Hinds Feet on High Places,* a book of inspiration by Hannah Hurnard. I'll never forget the epiphany I had one day while reading her book, realizing that had I not struggled through my own pain, grief and agony, I would not have understood her powerful words.

Early on in Ron's addiction, he was real adamant that I not tell anyone he was in treatment-especially not family and friends. It wasn't until I explained how much we need prayer, and how I especially could never have survived the pain of seeing him struggle without the help of prayer, that he finally began to understand. He allowed himself comfort in knowing that my prayer partners and family members were praying for him.

When he was going through his second treatment program, Ron received a letter from his Aunt Margaret, who prayed for him faithfully. "Aunt Mog," Ron used to say, "has a direct line to heaven." Ron wrote her back, and Margaret gave me a copy of his letter. I found it among my journals after his death. I thought I'd share that letter with you:

Dear Margaret:

I want to thank you for the inspiring letter. It was a big lift. I don't have much time to write here, but I wanted to let you know the Lord has come back into my heart, cast evil away and has given me a new life and purpose here on earth. Thank you so much for praying. Prayer has been answered. You and a select few have played a key part in my life. I will be coming home soon and will be able to share more. I cannot write on paper what I feel in my heart, but before I sign off, I want to leave you with this blessing:

May the road rise up to meet you
May the wind be always at your back
May the rains fall softly on your fields
And until we meet again . . . May God
hold you in the palm of his hand.
(Copied) Irish Blessing

Love, Ronnie

Looking back, I can see how God knew exactly what I was going to need to carry me through the many days, months, and years to follow. My prayer partners would not only help me cope with the loss of my sister, but give Brooks and me the strength that we'd need as we walked through the years of Ron's addiction.

* * *

Not long after taking up with the biker gang, Ron started experimenting with harsher drugs. It was during this time, he would later admit, that he experienced his first shot of cocaine. Soon he began to shirk all responsibility. He moved out of the family house, took up with a girl he hardly knew, and exhibited other forms of irrational behavior that Brooks and I found increasingly frightening. There was a drastic change in his behavior. Suddenly he was nothing at all like the Ron we knew-the buoyant, happy Ron that grew up enjoying family activities and sports. Suddenly he had become someone else, a hardened, embittered young man who no longer seemed to care about anything.

Ron was running with a dangerous crowd, but he couldn't tell the difference-not when he was using, anyway. Instead, he seemed to thrive on the adventure of the wild life, even as it put him in increasingly dangerous situations. He would be gone for days, never calling us, coming home long enough for a change of clothes at most before walking back out again. We feared that we had lost him, and prayed every night that God would watch over him and somehow bring him back to us.

When a dealer friend suffered a fatal overdose, we had hoped that might be the dose of reality Ron needed in order to snap out of it. Unfortunately, that incident only served to drive him further and further away:

For some reason, one night, this girl and I had something else to do. I got a call the next morning that [my friend] had overdosed on cocaine and was in a coma. He died a few hours later.

I was crushed. I felt scared, lonely, angry and guilty, that if I had been there maybe it wouldn't have happened. My relationship with this girl ceased and we went our separate ways.

At this point, I ran. I would stay gone weeks at a time, no one knowing whether I was dead or alive. My parents were worried about me and put a lot of pressure on me. They had not turned me over to God yet. I would come home periodically for selfish reasons, when I needed something. This made me feel ashamed and my self esteem even lower. This made me run harder and faster. I was in search of something, but I didn't know quite what it was. I felt locked in and all I knew to do was run.

Meanwhile, as Ron continued to run rampant, Brooks and I stood helplessly by, desperately wanting to help our son, but not knowing what to do... or where to turn.

Bear in mind that was still early in the 1980s. Drug awareness on a nationwide level was still in its nascent stages. The level of resources and education that are readily available to parents today simply did not exist at the time.

We didn't know it at the time, but in many ways, this marked the first step of our own journey through the ordeal of Ron's addiction.

CHAPTER SIX

The Descent Begins

R on remained rudderless as he turned 21. With his lingering
insecurities and low self esteem, he appeared to be living
simply to seek excitement and personal satisfaction without ever
considering the danger or consequences of his actions. All the while,
he was further isolating himself from the rest of his family. This
continued for several years. Occasionally he'd come home, hoping
to find stability in his practice of the martial arts, but even that was
more like a tease. Just when you thought he was about to settle
down, he'd get restless and bolt out the door. Every time we tried to
bridge the gap, he would quickly cut us off, as he explained in his
journal from 1987:

> *My family scared me. Their goals and expectations just
> seemed too far out of reach. I felt very lonely. I would meet
> up with another girl, but it was always the wrong kind of
> girl. Before you knew it, I was off the beaten path again. My
> life had no direction. I had no idea where I was going.*

Then one day, Ron met a biker girl, a former heroin user with
whom he fell "madly in lust." It wasn't long before the two of them
decided to marry.

I'll admit, Brooks and I did not care for this woman at first, but
she eventually won us over. She held down a good job, and seemed

genuine in her effort to renounce her former lifestyle. That in turn inspired Ron to stay clean and to become productive once again. He resumed working his job at Davis Steel, while also starting up his own martial arts academy, Tomiki Aikido of America. They rented a small house in the country, and in general seemed happy together.

After years of emotional turbulence, Ron finally seemed ready to settle down. Believe me, that was a relief. Gradually I began including his wife in on some of the ladies' activities at the church. To my surprise, she became inspired and expressed a desire to join our faith. Before long, she asked me to accompany her to the Pastor's office and informed him she was ready to make a profession of faith. She accepted Christ and was soon baptized at Mount Harmony Baptist Church. Looking back, I see how God gave me an opportunity to be a witness to this woman and mentor her in various ways, which in turn planted some seeds in her life. She and Ron would attend church frequently throughout this time.

Still, I always had misgivings about this girl. Brooks and I couldn't quite place it, but something about her set off an alarm that we could never quite shut off.

Then again, you always want to give people the benefit of the doubt until proven otherwise, especially where your loved ones are concerned.

I guess you could say we were cautiously optimistic about this girl. Ron's happiness was all that mattered. By the end of their first year together, he finally appeared to have settled down. His marriage seemed solid so far as we could tell, and his career was beginning to take off. He was invited to participate in a martial arts seminar in Chicago, where he was recognized as the youngest "sensei" (that is to say, "master") on the East Coast. This honor led to some wonderful media exposure for his Tomiki Aikido Academy, including a profile in one of the local papers and a short feature story on television about Ron and the school.

While this was clearly an exciting time for Ron, it also proved to be a bit of a trap. The more successful he became, thinking that material things alone would make him happy, the more he lost sight of what really mattered-his marriage and his spiritual life.

I became obsessed with getting ahead. I worked longer hours and spent a lot of time at my martial arts school. Being so wrapped up in my work and school, I started neglecting my wife.

Unfortunately for Ron, his young wife still had some serious issues of her own to work out, above and beyond the usual everyday ups and downs that usually come with married life. For instance, Ron always encouraged his wife to take part in his aikido class. There were many other ladies in the class, and he saw it as a good opportunity for her to meet people as well as learn self defense. Yet she would always refuse. Whenever he pressed her about it, she was never forthcoming, other than to say that she liked her free time and looked forward to being alone.

Ron didn't know it, but she was actually seeing her former boyfriend on the side-as well as using drugs again. Before long she would throw their marriage away, and nearly Ron's life along with it.

I'll give her this: at least she was discreet about it. None of us knew the truth for a long time, although Brooks and I remember when we first had suspicions.

Ron's house was located in back of our shop in an area very close to the railroad. Brooks and I had purchased the house and adjoining property some time before, and in fact we still own it today. Only a small stretch of woods separates the house from the railroad, making it a sort of buffer between the shop and the neighborhood. Other than the narrow winding road along the tracks, there's no other access to the house.

Early one evening, while Ron was teaching his class, my dad, Barney, decided to drop by Ron's house to see their garden. It made Dad happy that they had a garden, because he loved tilling the earth himself. As he pulled up, he noticed a strange man on a motorcycle zipping down the railroad track, instead of out of the drive. (Though that seemed odd to us, we said nothing about it at the time. No one wanted to upset Ron without knowing anything for sure.)

When Ron finally learned the truth in an awful way, his world once again fell apart.

Ron had gone to the gym one night to teach a martial arts class. By the time he arrived he discovered that a water pipe had just burst, flooding the entire gym. With no other place to hold the class, Ron decided to invite the students over to his home. He had just finished building a brand new extension, a sizeable room with a cathedral ceiling. As there was no furniture yet in the room, that made it large enough to accommodate up to ten people-perfect for a small class.

As Ron came up to the house, he encountered a black truck peeling out of the driveway. The truck sped so close and so fast, it nearly hit Ron as he pulled up in front of the house. Needless to say, that made Ron suspicious. So did the fact that the door was wide open, the phone was off the hook, and his wife was nowhere to be seen.

By this time, the rest of the students had arrived, including two men who also happened to be police officers. Ron asked them to go after the truck, while he sent the other students home. Ron called me, asking frantically if I knew where his wife was.

As it happened, she had also raced into the woods as the truck sped out of the driveway.

"I was crushed," he would later recall in his journal.

I put the blame entirely on her and felt like my world had crumbled. I could not take the pain. I was not willing to go through a crisis like this in my life, scared of the pain and the truth.

Ron immediately asked his wife to leave. Sometime after this incident, one of the man's cousins and an acquaintance of Ron's came by his house with a large amount of cocaine.

Ron did not realize it, but he was about to fall into another trap.

Ron discovered later on that this person had been sent to him that night by the man who was secretly seeing Ron's wife-a man who was very much aware of our son's prior history with drugs. It was a lowdown, underhanded, and insidious attempt to strike Ron at his most vulnerable point.

Unfortunately, the plan would work beyond anyone's wildest imagination.

Sure enough, the minute he saw it, all Ron could think of was the enormous rush cocaine had given him whenever he used it before. Cocaine was made for moments like these. He was devastated, he felt isolated, and he desperately wanted to escape. Suddenly he wanted it more than anything in the world, and suddenly there it was.

> *My mind recalled cocaine, the euphoria it brought me and my cravings for it. I ran straight for it, thinking I could handle it, thinking it would bring me escape, like before.*
>
> *If only I knew how wrong I would be. If only I knew this insane decision would eventually lead to a life of pure hell on earth.*

Ron was a very private person, and it would be years before he finally told us the full story-how the entire incident was a set-up. Ron had desperately wanted a wife that would fit into the family, and it devastated him to know that he could be so wrong.

For years he would always refer to this marriage as something "totally out of the will of God." He knew it was a hasty, unwise, and tragic decision made entirely out of loneliness and insecurity.

Unfortunately, Brooks and I had no idea just how tragic the consequences of this decision would be. This incident would mark the real beginning of Ron's addiction-a vicious cycle from which he would never fully escape.

Family and friends urged Ron to seek help, but he simply refused to listen. Once again he would prove to be his own worst enemy:

> *My ego wouldn't let me. I felt I could fully escape my pain and fear with the help of cocaine. I was shooting up 'round the clock, partying with girls, staying up for hours on end. I would run from motel to motel, hiding, terribly out of control, too insane to tell the details. I felt nothing. Nothing else mattered to me but cocaine 'round the clock.*

Then one day, Ron's best friend Johnny drove into Charlotte for a visit. Johnny, by his own admission, was a ne'er-do-well in high school, but he got his act together once he joined the Marines. I don't recall where he was stationed at the time, but he often stayed with Ron whenever he was in town.

After relaxing for a while, Ron suggested they go into town and look for some action. Only Johnny wanted to take a nap first, because he was still tired from being on the road all day.

Ron said fine, but it wasn't long before he started getting restless. While Johnny was sleeping, Ron went inside the bathroom to do a shot of cocaine.

They say the Lord moves in ways we do not always understand. In a sense, there's no better example of that than what was about to happen next.

No sooner had Ron shot up when suddenly he began to panic. "The shot was too big," he would later explain.

I had been up for days and my system just couldn't handle it. I knew what was happening. I was overdosing. This was it.

All at once, I became scared to death. I cried out for Johnny, asking him for help-and for the first time in a long time, I prayed to God: "Please save me.

I want to live."

Johnny rushed Ron to the emergency room, where our son was immediately treated with valium.

I told myself I would never do it again. But I knew I was really insane, and completely out of control, when as soon as I got home from the hospital, I started shooting up again.

I realize it may sound strange to say this-especially since it would take years of hard work on Ron's part, and patience on ours, before he had any semblance of control over his condition. But as Brooks and I think back on that night, we could see how God was watching over Ron, even at the height of his addiction. Because, if Ron had been alone that night-had Johnny not been there to take him to the hospital and get him treatment for his overdose-our son may not have made it. He would have never lived to see the progress he was able to make and the victory he would achieve when he finally gained sobriety. He would not have enjoyed the second lease on life that sobriety would give him in just a few years' time.

Nor would he have touched the lives of those he graced along the way. Nor would Brooks and I have experienced the many valuable lessons (and, indeed, miracles) that eventually came our way as a result of our own journey through addiction.

It may be hard to understand, but had God not intervened that night, we would have lost our son right then and there.

In many ways, that would have been an even greater tragedy.

CHAPTER SEVEN

Awaiting the Bottom

W ith Ron so clearly out of control, it was imperative that Brooks and I step in and do something before it became too late.

Unfortunately, as we both came to realize, that's a lot easier said than done.

By this time, of course, Ron was well into his 20s. He'd been married and on his own for several years, which made it all the more difficult for us as parents to try to get him the help he needed. More to the point, it would take a while for us to understand that when it comes to drug intervention, Rule No. 1 is that you can never *make* an addict do anything. Only after the addict realizes that he has hit rock bottom will he ever be open to the possibility of help. And since no two addicts are alike, consequently no two addict's "bottoming out" point is ever the same, either.

Even more frightening was the fact that we were so clearly out of our element. We did not know what to do or how to help him. As I said before, this was the mid '80s. We didn't have the Internet, nor did we have the vast amount of information on drug addiction that is so widely available today. We were truly on our own. . . literally, as well as figuratively.

This was also one of those subjects that you simply did not talk about in the company of your friends or among the members of your church. Not in our community, anyway. Drug addiction was one of those dirty little secrets that only happened to "other people."

And when you're raised to believe, as we both were, that image is everything and reputation is all, which makes the problem even more difficult to accept.

It was certainly that way for me. I simply refused to believe this was happening to my child. I wanted to look the other way, hoping it would disappear. Only instead of going away, it became progressively worse.

Then after denial, feelings of guilt started sinking in. Brooks and I looked at each other, wondering where we could have possibly gone wrong.

Our way of dealing with it early on was to try to confront him. Ron would come home, and I would preach to him: "Don't you realize what're doing? Don't you realize how much you're hurting us?"

Big mistake. Every time we tried that, we'd only end up arguing and getting more upset. Ron would storm out. I would cry or feel sick. The walls would go up again. Nothing would ever change.

It wouldn't be long before pride and anger set in. As the situation went from bad to worse, so did our level of communication. The harder we pushed Ron, the further away from us he ran.

Little by little, though, you find your pride stripped away, to the point where you no longer care what other people say. You finally realize that's something you really can't control, so why bother worrying about it? Besides, it's all you can do to hang on yourself and deal with the pain of seeing everything your son has worked for slowly slip away.

As agonizing as it is, there's really nothing you can do. Nothing, that is, except learn everything you possibly can about your child's condition so that you're ready to act the moment he's ready to listen.

There were so many times, as we anxiously waited for Ron to hit bottom, where Brooks and I so desperately hoped for someone, anyone, we could talk to who could understand our pain. Because unless you've been there, unless you've become educated on the matter and understand that addiction is an illness first and foremost, it's easy to dismiss it simply as a sign of weakness. It's easy for others to think it's just a moral issue, and say, *"Why is Ronnie doing this to you? Why doesn't he just stop?"* It's easy to focus on the behavior without really understanding what's going on.

That's what we did at first. That's how little we knew.

We badly needed a shoulder to cry on, someone who could comfort or help us. But as I say, unless you've been there, you can never quite understand what someone's going through.

Unfortunately, none of the pastors at Mount Harmony Baptist Church had any experience with drug addiction or drug counseling-not at that time, anyway. They just weren't equipped to deal with a situation quite like ours. Consequently, we continued to feel very much alone. Were it not for my prayer group, as well as our friends Nonia and Jimmy Polk, I'm not sure how we would have coped.

We pressed on as best we could. Brooks would go to the office, or we would go to church or social functions, smiling on the outside but dying on the inside. Well-meaning but otherwise blithely unaware parents would go on and on about how well their children were doing, without realizing how much our heart ached over our son and his lifestyle. (We had been praying so hard for a solution, it truly hurt.)

That said, we never felt jealous of or begrudged anyone their good fortune.

We knew that all of us face obstacles in this life, and not all problems and hurts are the same. We were happy for those who celebrated their children's accomplishments and appreciated them for including us in their activities.

Some mothers, however, did insinuate that their son "would *never* do anything like that." One woman made a remark that was really insensitive: *"Well, I'm glad that none of my children ever defiled me."* Now, this was a mother who had seen the marriages of several of her children end badly in divorce, so you'd think she'd be a little sympathetic. Yet somehow in her mind, we were the ones who bore the scarlet letter.

If only she could have stopped and realized that but for the grace of God, it could have been her child instead of ours.

That said, in the years before and since Ron's death, Brooks and I have shared our story with many families. We speak before groups occasionally, and also get calls from people asking our advice or seeking information on treatment centers. As a result, we've come to know many other parents whose children struggle with addiction. We've seen it happen to the best of families, as well as the worst, and we've seen many children overcome it. We have a friend whose son once went to a 30-day program. That was over ten years ago, and he has remained clean and sober ever since. We are so proud for them. We also admire children who come out of the worst family situations, never to succumb to drugs, and who go on to lead successful lives and careers.

If you're open to it, a wondrous kind of growth can happen as you help your child overcome his dependence. Not only does the experience strip you of pride, it teaches you to be more compassionate of others and less judgmental. We have also sensed that in sharing Ron's story, we may have helped other families take pride in their accomplishments, knowing that despite the pain they're going through, they have still done the very best they knew how.

* * * * *

We were also grateful for the strength that is only possible through the power of prayer. Through prayer we can build faith. With faith we can always have hope.

As children Brooks and I were raised to believe that God is always with us, especially in moments of desperation. One of the cornerstones of our faith as Christians is our belief that God provides us with what we need at precisely the moment we need it.

I mentioned earlier how we had seen the hand of God acting in the person of Ron's friend Johnny, and how if Ron had been alone on the night he overdosed he may never have survived. Well, not long after that, at a time when Brooks and I were at our wit's end and didn't know what to do or who to turn to, we somehow learned about a man who was with the drug addiction program at Mercy Hospital here in Charlotte. He was a recovering addict who had retired from the military sometime before. We made an appointment with him to learn about intervention. Through this man, Brooks and I began learning some of the important things we would need to do in order to help our son.

Once again, God saw to our needs at exactly the right moment.

We began learning how to intervene by getting advice, reading material on intervention, and asking lots of questions. We began to understand that when it comes to intervention, timing is everything. In most cases, the best time to step in is when the addict has exhausted all of his resources and has nowhere else to turn for help. Even so, there's a right time to approach and there's a wrong time. For one, never try to discuss the matter if he's drunk, sick, under the influence, or going through withdrawal. Depending on his condition, he may agree to *anything* at that moment without really meaning it, simply to get you off his back. Secondly, don't begin your presentation unless you have the time and information you need to complete it. If you try to tell him things piecemeal over the course of several days, he may well have rationalized away and forgotten the first part by the time you bring up the later points.

Spell it all out, clearly and calmly: first, the diagnosis fitted to his behavior, then the prognosis, if he continues without treatment and the plan for recovery. Remember, you're not bluffing or threatening, nor are you asking his permission. You are simply laying out the facts of his present life. You don't want to kick him out of the house, or see him lose his job or sink deeper into debt anymore than he does. But you know-and he needs to know, too-that unless he takes action and gets serious about recovering from his illness, no one can prevent these things from happening.

That said, be aware that you may well be confronting him at his darkest and most depressing hour in a long time. So be positive. Give him hope. Express confidence in his ability to recover with the right kind of help. Remind him that his life can change if he wants it to. Thousands of people recover every day, some of whom he probably even knows. Be prepared to put him in touch-immediately, if he agrees-with people who can give him further help or share with him their own experience.

At the same time, be firm. Don't bargain with him or get into a debate. Set deadlines, lay out conditions-and stick to them. Otherwise, the whole plan may go down the chute. Give him a few days, but no more than that, to decide what he is going to do. Be sure you've had a few places checked out for treatment, because depending on his condition he may not be physically and mentally able to do so himself.

Finally, once he's ready, have him pick up the phone and call. Most treatment centers require the patient to contact the facility directly and register themselves. That, and only that, shows them that he is serious about getting help.

Brooks and I would also learn all about the concept of "tough love" and how that doesn't mean you stop loving them, but rather that you stop "enabling" them-staying out of the way and letting things happen in order for them to reach their bottoming point and realize they need help.

Practicing tough love was without question one of the hardest things I've ever had to do, because it goes against a mother's every instinct. It's not easy standing by and watching your child destroy himself. However, if you keep bailing him out of trouble, paying for everything and cleaning up his messes, he will never see the need for help. Once again, timing is everything-and Brooks and I didn't always agree when it was right to practice tough love and when it wasn't. We had to learn to trust each other's instincts on the matter and allow ourselves to make mistakes. Fortunately, we did. Had we not, it could have easily destroyed our marriage.

I remember the time early on in Ron's addiction when we had to allow his car to be repossessed. Brooks and I both knew how much pride Ron took in his car and how he absolutely loved to drive. He would become terrified and practically paranoid at even the thought of not having a means of transportation. So when he fell behind on his car payments, it was difficult for us both to stand firm and refuse to offer help.

Naturally, Ron was very angry at us at the time, but he would have an entirely different attitude about it once he became sober. As he grew serious about fighting his addiction and understood how destructive his past behavior was, he knew taking the car away from him was something we had to let happen. It would be years before he could have this stricken from his credit report. Came the day when his credit record was finally clear, he was truly a happy guy.

Also early in his addiction (I believe it was around 1984), he maxed out his credit card, which had something like a $1,000.00 credit line. He would live 13 years after this experience and would never apply for a credit card again. Brooks and I were glad that he had disciplined himself not to run up a charge account again. Granted, that made it a little embarrassing or inconvenient for him at times-credit cards, after all, are often used as a secondary means of identification, or to hold a reservation at a restaurant or motel. However, those paled in comparison to watching him con and manipulate us, as Ron would often do in order to feed his addiction.

None of this came to us overnight. Like so many things in life, intervention was a process, and Brooks and I had a huge learning curve. We made our share of mistakes, but we always tried to learn from them.

Waiting for your child to hit bottom is truly painful, for you as well as for him. You have to exercise patience. You have to remind yourself what's really going on as your child spirals downward. You have to remember that the irrational behavior you're witnessing is not indicative of your real son, but is rather the effect of the drugs on him.

* * * * * *

By now Ron had long since quit his job at Davis Steel, and his martial arts school had also folded. He no longer cared about anything, pawning off responsibility on others while living only for the next high. Brooks and I grew increasingly concerned, to the point where it was affecting our emotional well being, making it difficult to keep our minds focused on other things. At that point we learned about Fenwick Hall, a private drug rehabilitation facility in Charleston, South Carolina. We decided it was time to intervene and admitted Ron for treatment.

Ron lasted all of nine days before he finally bolted.

A short time later, Brooks and I were away at a convention when he overdosed again. Fortunately, he had the presence of mind to call his brother Rick. Thankfully, Rick was home that night and was able to get Ron to the hospital-otherwise, who knows what would have happened.

It was a rather awkward episode, though. Apparently Ron had a girl in the house at the time, and Rick had never dealt with anything like that before. "I felt badly for embarrassing him," Ron would later write.

It was a lot worse than the last time; I was having to deal to support my habit. I was scared to death and I had to stop this, because I knew if I got locked up, I could not handle it. I was claustrophobic as a child and I couldn't take being locked up. I did stop [and yet] I had a bad habit to keep up.
This is when my problems really snowballed.

To his credit, Ron did agree to return to Fenwick Hall-only this time, he stuck it out. It was an intense 30-day program implementing the 12-Step principles of Alcoholics Anonymous.

In addition to the 30-day program for drug addiction, Fenwick also offered a special three-day seminar for parents, spouses, siblings, or any other family member who chose to attend. From an educational standpoint, it was invaluable. Of all the family programs we attended, Fenwick Hall was the best. Not only did it put you directly in touch with rehabilitation professionals, it gave you many opportunities to benefit from the experience of other families, especially in the sessions where everyone spoke openly and freely about their situation.

Brooks and I were fortunate to be in group sessions and hear family members make restitution with each other, as well as recovering addicts who spoke honestly about their problems. It soon became apparent that these were people who were ready to deal with whatever it was buried deep inside that caused them to drink or do drugs.

One particular story has always stayed with me. There was a young man in one group meeting who shared with all of us a heart-wrenching story about how he told his parents that he had always blamed himself for the death of his younger brother. The boy died in a drowning accident, and for some reason he blamed himself for not being able to save him. The guilt became so overwhelming that he turned to alcohol to kill his pain. He kept this from his parents for a long time before finally leveling with them. Unfortunately, the mother and father had become deeply split over their grief, making it difficult for the son to talk to them before-which only exacerbated his condition.

This experience reminded us not only how tragedy can lead to addiction, but how it can rip even the strongest of families apart if the lines of communication are broken. It isn't always just the addict who needs help. Sometimes other members of the family need it, too. The programs offered by facilities such as Fenwick provide a wonderful opportunity for families and loved ones to learn about and understand addiction so that everyone can heal.

Brooks and I had hoped this 30-day program at Fenwick Hall would cure Ron of his addiction once and for all. Goes to show just how ignorant we were about addiction at that time. We had no clue what else was in store-for ourselves, or for Ron.

As Ron himself would later put it:

> *I came out [of Fenwick] an educated drug addict, knowing it all. I knew I [was fully capable of not using] coke, and yet I still had an ego that got in the way.*
>
> *I was not willing to get honest with myself. My disease told me I could have an occasional drink as long as I stayed away from cocaine.*
>
> *I went on vacation as soon as I got out of treatment. [Sure enough, the first thing I did was] have a couple of drinks and run straight for the cocaine.*

Ron's problem only intensified by the time he returned home.

> *I still had not found a real bottom at this point. I think I was in a blackout period for a while. I do remember getting off somewhere shooting coke, becoming very ill. I was hallucinating and having chills. There again, I thought I was going to die.*
>
> *I drove to my parents' house, making it there only by the grace of God. I had to level with my parents and tell*

them what was going on, because I knew I was going to have to go to the hospital. From there, all I remember was being wheeled into the emergency room, vomiting and blacking out.

Brooks and I drove Ron to the hospital. He woke up in a private room, praying to God and thanking Him for sparing his life. We later learned that he was diagnosed with trash fever and that he had at best a 50/50 chance to live.

A few days later, we admitted Ron to a treatment facility in Pinehurst, North Carolina, two hours away. He felt "doomed" at the time, as though he were fated to live the rest of his life in and out of treatment. After completing the 30-day program, he moved to another town with a friend he had met while in treatment. Brooks and I had hoped this would provide our son with the support he would need in his effort to remain sober.

Little did we know he was still on the road to a much further bottom.

CHAPTER EIGHT

Let Go and Let God

From the time he first sought treatment in 1985 until his brutal murder 12 years later, Ron would be in and out of rehabilitation no less than 18 times. Brooks and I would have to learn to forgive our son many times along the way. . . but we also had to forgive ourselves. Not only that, we had to learn how to let go of the resentment we had harbored against those who had led Ron astray. This breakthrough didn't happen overnight-nor did it happen for either of us at the same time. In fact, it would take a lot of soulful reflection, and many hours of prayer, before we both could finally let go of our anger and again put our trust in God.

When Ron began his period of rebellion, it puzzled us both that he would suddenly choose to spend his time with a crowd of people who seemed so completely removed from him-people who shared none of his previous interests, such as sports, martial arts, and church. We could not understand why he would distance himself from his family. At first we tried preaching to him, but as you can imagine that only lead to frustration. The more we confronted him about it, the more determined Ron was to do things his way. Brooks and I could see where he was headed, yet there was nothing we could do to stop him.

For years I was angry at the people who were an influence on Ron, especially the man who ultimately sprung the trap that would mark the real beginning of Ron's addiction. The further Ron spun out of control, the more bitter and angry I became. With God's help, I had to let go of those feelings and realize that like it or not, Ron was making his own decisions-and that while I may not have cared for his decisions, I had to accept them as a matter beyond my control. God was helping us both grow in ways that we probably would have never learned otherwise. In that same spirit, Brooks and I would have to forgive our own son over and over again.

Now, I'm sure some of you might wonder why we even bothered. I know some of our friends and family felt that way, as well as other people in our community. We've heard it said more times and in more ways than you can imagine: *"Why do you put up with Ron's behavior? He shows no concern for anyone but himself. Why don't you just disown him?"* I'm sure there were also those who thought we should have just given up.

We never lost hope and neither did Ron. You don't give up on a loved one. Regardless of what happens, there's a peace that comes when you know you've done all you can do. God has given us that peace.

God never turns His back on us, no matter how many mistakes we make.

God's love is steadfast and unconditional. None of us are really worthy of it. Yet God loved us so much, He sent His only son to die for our sins. He still loves us, despite our failings. He doesn't love the sins we commit, but He loves us just the same.

There's a passage from the Old Testament that I came across during one of our darkest moments of despair. It spoke to me so much at the time that it remains some of my favorite verses from scripture.

Yet there is one ray of hope, his compassion never ends.
It is only the Lord's mercies that have kept us from complete
　　destruction.
Great is his faithfulness; his lovingkindness begins afresh
　　each day.
My soul claims the Lord's inheritance; therefore I will hope
　　in him.

Lamentations 3: 21-24(LB)

With the dawn of each new day, God shows his capacity to forgive us. All we have to do is ask.

This isn't to say it was easy. Trust and forgiveness are no different than any other skills. They both take time to learn, and they both must be practiced every day.

I know for a fact it wasn't until after Ron had gone through several treatment programs that I finally allowed God to begin working on me and was able to truly, truly let go. (There's a song titled "God's Still Working On Me." How true with us all.)

I still remember when it happened. It wasn't anything dramatic. The earth didn't move. There was no flash of light, nor any parting of the seas. It was more an epiphany than anything else. I simply realized that what I had been demonstrating in my anger was certainly not God's peace in the middle of the storm. In His Word he reminds us that

In quietness and confidence shall be your strength.

Isaiah 30:15

Better is a dry morsel and quietness therewith, than a house full of sacrifices with strife.

Proverbs 17:1

I had to go through some deep valleys before I could finally let go and totally trust God. Brooks and I know there will always be things that cause us fear, frustration or anxiety. Yet we also know that if we take the time to reflect on God's promises, that strength and victory will no doubt come. This idea is expressed so well in the following verses:

Be not afraid nor dismayed by reason of this great multitude, for the battle is not yours, but God's.

2 Chronicles 20:15

Casting all your care upon him, for he cares for you.

1 Peter 5:7

> Wait on the Lord, be of good courage, and he shall strengthen thine heart, wait, I say on the Lord.
>
> Psalm 27:14

I also remember the day when I could finally look Ron in the eye with gentleness in my voice and say, "You are accountable to God. I cannot change you, but I can pray for you. You belong to God and are a purchased possession by His shed blood on the cross."

You should have seen the look on his face. All the tension that hung in the air between us slowly evaporated.

From that moment on, our relationship changed. Slowly, gradually, came the time when we could sit down and talk to each other, trust each other, and communicate with each other with love and understanding in the way a mother and son should.

That never would have happened had I not allowed God to work through me and show me his peace. Even though there were many rough times ahead in practicing tough love and intervening to get Ron to give in for more help, there was still that understanding deep down inside that always remained between us. Eventually, Ron would say to me, "I can't believe I can talk so open to my Mom about anything," and "My Dad is my best friend."

Brooks and I retained this bond with Ron until the day he died. Without it, I can't imagine how we could have possibly endured the challenges we would face together in the years before his death.

I was also fortunate to have a husband to help me carry the load. Addiction can put tremendous stress on a marriage. Not every marriage survives the crisis. A spouse or family member can easily become devastated without emotional support. We've seen it happen far too many times.

Brooks and I still remember the time we laid in bed one night praying, "God, he's yours, even as unto death. If he doesn't make it, please don't let him bring harm to someone else in an automobile accident," etc. Thankfully, that prayer was answered.

Brooks and I did not always agree on everything, but we did try to be understanding of each other. We realized that with each decision we made, if the results were disastrous, we'd always have to live with ourselves over that decision.

It still amazes me how when one of us was so distraught that we could hardly function, the other was strong and vice versa. We were truly blessed in that way.

Still, there are some matters where forgiveness would seem out of the question. Forgiving the person who sold your son drugs is one thing. Forgiving the person who took your son's life is quite another.

To be honest, I've never thought about bitterness or unforgiveness toward Michael LeJeune. It was enough of a struggle trying to cope with the legal hearings, the judicial system, the details of the criminal investigation, and everything else leading up to the trial. Neither one of those thoughts have really crossed my mind. Perhaps someday, they will.

I'll tell you this, though. I would like to see some remorse from that young guy, but so far that's never happened. Maybe with the help of God, some day it will.

CHAPTER NINE

"Teach a Child in the Way
He Should Go . . ."

By the end of 1985, Ron had been through programs at two 30-day drug treatment centers, only to revert back to his old habits immediately upon release. Brooks and I soon realized that if he stood any chance of achieving long-term sobriety, he needed a change in environment and a long-term commitment to treatment.

Only we didn't know of any long-term treatment facilities. Once again, we were flying blind.

Fortunately, God once again saw to our needs at precisely the right moment.

It was around this time we first heard about New Vine Fellowship, an addiction support group that regularly met at PTL, a Christian theme park in Fort Mill, South Carolina, not far from where we lived. We asked Ron to attend a meeting with us, and were pleased when he agreed.

There was a large gathering that night, and we spoke to a lot of people. I don't remember many details, however, other than being pulled aside by the leader of the group at the end of the meeting. He handed me a business card for a place called The Shoulder, a year-long Christian rehabilitation facility in Houston, Texas established by a man named Don DeVoss.

"Mr. DeVoss has spoken to our group before," the leader told me. "If you ever have the need for such a place like this, I would give him a call."

The Shoulder ministered to the total person: mentally, physically, and spiritually. In many ways, it would prove to be just the right place for Ron. Unfortunately, it just wasn't the right time yet. As painful as it was for Brooks and me to see, Ron would have to spin even further out of control, to the point where he was no longer able to function at work or at home, before he was finally ready to make the call. As he would later write in his journal:

I wrecked my car, money ran out, things bottomed out completely, life was totally unmanageable. I tried going to a few meetings, trying to convince my parents that I was okay, but things just got worse.

In the meantime, Brooks and I stayed in touch with the group at New Vine Fellowship while also praying for guidance. Every night I returned to my devotional book, *Streams in the Desert, By LB Cowman* I would always go back to the following passage for hope and inspiration:

Believe ye that I am able to do this. Matthew 9:28 (KJ)

God deals with impossibilities. It is never too late for Him to do so, when the impossible is brought to Him, in full faith, the one in whose life and circumstances the impossible must be accomplished, if God is to be glorified. If in our own life, if there have been rebellion, unbelief, sin, and disaster, it is never too late for God to deal triumphantly with these tragic facts if brought to Him in full surrender and trust. It has often been said, and with truth, that Christianity is the only religion that can deal with man's past. "God will restore. . . the years. . . the locust hath eaten." (Joel 2:25), and He will do this when we put the whole situation and ourselves unreservedly and believingly into his hands. Not because of what we are but because of what He is. God forgives and heals and restores. He is "the God of all grace. Let us praise Him and trust Him.

As I continued to reflect on these words, I tried to remind myself that everything laid in God's hands.

I mentioned before how angry Ron became at the notion of long term treatment. Looking back, Brooks and I both realize that this was more fear and insecurity talking than anything else. Up to that point, Ron had never really been away from home for an extended period of time. Even as a child, he never strayed far from home for fear of somehow getting lost.

Finally came the time when we knew we had to intervene. Late one night, around two in the morning, we heard Ron downstairs in the kitchen fixing him a snack. Brooks and I got out of bed, made our way down to the den, and waited until he was finished.

As Ron walked passed us, we asked him to sit down. Then we started our intervention the best way we knew how. We confronted him with all his irrational behavior and his inability to pay his bills. We told him point blank that he was out of control and that we would no longer be able to help until he started to help himself. To make sure he got the message, we told him we were going to have his car repossessed-and that he could no longer live with us unless he got help.

Then we presented him with hope, just as we had learned. We assured him that we believed in him and believed that he could over-come his addiction, if he was willing to do the work.

It was the hardest thing Brooks and I had ever done, and it didn't go well at all. All Ron did was stare coldly at us for the longest time before he finally mustered a reply.

"Do you honestly expect me to go halfway across the United States?" he asked in anger. "NO WAY!" Then he stormed up the stairs and slammed the door to his room in disgust.

I didn't sleep very well that night. I kept replaying the conversation and wishing that somehow it could have gone better. The more I thought about it, the more depressed about it I became. This was our opportunity, perhaps our *only* opportunity to help our son, and I was convinced we'd blown it.

The next morning I was supposed to meet with my prayer group for our monthly session together. As badly as I wanted to be with them, I just had to cancel.

I was too weak to even pray.

A few hours later, Brooks and I went upstairs to check on Ron. He was still asleep. We woke him up and handed him the card with the phone number to the Shoulder. "When you're ready to make your decision," I said, "this is the number to call." Then we went back to the kitchen.

Next thing we knew, Ron was on the phone talking to someone in the Intake Department.

Brooks and I looked at each other with pride and relief. As I mentioned before, with any long-term treatment facility, the patient not only must go willingly, he must also apply for admittance himself. That, and only that, proves that he is serious about fighting for his recovery. The fact that Ron picked up the phone and made the call was the first real sign of progress.

By mid-afternoon, he had packed everything he owned and was on a flight to Houston, Texas. It was the 8th of December, 1985. It would be the first time Ron would spend Christmas away from home. A few years later, at the testimony he gave before the congregation at Mount Harmony Baptist Church, he said it "was not like it was me picking up my feet to get on that plane-it must have been the Lord." He recognized then and there that it was the power of prayer.

When Brooks and I returned from the airport, the first thing I did was call my prayer partners, as well as the director of New Vine Fellowship.

"Praise the Lord!" the director exulted. "God will restore the years the locust hath eaten."

As I had been reciting that verse in the *Streams in the Desert* devotional daily, I continually claimed that promise from God's word for Ron's life.

* * * * * * * *

The Shoulder was a sizeable treatment center with facilities for 300 patients (or "clients," as they were known). One building housed 200 men, while approximately 100 women had quarters in another. The program lasted one year, though some patients were allowed to stay on longer if necessary to continue their fight against addiction. Like many long-term programs, The Shoulder knew it took more than 30 days to lose control of your life, and it would take more than 30 days to take it back. You can learn all the tools in the course of the year, but recovery is ultimately a process that requires a lifetime commitment.

Ron thrived at first, sticking with the "winners" in the program and learning from their example. Within three months, he was promoted to Intake Supervisor. His main responsibility was to interview each client by phone and as well as when they arrived. Because some addicts might end up in jail before reaching their bottoming-out point, he was also required to spend some time going to the courtroom to evaluate prospective clients to determine whether they were for the program at the Shoulder. During this time, Ron also worked closely with the director of the facility, Lynton Ellisor, a deeply spiritual man who took Ron under his wing.

There is a scripture verse that says, "Train up a child in the way he should go, and when he is old, he will not depart from it." *(Proverbs 22:6)* How many times have people, for whatever reason, let the roots of their spiritual upbringing wither away, only to somehow bring them back to life later on? That was certainly the case with Ron. As part of the daily structure, clients at the Shoulder participated in Bible studies and regular gatherings of group prayer. It was during this time that Ron's spiritual life began to take root again.

As it happens, Lynton Ellisor was an accomplished pianist and soloist with a deep love for traditional Gospel hymns. It was Lynton's music that particularly drew Ron closer to God and rekindled his faith from long before. He began studying the Bible again and growing stronger in his faith. And though he would relapse time and again in the years to come, Ron would never totally lose sight of God again. No matter how many times he stumbled, he always found strength through prayer to continue "walking the walk" (as he liked to put it) throughout the rest of his life.

While at the Shoulder, Ron regularly attended services at First Baptist Church in Houston. He liked the church community there, and at one point moved his membership there from his home church in Matthews. First Baptist Church was where Ron first heard a concert by Steve Green, the renowned Christian recording artist who has always used music as part of his ministry. Ron loved Green's music so much, he would later use one of his songs, "Household of Faith," when he married his second wife in 1990.

Brooks and I flew out to Houston for a visit in January 1986, a few weeks after Ron began his stay. Right away we saw evidence of our son's newfound spiritual life. While we were there Ron took us to the chapel, where he asked Lynton to play a medley of old hymns for us, including "The Lily of the Valley" and "What a Friend We Have in Jesus."

I sat there listening with tears in my eyes. In a profound way it was as though Ron had finally come home, and I immediately thanked God for that. The seeds we had sown in his youth by raising him in a Christian home and church may have scattered, but they were clearly not forgotten.

Though Ron took to his surroundings well early on, one aspect of rehabilitation proved difficult for him to accept. By and large, the rules of the Shoulder prohibited him from participating into recreation activities at First Baptist (or for that matter, socialize or even become acquainted with other members of the church) until after he completed the program. That was odd, considering that, like other clients at the Shoulder, Ron could go to movies and other kinds of group outings, and was also entitled to the occasional weekend pass. (If memory serves, the rationale behind this rule was that some clients might somehow take advantage of the good nature of church members who, not knowing any better, might find themselves conned, manipulated, or otherwise taken advantage of by the addicts. This, of course, would be more likely to hurt the clients, thus causing them to relapse, more than actually help them.)

Be that as it may, Ron knew from his youth that fellowship outside the church was also an integral part of the spiritual experience. In that respect it especially hurt him not to be able to participate in recreational activities with his fellow church members. As a result, that made him very lonely.

Ron's progress was also impaired once again by tragedy. My father Barney had been diagnosed with cancer a couple of years before Ron entered The Shoulder. His condition worsened in early 1986, to the point where he only had a few months to live. Because I had to help take care of Dad, Brooks and I could only go to Houston that one time before Dad finally died in June. Fortunately, Lynton allowed us to fly Ron home in April so that he could have one last visit with his "Paw-Paw."

I've talked before about how close Ron was to my dad. Only after Barney's passing did we realize just how close they were.

As outgoing as my father was with people, it wasn't easy for him to express the affection he had for his family. We knew he loved us, and that if he couldn't always say it in words, he would somehow show his love through the many little messages he conveyed through his hands. One example was planting and harvesting lots of vegetables for us during the summer. Another was to go flounder gigging at the coast and catch lots of fish. He would freeze them and later cook them outside on a gas burner. He did that all the time for family get-togethers. Also once a year, he would bring all his equipment over to Davis Steel and fried flounder for everyone at lunch time. He would just beam to see how everyone enjoyed them.

Like most kids, I suppose, I never really came to truly appreciate my dad until I became an adult. He really was a very unique person.

Barney was also private, at least in the sense that in those final months there was only one person he confided in. That person was Ron.

Ron was the only one that Dad talked to about dying. He otherwise never discussed it with any of us-not even Mother, other than a comment or two at the very end (and even that was more along the lines of giving her instructions as to his final wishes). In a way, God used Ron to have a prayer time with Barney during his visit home, and together they prayed for each other. And no matter how often Ron continued to struggle, he would always find strength and encouragement from the last words his Paw-Paw said to him that day: "Ron, keep on keeping on."

Keep on keeping on. This simple phrase would remain Ron's personal anthem throughout the rest of his life. He would always tell us how whenever he felt discouraged, "I can hear those words ringing out in my ears."

Still, it wasn't easy at first. Grieving over his grandfather without any family while also trying to rehabilitate him-self would ultimately be too much for Ron to take. Back home we had each other, but in Houston he was alone-and he simply wasn't strong enough to handle it. He became increasingly stressed out and easily discouraged, to the point where

I wanted to pull my hair out. I felt like I was never going to get out. I really felt locked in and was tired of being around drug addicts and alcoholics.

Finally, eight months into his rehabilitation, he decided he'd had enough. Ron headed out on a weekend pass and never headed back.

Needless to say, it broke our hearts to hear that he had quit. Ron had promised Brooks and I that he would stick it out for a year. He knew we would be disappointed, which no doubt accounts for his decision to remain in Houston rather than come home and face us.

CHAPTER TEN

Reaching the Bottom

Ron spent the next several weeks living on the streets of Houston. The city's economy had bottomed out, and the area where Ron found himself was as violent and dangerous as any in the United States. This was 1986, about the time crack cocaine first hit the streets there. Because crack was cheaper to buy, that made it readily available (and consequently, even more addictive) than cocaine. Up until this time people who used cocaine generally snorted it or injected it. Soon afterwards, though, addicts started to free-base crack.

I remember Lynton Ellisor, the administrator at the Shoulder, once mentioning crack to us. Brooks and I had known nothing about it at the time.

While in Houston, Ron

> *. . . saw everything imaginable. I almost died again. I experienced hunger for the first time in my life. REAL HUNGER!*
>
> *My family had a private investigator to track me down. I was taken to a homeless shelter. I could have something to eat, sleep there and at 6:00 a.m., they would vacate the place. I knew I was definitely a drug addict, totally out of control, and my life was completely unmanageable.*

Brooks and I decided not to go out to Houston ourselves, but with the help of the private investigator, we arranged for Ron to find treatment at a rehab center outside of Dallas called Slick Ranch.

An offshoot of PDAP (Palmer Drug Abuse Program), Slick Ranch offered a 12-step program for adolescents and young adults that was modeled after Alcoholics Anonymous. Based in Texas, New Mexico and Oklahoma, PDAP was co-founded by Bob Meehan, "The Father of Drug Intervention" and the author of the best-selling classic *Beyond the Yellow Brick Road*. A former addict himself, Meehan is renowned throughout the country for his continuing efforts in training counselors and helping parents who want to keep their children off drugs.

Once Ron began the treatment program, though, Brooks and I did go out to visit him in Dallas. At this time we were able to learn more about the program (Slick Ranch was the only treatment center we did not locate and investigate for ourselves). Most times like this, it was a matter of life or death.

Ron successfully completed the program at Slick Ranch and came home chemical free in December 1986. He went back to his old job at Davis Steel and had every intention of moving on with his life. He'd go to work, come home, watch TV with his Dad, and go back to work the next day. Beyond his family and an occasional AA meeting, he saw no one and rarely left the house. He was so mindful of the mess he'd made of his life and the impression he left on the community, it was as though he was afraid to go out on his own for fear of using again.

He did manage to make it through Christmas, though. Christmas was always Ron's favorite time of year, and somehow, someway he just had to buy presents for everyone in the family. Remember, he had spent the previous Christmas away from us at the Shoulder in Houston. I'll never forget him calling that year and telling me about this guy he'd met who had no family. Always a soft touch, Ron insisted that I use some of the money I had planned on spending on him to buy this man some boots for the winter.

Finally after the holidays, he did go back to church with us... but he never felt comfortable around people in the community. They walked on egg shells, not knowing what to say. Ron tried to be brave about it, but deep down we knew he was struggling. Things were not going well at all.

It was at this point we thought of Bethel Colony of Mercy in Lenoir, North Carolina, a Christian-based treatment center run by a Baptist minister named Paul Ritchie. This was a place Brooks and I had first come to know about a year before, during a weekend retreat we attended at Mount Harmony Church. One of the speakers at that retreat was Dr. Clifton Wood, a staff counselor from Calvary Church, a large, spirited, non-denominational church located in Charlotte. This was a time when we were grasping at straws, desperately seeking answers that could help us help our son. With nowhere else to turn, I called Clifton after the retreat, and it was during that conversation that he told us about Bethel Colony of Mercy.

A short while later, Brooks and I visited Bethel Colony of Mercy and came away impressed by the spirit that was so evident there. We knew in our hearts it was the perfect environment for Ron. Brooks even went so far as to say, "I'm not an addict, but if I had the time, it would be a wonderful place to go for two months of Bible study."

That was in 1985. Never in my wildest imagination would I have thought that nearly 20 years later, Brooks and I would be members of the same church where Clifton Wood worships. (While Mount Harmony Baptist Church will always be part of our lives and our hearts remain with the ministry and community there, for personal reasons we decided to seek a new place to worship in 2000. After looking around and attending services at a few other churches, we settled on Calvary Church. Once we first took part in the Sunday service, we found Calvary to be a warm, friendly and inspiring place to worship.) We will always be grateful for Clifton and the role he played in our lives, leading us first to Bethel, then later meeting up with him at Calvary Church.

Yes, indeed, God works in mysterious ways.

* * *

Clifton Wood led us to Bethel Colony in 1985, but we knew we'd have to wait until the time was right to approach Ron about it. One year later, with Ron once again struggling without the right kind of support, Brooks and I knew it wouldn't be long before he went down the same path he'd been on so many times before. Perhaps the time had come to talk to him about Bethel.

Ron flatly refused-a decision that did not completely surprise us. He said that he preferred to try AA instead over the confines of yet another controlled environment. While he knew he needed help, he simply believed there had to be another way of finding it without entering another long-term treatment program:

> *My parents wanted to send me to another rehab, but I knew I had to take action. I was becoming a treatment burnout. I knew I needed a complete change and the support of AA. I knew AA worked and had seen the results in other people's lives. It didn't work for me in the past because I wasn't willing to get honest and I didn't work the simple program.*

Remembering a young man named Jon Swickard, a recovering addict from Rancho Santa Fe, California with whom he rehabbed at Slick Ranch in Dallas (and whose family immediately took to Ron when he came out west for a visit), Ron gave the Swickards a call. Besides Jon, Jim and Nancy Swickard also had a daughter who had struggled with addiction. Ron knew that the whole family had been deeply involved with AA and Al-Anon, and that those programs had helped their daughter turn around. Ron told Jim and Nancy that he was not doing well here in Charlotte, so they suggested that he catch a flight out to their house immediately and live in their guest house. He could go to AA, find a good sponsor, get a job, and hopefully move on from there.

Brooks and I weren't quite sure that was the best decision. But we had also seen firsthand how he struggled outside of treatment whenever he completed a program. What mattered most was that he was willing to try, and that we supported his efforts. (As it happend, Ron would eventually give Bethel Colony a try in 1988.)

* * * * *

Jim and Nancy Swickard loved Ron. Brooks and I will never forget the kindness and compassion they extended to him. They took him into their home at a time when their own son, Jon, was back on the streets again.

The Swickards helped Ron get established in an AA group, and they helped him find a sponsor. For those who are not familiar with AA, a sponsor is a person who has achieved long term sobriety: someone that you can talk to when you find yourself struggling, someone that you can hold yourself accountable to.

Once he was settled, Ron landed a job as a salesman at a BMW dealership. At first he thrived in his new environment. He sold three cars his first week on the job, and the Swickards treated him well at home. They took Ron on weekend trips in their motor coach to Mexico and treated him as if he was their own son.

But as the weeks went by, I could detect the ache of loneliness in his voice every time he called. He became increasingly despondent, and unfortunately he wasn't strong enough to handle it on his own. Brooks and I felt that it was only a matter of time before he stumbled once again and reverted to that same old pattern from childhood: insecurity, lack of patience with himself, and an inability to stay focused. Unfortunately, our suspicions were true, as Ron himself explained in his journal:

> *After a while, loneliness set in and the rest is history repeating its cycle. My cycle has been I have not been willing to lower my ego and take direction.*
>
> *I would be too impatient to give myself time, especially in a relationship.*
>
> *I couldn't seem to stay focused.*
>
> *I had been very lonely since my wife and I split up and instead of giving myself time to recover and being honest with myself, I would run for a quick fix and use cocaine.*

As I said, the Swickards were truly wonderful people. But once they realized that Ron did not come home one night-which they knew from their experience with their own children was an instant danger sign-they knew what they had to do:

I went out one night and when I came home, I found my quarters to their guest house locked and my clothes setting outside. This family was wonderful to me, treated me like their own son, but they knew how to practice tough love.

With nowhere else to go, Ron ended up on the streets of San Diego. He stood in food lines and otherwise scrounged for food wherever he could find it. It was only by the grace of God that he lived and survived this experience.

Occasionally he would call home and ask for money. As painful as it is to say this, we had to tell him no-not until he reached bottom, not until he was honest with himself and realized that he needed help. I'll never forget sitting down to eat, knowing that he was somewhere out there hungry. . . I would get weak and nauseous, and I felt that my heart would break.

At some point, a stranger took him in and called us. I will not even attempt to describe the horrible details. I'll leave that for Ron:

I slipped to an even lower bottom. I went wild with cocaine on the streets of San Diego. I was around a lot of insane situations. The disease started taking a toll on me physically and this time it was noticeable. I almost died on the streets again. My automobile was taken and I got cut up badly and taken to the emergency room. I went to another homeless shelter where I felt hopeless and left, back to the streets after I got rested up. From there, I went to a halfway house that was [run so poorly and ineffectively, it was] a joke.

[I was so despondent, I felt] I was going to die and was willing to try anything.

At that point Brooks and I felt Ron was ready to surrender for help, so we flew out west to search for another place to take him for help.

This was a hopeless, heartbreaking situation. There was no way we could bring Ron home in that condition, but we knew of no place in California where we could take him, either.

Fortunately, God once again saw to our needs. We got in a

car and just drove and eventually wound up at Schick Treatment Facilities at Long Beach Hospital, a few hours north of San Diego. Brooks and I got Ron admitted there, flew home to Charlotte, and returned two weeks later at the end of the program.

At Long Beach Hospital, their idea of treating addiction was to make the addict so sick of drugs or alcohol that he would never try them again. It was an innovative approach which Ron had never seen before. But he would find that it just didn't work, not without the support of any friends or family. Yet at the same time he refused to go back to Charlotte. He kept insisting, "I must walk the walk before I go home." He knew he had already disappointed a lot of people, and his self esteem was at about its lowest ebb.

Brooks and I again felt helpless, but clearly Ron had made up his mind. We spent some extra vacation time with Ron, sightseeing, going to movies and simply spending time with him. Ron seemed so grateful for that. It was during times like these that, even though things were nowhere near what anyone of us wanted them to be, we were developing a close bond and a deeper respect. So we helped him rent a small furnished apartment at Huntington Beach. Brooks flew home while I stayed out west for a week to help Ron get settled as he also looked for a job.

I'll never forget how apprehensive I felt the day Ron took me out to the airport. We had talked the night before, and he sat there with the most serious, forlorn look on his face I had ever seen. He was scared because he knew I was going home the next day. And he said, "Mom, I'm fearful, but I think it's a good kind of fear." And what he meant by that was, "I'm fearful enough that I won't ever use drugs again."

As much I wanted to believe in him, I just knew this wasn't going to work. Ron knew absolutely no one in Huntington Beach. In my heart I was afraid it would be only a matter of time before he was using again. But we had done all we could do. We knew we just had to leave it in God's hands.

That morning before he drove me to the airport, I gave Ron some spending money-which, by the way, is something you should only do with great discretion. "Tough love" reminds us that if you're not careful, giving the addict money may end up "enabling" his addiction, instead of helping him try to stop it.

Ron put some of the money in his billfold and taped the rest underneath the drawers of his dresser. Then we left for the airport.

I cried silently on the airplane all the way home, feeling so sad and totally helpless.

One night in the middle of the night, I had this terrible dream and sat up in bed. Something was telling me, *"If you want to see your son alive, you must go to him now."*

The next morning, Brooks and I flew out to Los Angeles, rented a car and drove out to his apartment in Huntington Beach. We arrived to the most pitiful looking sight I had ever seen.

I had a key to the place-I mean, I always had sense enough to have an extra key made for myself to wherever Ron was staying-but knocked on the door first. An older man answered the door. Apparently he had been sleeping on the sofa. He led us inside, and to our horror, the entire apartment had been stripped clean. He mentioned that drug dealers had taken everything-the TV, stereo, even simple things like green plants. All we had purchased to help him get settled was suddenly taken away.

Meanwhile, Ron laid there quietly on the bed, weak, sick, and depressed to the point where he no longer cared. The moment we both had long dreaded had finally arrived. Our son had hit bottom.

This time, it was an even lower bottom, which was going to be death. If my parents hadn't intervened this time, I would have died. I had lost all hope, no self esteem whatsoever. One thing this time, my ego had been crushed to crumbs.

I was bankrupt on life. I was a broken person totally. I had filed Chapter 11 in life. I admitted I was powerless over people, places and things and that my life was totally unmanageable.

Ron could barely sit up on the side of the bed. There was not one particle of food, nor anything to drink in the apartment. We had thought to stop and pick up some fast food and drinks. He ate like he was starved. We gave the man something to eat and he left. We slept in the living room and stayed a night before we could move him, and then we had to take him by the emergency room of a hospital for some antibiotics. We drove south to Dana Point and got one motel room, where all we could do was feed him, give him the medication, and wait until he got strong enough to take him somewhere else. Some places do not have medical facilities to detox patients, so we had to take care of this ourselves by keeping him in a controlled environment. Neither of us left at the same time, but one would go for food and bring it back to the room. We did what was necessary and kept him surrounded until he was detoxed.

Brooks and I were grateful to have each other. It would have been very difficult for one person to handle a situation like this, because if left alone, while going through withdrawals, Ron probably would have bolted, even if it were on foot. We had to stay in this motel room for several days, and our first attempt to move him failed. He was still too sick.

I cannot even remember how we found out about Rancho L'Abri, a 60-day treatment program out from San Diego. Ron said that God protected his mind from secular psychology in places like this, and he was ridiculed and called a Southern gentleman. When he left this program, he insisted on stopping off in Houston to see the administrator and a couple of other guys on the staff.

Ron finally returned to Charlotte in October 1987. He once again resumed working at the family business and went to our church minister every week for counseling.

That Christmas, he wrote Brooks and I each a special letter which we still cherish to this day. This is what he wrote Brooks:

Dear Dad,

I pondered a long time on what to give you this year and it came to me what you would want more than anything else in the world. I got down on my knees and decided to let it go. It would be much easier to go out and buy a cheap gift. I'm working on my third step (12 steps of AA) with the pastor. It's been the hardest, but with help and a lot of prayer and a long time coming, it's finally here. I'm turning my life and will over to the care of God through the Lord Jesus Christ.

As you know, a lot of things have happened on the eighth day being the day of change. This new year being 1988, being no coincidence sums it up. It's a real task to write this letter, as you know, it's not one of my better traits. I've also decided to move my church membership back to Mt. Harmony and I'm going up for rebaptism. It's easy to let the devil come in and start feeling sorry for myself, when I think of how the lessons I've had to learn had to be such hard ones. I want this to be the best Christmas we ever had and I want you to know words can't express how much I love you and appreciate you.

With love on December 25, 1987
Your son, Ronnie

CHAPTER ELEVEN

"Grateful for My Addiction"

In March 1987, four months after he returned home from his rehabilitation in California, Ron felt it was important that he speak
publicly about his addiction while also rededicating his life to Christ.
He even asked me to take him out to the Upper Room at PTL in
nearby Fort Mill, where there were ministers on staff 24 hours a day,
and arranged for one of them to pray with him and anoint him with
oil. Ron believed in his heart that this would give him the strength
he'd need to finally free him from his addiction to cocaine. In the
days leading up to his testimony, he prayed for deliverance with a
seriousness and intensity Brooks and I had never seen before.

At the Sunday morning worship service on March 8, 1987, Ron
stood before the congregation at Mount Harmony Baptist Church
and gave his testimony. He had asked his friend Lynton Ellisor,
the Director of the Shoulder in Houston, to join him that weekend
for moral support, as well as to share the beautiful music that had
touched Ron at the Shoulder. Besides giving two musical concerts at
the church that day (one at the morning service, followed by another
in the evening), Lynton also gave a few words about his work at the
Shoulder. Then it was time for Ron to speak:

*My name is Ron Davis. I grew up in this community. I went
to church here-only it wasn't this church. It was just this
building. And in a way, that really pleases me. You see, for a*

long time I had Christianity and religion and a lot of things mixed up. I was a back sliding Christian. But as I look back on it now,

I really don't know if I was a Christian or not because I really didn't have a personal relationship with Christ back then. And today, I do.

I'll tell you, the devil has done everything imaginable to keep me from standing here in front of you today. From four or five life attempts, to the syndicated drug world, to two overdoses under the bondage of cocaine, and things I can't even mention. . . it's been unreal.

I'm a miracle. Only by the grace of God can I stand up in front of you today.

I'm just thankful for today, for life-I'll never take another day of life for granted again. And I'm thankful for this community and for all the "prayer warriors" that prayed for me when I couldn't pray for myself.

I am grateful for my addiction to cocaine because it brought me to my knees.

And I know a lot of you can't understand that. But I'm really grateful for it.

I went to four drug and alcohol treatment centers. The first two, I just came out an educated drug addict and a better con than I was when I went in. I had it up here in my head, but I didn't have it down here in my heart.

And then I went to the Shoulder-I don't know how I got there. I mean, when I stepped on the plane, it wasn't even my feet picking myself up and moving. I met Lynton Ellisor there, and later on I became part of the staff at the Shoulder, and worked for Lynton as Assistant Administrator and Intake Supervisor there at the Shoulder.

Things didn't even come completely together then. But what I had gotten from the Shoulder finally hit me. And everything in the world is looking up.

I don't know how to explain it to you. But I had to step up here today. I wasn't free until I put my foot up on this stand. But I know it's going to be okay now, I'm telling you. Maybe in time, I'll have time to share my story-how it was before, how it was then, and how it is now. I'm just lost for words now. I don't know what to say, other than I'm taking this stand today for Jesus Christ, and not for me.

There are a lot of other things that went along with addiction of cocaine. One on one, I'll be glad to share, but I'd have to pass the cotton out and put it in your ears to share the whole story. And the problem was me.

You see, I had an ego you couldn't fit in this church, and I had a self-esteem you could not see. I have had to humble myself and bail my ego, and I feel good about myself today.

I'm not worried about risking my reputation in this community or with anybody here. If my testimony can help one soul in this church, I'll be glad to take a stand because only by the grace of God and others' loving and caring and reaching out to me, do I stand here today. Like I say, the devil has thrown every obstacle in the world to keep me from coming up here today. And I didn't think I was going to make it. I've run from it. But I'm here. And I'm rededicating my life to Jesus Christ. I'm going to live for Jesus Christ.

After I left Houston, I went to Dallas for about three months before I came home. It was the first time in my life I was ever really persecuted for being a Christian. You know, I'm really proud of that. I'll stand up for my Lord and personal Savior any time. And I just praise God that I'm here and I praise God that you are here. I don't want to leave anyone out and start naming names, but I especially would like to thank my aunt Margaret, and Nonia Polk, and my brother Rick and Dana, and my mother and father, and Lynton, and my grandmother, and my grandfather-he hears me today. I just praise God. Thank you.

The church always recorded each Sunday service. I'm so glad I was able to get a copy of the tape of the morning Ron spoke. I cherish that tape even more now, because I have it to listen to his voice.

I wish I could say that he remained clean and sober from that day on, but unfortunately that wasn't the case. He would have to stumble yet a few more times before long-term sobriety came.

CHAPTER TWELVE

New Beginnings

Because Ron continued to struggle even after giving his testimony at church, Brooks and I thought the timing was right to approach him again about Bethel Colony, the Christian-based treatment center in Lenoir, North Carolina that we'd told him about the year before. Though Ron had refused to go the first time we spoke to him about it, we felt that after rededicating himself to Jesus he might be more receptive to the Bible Study, the Christian counselors and the wonderful program Bethel Colony had to offer.

Thankfully, our instincts were right. Ron contacted Paul Ritchie, the administrator in charge of Bethel Colony, and got on their waiting list.

In the interim, some missionaries with the Jungle Aviation and Radio Services (the world-renowned Bible translation service better known as JAARS) approached Ron at church and invited him to stay with them and do volunteer work at their headquarters in Waxhaw, North Carolina. Ron was excited by the idea. Waxhaw was not far from Charlotte, so he knew he'd be close to home. Plus he believed this would help support him in his efforts to stay sober. He even gave thought to working as a JAARS missionary in a foreign country in hopes of escaping drugs.

Unfortunately, it wouldn't be long before fear, loneliness, and anxiety would once again drive Ron back to cocaine. Once again, however, God intervened at just the right moment. On April 8, 1988,

Bethel Colony of Mercy called to say that they had space available to Ron. This time, he went willingly.

Ron loved the staff at Bethel Colony and did well in the program. On Mother's Day, Brooks and I visited him there and attended church in the small chapel on the grounds. Ron spoke at the service that day of how grateful he was to Brooks and I for never giving up on him. He also mentioned how thankful he was just to be alive, considering that the year before he had been alone in California, living on the streets.

As we left for home that day, Ron handed me a small book and said, "I went over to Fruitland Bible College with one of the guys here. I saw this book about the Book of Ruth in the Bible and thought you might enjoy reading it."

When we returned home, I immediately sat down and started reading the book. The very first sentence of the first chapter said:

It is no mistake that the book of Ruth is lodged lovingly as the eighth book of the Old Testament. It is a story of new beginnings.

It really surprised me to read that. Immediately I went back to some notes I had kept in my calendar. (I have kept all my desk calendars dating back to 1980.) Good thing that I did. To my amazement, this is what I discovered:

September 8, 1985. Ron left treatment in Pinehurst and went to Durham to find a job in order to be around support.

October 8, 1985. Ron came home on my birthday and stayed four weeks.

December 8, 1985. Ron left for the Shoulder in Houston, Texas.

August 8, 1986. Ron left the Shoulder after eight months.

September 8, 1986. Ron called home, saying, "I have hurt

long enough," and that he was ready for help. Soon afterwards he would go to Slick Ranch, Dallas.

December 8, 1986. Ron returned home and went back to work at Davis Steel.

March 8, 1987. Ron gave his testimony at Mount Harmony Baptist Church.

April 8, 1987. Ron telephoned us to say he was hired on a new job at Harloff BMW-Chevrolet in California. This was the first time he had to find a job on his own. Prior to that time, he had always worked for the family business.

May 8, 1987. Ron moved from the Swickard family's home.

July 8, 1987. Ron entered a California halfway house.

April 8, 1988. Ron is accepted at Bethel Colony of Mercy in Lenoir, NC.

I was amazed at how many significant events in Ron's life happened on the eighth day of the month. All of the events marked a beginning in one way or another.

I immediately called Ron to tell him what I had discovered. As we spoke, this verse from the Scriptures came to mind:

And on the seventh day, God ended his work, which he had made, and he rested on the seventh day from all of his work, which he had made.

Genesis 2:3. (KJ)

So in a way, the 8th is like a new beginning. At least, it has certainly been that way for Ron and me.

* * *

Ron stayed two months at Bethel Colony, and as I mentioned before, he did very well. But once the program ended, he felt he had nowhere to go but home, back to the same routine. Bethel did not promote AA, and since Ron had fallen so many times, he did not feel accepted at his own church in Matthews. So he stayed in Lenoir, rented an apartment and tried to make it on his own. Unfortunately, it wasn't long before he found himself lonely and struggling again. Next thing we knew, he was back in rehabilitation, eventually ending up at a halfway house called Jellinek Center in Knoxville, Tennessee. He stayed there for six months while working some in a small iron shop close by.

Ron would have to spend Christmas at Jellinek that year. As much as he loved the holidays, that was definitely hard, but he managed to make the best of it. I'll never forget on Christmas Eve, he was driving in his Blazer to pick up pizza for all of the men, when a girl ran a stop sign and hit his car. The woman had no insurance. Ron never told us about this until after Christmas, because he didn't want to spoil our holiday. The way he saw it, it was bad that his had already been spoiled.

Another facility where Ron would spend time during his struggles was Bethel Christian Home in Atlanta. He rehabilitated there on three different occasions. The director of Bethel was a recovered addict named Larry Owens. Larry and Ron became good friends-which was quite unusual, insofar as very few drug counselors allow themselves to become that close to a client. However, as Brooks and I were told many times by individuals in the various treatment centers where Ron rehabbed, our son was not your usual drug addict.

For one, as I mentioned before, most addicts either have no family of their own, come from a broken home or a home where a parent is an alcoholic. Ron, of course, came from a solid, loving family background. He also had a winsome personality and was caring and compassionate, always encouraging others to "keep on keeping on" wherever he went.

Just as important, Ron, like his grandfather Barney, was the kind of person to whom people naturally gravitated. Larry Owens told us all the time of how other clients were drawn to Ron because of his earnest nature, his good humor, and his fierce dedication to succeed.

"He would tell the others, 'Guys, we're not here because we won a trip to Disney World,'" Larry often said. "Then he would stare into them with his big, blue eyes, so that they knew he meant business."

Larry also told me that Ron led the Bible Devotions each morning at Bethel, which was something I did not know about. Larry also says that he still uses Ron's line about Disney World when he counsels addicts today. That's something I know would make Ron particularly proud.

A few years after Ron's death, Brooks and I would meet and become close friends with Ketta Guy, one of the drug counselors at Bethel. Ketta told us that Ron had a knack for bringing order in a group quickly whenever things got out of hand. She also pointed out what a gentleman he always was. If someone ever used bad language in Ketta's presence whenever she led the group, Ron would be quick to silence them.

It was while Ron was at Bethel Christian Home that the scripture Isaiah 40:29-31 became one of his favorites:

> He gives strength to the weary and increases the power of
> the weak. Even youths grow tired and weary, and young
> men stumble and fall.
> But those who hope in the Lord will renew their strength.
> They will soar on wings like eagles.
> They will run and not grow weary.
> They will walk and not be faint. (Isaiah 40:31) NIV

Ron loved to tell the story of how this scripture came alive in his heart while in treatment. He was doing his Bible study at Bethel while a nature program on television played softly in the background. At that particular time, he was once again experiencing all the guilt, shame, and remorse over the things he had done while on drugs, wondering, *"How am I going to go home again and face all my family and my community?"*

At that point in the TV program, the narrator began to explain how the eagle can sense a storm hundreds of miles away, and that it will "stick out its head, spread out its wings and soar above the storm."

Once again God made His presence known to our son at a time when he needed Him the most. It was as though God were saying, "Ron, I'll help you soar above the storm. All you have to do is just trust in me."

Ron called me immediately with a real sense of peace and shared this experience. This story meant so much to him that later on, a picture of an eagle hung in his home with that very scripture engraved on it. That same scripture would appear on his monument after his death.

Chapter Thirteen

Clean and Sober

After a five-year struggle in and out of treatment, Ron finally became chemical-free in 1990 and would remain that way for several years. Renewed in his faith, bolstered by a new marriage, and strengthened by the love and support of his family, Ron grew closer to Brooks and me than he had ever been before. These years would yield many of the happiest moments of his life-as well as ours.

Seeing Ron so happy is a joy we will never forget. In many ways, it really was like the story of the prodigal son that we all know so well from the Bible. Certainly when Ron was under the influence of drugs, he was like another person, someone completely different than the son we had raised. Now that he was free of his addiction, it was as though he had come home at last. We were all so grateful to have him back.

In 1990, Ron married a young woman named Melissa, whom he had met the previous year. Melissa and I would become particularly close. She often told me how she believed God used me to help her grow spiritually. I, in turn, have always thanked her for providing companionship to Ron. Also, she was a wonderful cook and home-maker, and their marriage was truly one of the things that helped his sobriety.

When my mother moved to a retirement center sometime after the wedding, she decided to rent her home to Ron and his bride.

The opportunity to live in his grandparents' house would bring Ron great peace and joy. One of his favorite pastimes was sitting on the porch in his grandfather's chair, reminiscing about the many fun times he spent with his "Paw-Paw" as he was growing up, as well as remembering "Maw-Maw's" home cooking. I especially remember the time he told me how he liked to lay in bed at night with the rain falling on the roof. That made him so grateful that he was not on the street with no place to go, and that he no longer had to con or manipulate people in order to feed his cocaine addiction.

Shortly after Ron and Melissa's marriage, they became interested in horses. Ron's childhood friend Danny was a great support in helping them get started, as well as providing moral support. Danny spent many hours helping Ron remodel his grandfather's old barn, where they were living. Later on, with the help of his dad, Ron built a nice barn for their horses on the back of the property where they lived. Brooks and I could see the barn from our house, and it brought us a lot of joy seeing Ron and Melissa having so much fun and enjoyment with friends. Later, Danny's brother Steve, who was a lifelong friend of Ron's, decided to buy a show horse. Together the three of them enjoyed horse shows, training horses and riding them as well. It was like old times for Ron, because he had enjoyed many fun times with Danny and Steve growing up in the same community, church and school.

Ron, Brooks, and I were especially close during this time. He would call me almost every day. We had many, many long conversations on the phone during this time, whether it was discussing a devotional, a scripture, or simply listening to him share his hopes and dreams for the future. It was as if we were both making up for the time we had lost during those years of little to no communication. Ron had grown to love and respect us in ways he had never shown before. He was never angry or bitter over the actions we had taken out of "tough love," because he recognized our actions had quite possibly saved his life.

Several months after Ron and Melissa got settled into my mom's house, they went with us to a convention in Boston. We had connecting rooms. One night I remember hearing them talking in the next room, only it didn't sound like a normal conversation. Being some-what concerned, I went over to the door and listened. I could not hear what they were saying, but it wasn't long before I realized that they were praying. That brought great joy to my heart. By that time, Ron had developed a very strong prayer life-in fact, shortly after their wedding, he and Melissa both rededicated their lives to Jesus Christ and requested to be re-baptized. What a blessing it was to witness his spiritual growth. We had the privilege of seeing him back in church every Sunday morning and Sunday night.

Ron not only returned to the church where he had worshipped as a child, he began teaching Sunday school to young boys every week. Children were likewise drawn to Ron because he was so utterly open and honest about his life. He wanted desperately for the youth of the community to learn from his mistakes and avoid the pitfalls of drugs-so much so, it was during this time that he made the following request to his father:

Dad, if something should happen to me during your lifetime, and I don't have a family of my own, I would like you and Mom to take whatever I have, and whatever is coming to me, and use it to help those who are hurting and struggling. Most especially, I would like a part in helping to build a gym where young people will have an ongoing Christian place for activities, and for others to have fellowship and a safe place to walk.

Unfortunately, Brooks and I would end up following through on this promise sooner than any of us could have imagined. In the months following Ron's murder, we indeed donated the money from his profit sharing at Davis Steel, his life insurance and some money he would have inherited to help construct a gymnasium on the grounds of Mount Harmony Baptist Church-a facility not far from the building where Ron taught Sunday school during his years of sobriety.

* * *

Sometime in 1991, Ron, Melissa, Brooks, and I went to see a concert by the Gaither Vocal Band. Bill and Gloria Gaither are two of the most renowned and successful artists in the history of Christian music. The Gaither's have written, composed, and produced countless gospel songs over the past 35 plus years and have won many honors, including four Grammy Awards.

It was just before this series of concerts that the Gaither's assembled some of the greatest Christian singers of all time to sing some of their old songs together. The meeting was so special that later they decided to make the video tape available to the public and titled it "Reunion." Bill and Gloria knew the occasion would be special, but they had no idea just how special it would be. This vast collection of talent weren't just making music. They were truly expressing God's love in song and His holy spirit was felt among them.

The Gaithers were so moved by this experience, they began a series of all-star "Homecoming" concerts that continue to this day. All of these shows are available on videotape, and they continue to inspire people all over the world.

The concert we saw that night was one of the first the Gaither's videotaped. Brooks and I purchased that tape, and have since collected more than 65 of the "Homecoming" videos. The stirring power of these songs would not only provide us with many hours of comfort and inspiration in the years ahead, they would particularly lift our spirits at the weeks following Ron's murder. We can truly say that with the many artists included on the tapes, you can find the music and song to minister to any need that you may have.

* * *

Also during all this time, Ron was back working at Davis Steel-this time in the capacity of assistant shop superintendent. This was a good job for Ron because it showcased his many people skills, a natural strength which he had put to good use on many occasions during his years in rehabilitation. Ron liked his new job, and it showed. As a matter of fact, Brooks has always said that the shop never ran any smoother than it did during the years in which Ron was assistant shop superintendent.

After two or three years, Brooks built another shop building near Davis Steel to handle the fabricating of rebars and wire mesh. This is the steel which holds the concrete together in the foundation of a building. It has to be detailed from the engineer's drawings, and then the shop can cut and bend as specified on the blue prints. The job is estimated for quantity and price for the bid that is offered to the contractor. Ron was promoted to Vice President of Steelco, Inc., a position which saw him run the business.

During this time, Ron was very protective of us. Almost every time we went out at night, he would always call to see if we had arrived safely.

One memory I'll never forget happened several years before his period of sobriety, during one of Ron's worst struggles with addiction. Brooks and I were asked to be directors of a steward-ship campaign called "Expecting a Miracle" at our church. At that moment, Ron was on the streets of California and we didn't even know exactly where. Our hearts were crying out, *"No, we cannot take that position, there's no way we could function and do the job."* But as we prayed about it, we felt in our hearts that God was telling us, *"Brooks and Jean, you serve me, and I'll take care of the rest."*

Four years later, as we were celebrating the victory of paying off the debt for the church building project, there sat Ron and his wife, chairpersons of a 24-hour prayer chain. Truly a miracle.

* * *

One time after Ron and Melissa were married, he went shop-ping for a new car: his very first one. Brooks had offered him a company vehicle, since many of the other employees drove one, but Ron declined, insisting that he needed to "do this himself" and make payments on his own. After shopping around some, he had his heart set on a red Chevy Blazer. When he went to test drive the car, he noticed it had exactly eight miles on the speedometer.

Knowing how significant the number "8" has been in our lives, he said to me, "Mom, this must be the car for me."

Later on, he would name his barn "Circle 8." The sign on the inside wall still hangs there as a memento.

* * *

Ron's years of sobriety were indeed joyful times, especially for Brooks and me, and we thank God for these wonderful memories that cannot be taken away. After struggling with his addiction for so long, life was on an even keel again, and it looked as though it would stay that way forever.

But recovery from substance addiction is a lifelong process-a process where the rate of relapse can be as high as 90%. Even the most inspiring of success stories is capable of relapsing at any time, for any number of reasons.

That's a bitter pill for any parent to swallow, as Brooks and I were about to discover.

CHAPTER FOURTEEN

Relapse is Part of the Recovery

Statistically, the rate of relapse for substance abusers is 75-90 percent, mostly due to a number of symptoms that make it difficult for a recovering abuser to achieve sobriety. One such symptom is post acute withdrawal syndrome, a bio-psycho-social syndrome that results from the combination of damage to the nervous system caused by alcohol and drugs and the psycho-social stress of coping with life without drugs and alcohol. The damage done to the brain from substance abuse leads to a chemical imbalance that can leave recovering addicts susceptible to relapse in moments of tremendous stress.

Medically speaking, post acute withdrawal syndrome accounts for Ron's continued relapses throughout the mid-1980s. It is also the reason for his setback in 1995 after several years of sustained sobriety.

As Brooks and I continued to learn more about addiction, we came to see that addiction is not a moral issue, but rather an illness: an ongoing battle that every addict wages, one day at a time, every day of his or her life. An expert on rehabilitation once told us that it takes seven years for the addict's body to return physically and mentally back to normal-that is to say, before he started using. Compounding the matter is the fact that addiction is progressive. With each relapse the addict does not "start over," as one might think, but instead picks up where he left off.

Some addicts manage to overcome their illness immediately, never to crave again. Others, like Ron, are not so fortunate and struggle constantly as a result.

The obstacles that plagued Ron as a child (fears, insecurity, short interest span, and a problem staying focused) became even more difficult to hurdle as he coped with his addiction as an adult. Because drug awareness is much more prevalent in our country than it was 20 years ago, parents have more information and resources at their disposal these days. If you feel your child has a problem with drugs or alcohol, there are places you can go and answers you can find that simply weren't available when Ron was young. To this day Brooks and I believe that with the right help and medication, we could have prevented a lot of his struggles when they first began to surface.

Relapse does not begin with the first drink or use of drugs. Relapse begins in a behavioral dynamic, which reactivates patterns of denial, isolation, elevated stress, and impaired judgment. You might call attention to the addict's mood swings, but there's not much you can do once you recognize the symptoms, unless the addict runs for support.

Here are some of the most common warning signs of relapse:

Apprehension about well-being. Fear and uncertainty about the ability to stay sober.

Compulsive behavior. The tendency toward overwork and compulsive behavior in activities begins to appear. In Ron's case, this was particularly exhibited in the increasing number of hours he put into training his horses. What began more or less as a hobby became an obsession, one in which Ron set impossibly high expectations.

Impulsive behavior.

Tendency toward loneliness and isolation.

Tunnel vision. Focus entirely on one area in life, to the detriment of all others.

Depression, often manifested by habitual oversleeping.

Loss of constructive planning. When he wasn't using, Ron was always a very organized, detail-oriented person. Every day he would keep a list of important things to do and check them off when completed. Then all of a sudden, it was as if he didn't care as much about anything. All attention to detail would begin to subside.

Feelings of hopelessness, as if nothing can ever be solved. Ron's short interest span would kick in. He'd become discouraged at even the slightest problem.

Irritation with friends/social involvements.

Easily angered. Increasing episodes of anger, frustration, resentment and irritability, which fueled Ron's level of stress and anxiety.

Irregular eating habits. Would begin overeating or under eating, often skipping meals altogether and binging on junk food. Tremendous appetite, eating continually when coming off drugs.

Listlessness. Inability to concentrate, anxiety and severe feelings of apprehension. With Ron, it was often a vicious cycle. He would often feel rushed, overburdened and overwhelmed, as if he didn't know what to do, when in fact he probably did. But because of his dependence on drugs, he was unable to follow through and take the steps he needed to take to overcome his feelings of tension, frustration, fear or anxiety.

Progressive loss of daily structure/Irregular sleeping habits. Daily routines would become haphazard. Regular hours of retiring and rising disappeared. While using cocaine, not eating or not sleeping for several days. Coming off of a cocaine binge, Ron would crash and sleep for several days.

Irregular attendance at support groups or attending church.

Periods of deep depression. Depression became more severe, more frequent, more disruptive and longer in duration.

Development of an "I don't care" attitude, masking a feeling of helplessness and extremely poor self-image.

Open rejection of help.

Self-pity.

Thoughts of using drugs or social drinking, hoping that it would alleviate many of the feelings and emotions he was experiencing. He may feel as though he is faced between feeling hopeless or returning to drugs. This is again a vicious cycle. Once the addict seeks comfort in drugs or alcohol, he deludes himself into thinking that perhaps he could use again provided he does so in a controlled fashion.

Constant lying, deception and conning.

The kind of friends they are associating with.

Always asking for money. Either the addict never has any money, or will pawn personal items for money and spend it immediately on drugs.

Appearance. Ron was usually neat and clean, a perfectionist about how he dressed. When he was on drugs, however, his unkempt appearance was evident. Sometimes we could tell he was using by looking at the pupils of his eyes.

Lack of accountability, promising faithfully to be back home at a certain time or to be at work the next day, but when the time comes, he doesn't follow through.

Complete loss of self-confidence. Feelings of not being able to get out of the trap no matter how hard he tries.

Loss of control, eventually resulting in the resumption of using drugs or alcohol.

* * *

We also discovered through our experiences with Ron that the loss of control in relapse is generally influenced by three factors:

Psychological factors, such as the level of emotional stress, the general attitudes a person has about himself, life, and other people, the strength of denial systems, and the strength of the person's self-image;

Physiological factors, such as the individual's tolerance level to drugs or alcohol, the stage of addiction, and the presence of other related illnesses which may affect tolerance, overall nutritional balance as well as levels of fatigue; and

Situational factors, including the intensity of stress situations, the number of social support systems for continued sobriety, and the number of influences toward continued using or drinking.

That's why it's important for a recovering addict to stay involved in a support group. If another former addict sees signs of relapse in your behavior, he or she won't hesitate to call you on it, because they've been there before. They can help you in ways that other people can't, because they know exactly what you're going through.

Ron certainly knew that. I mentioned how good he was in helping others in their struggle to overcome addiction. He was caring and compassionate, having experienced all the pain of his own addiction. In fact, sometimes he spent so much time helping other people that he forgot to take care of himself.

Still, Ron was able to help a lot of people during his years of sobriety, as well as later on. There were times at work when he and Brooks met with a salesman whose own son was on drugs. They spent hours talking to this man and praying with him for his son's recovery.

There was another time in which Ron and a friend of his who worked at Davis Steel suspected that another employee of the company was relapsing. They left work in the middle of the day and went to the man's home, only to find that he was preparing to take off somewhere and not come back to work. They intervened and brought him back to work. Ron kept the guy's car and keys. The friend let him stay at his house, transporting him back and forth to work for a week, until his family could get him back in a program at Bethel Colony of Mercy in Lenoir, North Carolina.

Ron knew every manipulation and excuse an addict used in order to find drugs to satisfy the craving. He'd heard them all, because he'd used them all himself.

The first several days of withdrawals can be sheer torment. Unless you're in a controlled environment, without any way of leaving, the craving will overpower you. So many times Ron had to be detoxed medically before he could enter another treatment facility, especially the ones that offered no medical attention.

I mentioned before how Ron had become interested in horses. He bought a paint horse and a quarter horse, while Melissa had also bought a horse of her own. They dedicated themselves completely to those horses, always making sure they were well-equipped and well-fed. Ron bought a brand-new horse trailer, along with a nice big truck to tote them in. He and Melissa put in a lot of time and work into caring for the animals and keeping their barn immaculate.

One of Ron's horses was a quarter-horse named C-50. He had paid a lot of money to a trainer and was led to believe that C-50 was going to be a big winner. Brooks and I went to several horse shows with Ron and Melissa, including one in Columbus, Ohio. Ron's trainer had C-50 there. It was a big disappointment-the horse did not show well at all.

As you can imagine, one horse (let alone, three) is a serious investment of time and money. To finance the deal, Ron and Melissa took out a loan from the bank. They always managed to pay their bills, but between their bank payments, the trainer's salary, and their other monthly payments, they never seemed to have any money left for anything else. That troubled Ron immensely. He had always been good about managing his money, especially during this period of sobriety. It wasn't long before the financial strain and feelings of discouragement finally took its toll.

We'll never forget the day it happened. Ron and Melissa were planning a barbecue at their barn for the Sunday School class that weekend. Ron came by the house briefly that night-he was supposed to be on his way to the caterer's to pay for the barbecue. I could tell from the moment I saw him that he was once again at the end of his rope. He just rode on off and did not go back home. Melissa called us about midnight. Ron had never failed to come right away whenever he ran an errand. You can imagine how sick we were in the pit of our stomach. Ron had relapsed once again.

Fortunately, Brooks and I intervened quickly and got him back on his feet in a couple of weeks. Ron and Melissa agreed to go for counseling, and they managed to hold things together for another year.

Then it happened all over again, this time so bad that Ron could never forgive himself. Before long, he would lose everything: his marriage, his horses, and worst of all, his self-esteem. All he could feel was embarrassment, especially after having gained back his reputation in the community where he had lived his entire life. *Now he was wrestling with the same old thing his father and I used to wrestle with: What do other people think of me? What are they saying?*

Loss of control can and generally does occur in every relapse, and usually manifests itself with one or more of the following symptoms: *irrationality, confusion, daze, poor judgment, inability to initiate action, bizarre behavior, physical unconsciousness, toxic psychosis, stupor and delirium, total inability to concentrate, progressive physical debilitation* and finally, *blackout.* There is a growing body of evidence that these symptoms are physiologically induced by the toxic effects of alcohol or drugs on the brain and central nervous system.

117

Once a total loss of control is manifested, outside intervention is generally required to interrupt the relapse. Effective intervention may require hospitalization or close supervision with massive support.

In intervening, a doctor once told Brooks and me that the addict's mind is like a window: you must catch him when it is open or the next thing you know, it is shut and there is no reasoning.

You must educate a person or family about relapse and necessary intervention techniques, as well as the early signs of relapse. Equally important, you must help the addict realize that he or she is in no way a failure for relapsing. As the statistics show, relapse is indeed part of the recovery.

* * *

Experiencing a loved one relapsing is like being dropped off a ten-story building. There is no way to describe the pain, horror and irrational behavior that is taking place right before your eyes. After watching Ron slowly lose everything he had worked so hard and long to build, Brooks and I once again had to work through the conning and manipulative behavior he would exhibit in order to feed his addiction.

I talked briefly before about blackout periods, those times when Ron would do things that later he wouldn't even remember. I don't see the benefit of going into specific details, other than saying they concerned matters that we would all like to forget. Once the addict is back on his feet and receiving treatment for his illness, the guilt and shame he feels once he does remember what he did during his blackout is almost always too painful to bear.

I remember one time back in the '80s, before Ron's years of long time sobriety, Brooks and I were driving him back home from treatment. He was sitting quietly in the back seat when he suddenly asked Brooks to pull over. We had no idea what this was about or what he was going to do. I'll admit, I thought the worst: for a moment, I was afraid he was going to get out of the car and run.

Fortunately, I couldn't have been more wrong. The minute Brooks pulled over, Ron reached up to the front seat with one arm around each of us and cried like a baby, telling us how much he loved us, and also how thankful he was that we never gave up on him. He had witnessed others in treatment whose families had given up on them.

That is one of the few times we had ever seen Ron cry. He had maybe shed some tears before, but never really cried. Later on, though, one of his counselors would tell us that Ron had grieved many times over the pain he had caused us over the years.

Around the time of one of Ron's relapses, I had a serious accident that required surgery: I fell and broke off a third of my knee cap. Because our house at the time had a lot of stairs and no downstairs bedroom, we had to rent a hospital bed for me to sleep on once I came home from the hospital. I lay suffering with pain, unable to get up or do anything without help-even going to the bathroom. Brooks would put out the bed pan where I could reach it during the night. My first night back from the hospital, I felt so helpless and distraught that I lay crying all night. Brooks, being upstairs, knew nothing about this, even though he had a monitor turned on in his room in case I called out for something. I sobbed softly, feeling nothing but despair, knowing that Ron was running rampant on drugs and that there was no way he could get off them until he went back to a treatment facility for help. He was still living at my mother's house at the time, which made it all the more painful to deal with. He was so close, and yet so far away. All I could do was lay flat on my back, feeling even more helpless than ever.

And yet, once again, God provided. I'll never forget how I felt the following morning at the first sign of the sun rising. Suddenly there came to me a song by Andre Crouch. It was as though it were coming as vibes from my throat: *Through it all, through it all, I learned to trust in Jesus, I learned to trust in God.*

At that moment, I felt a peace inside like calm in the midst of the storm. I knew God had given me that song to carry me through.

* * *

Sometime in 1995, Ron ended up back at Bethel Colony of Mercy in Lenoir, North Carolina. With the help and guidance of his friend Paul Ritchie, he was back on his feet in a few months' time.

But with his marriage over, and his horses and everything else that had been special to him gone once again, there was no way he could go back to his own community-not at that point, anyway. He knew from his own experience, as well as from talking to other recovering addicts, that sometimes you're not quite ready to re-enter society once you finish rehab. Sometimes you need a little extra transition before you're ready to take that next step.

Before he left Bethel, with the help of his friend Larry Bowman, Ron came up with a novel solution that would also help him piece his life back together once again.

CHAPTER FIFTEEN

A Three-Quarter House

One of the first things a substance abuser learns in rehab is how important it is to change their environment, as well as change their habits. With the help of drug counselors, and the encouragement of their fellow addicts, they practice these behaviors every day in a controlled environment. By the time they finish treatment and re-enter the real world chemical-free, they have all the tools they need to take back control of their lives.

That's the theory, anyway. For everyone like Ron, who always had a family ready to help him in the outside world, there are countless other recovering addicts who either are on their own or end up back on the streets. Without a support system to "keep them on their toes," these people return to their old environment and, inevitably, back to their old habits. That's one reason for the alarmingly high rate of relapse among recovering substance abusers.

But sometimes even coming back home isn't all that easy. That was certainly the case with Ron as he completed treatment at Bethel Colony in Lenoir.

Bethel did not promote the methods of AA. Rather, they encouraged their clients to reacclimatize themselves with their local church upon returning home and draw support from the fellowship of their community.

Unfortunately, even though Ron liked the program at Bethel and did very well there, he could not bring himself to go back home. He was so wracked with guilt and shame over his last relapse that he no longer felt welcome at his own church.

Let me clarify that. I don't mean to suggest that he would not have been accepted again into the Mount Harmony community. I believe in my heart he would have had he just given it a chance. It's just that when you've fallen from grace in the eyes of friends and family as many times as Ron had, you can't help but wonder whether people are ever going to accept you-especially when they walk on eggshells around you, as was often the case whenever Ron came back to the community before. People mean well, but when they treat you like a delicate object (instead of like a normal human being), they tend to do you more harm than good.

Ron had talked before of the need for additional transition after coming out of treatment. As helpful as it was for an addict to be surrounded by support in a controlled environment, it was somewhat frightening to step back into the real world. There needed to be an additional step available to those who weren't quite ready to re-enter society after completing treatment. Ron knew far too well that some addicts still need a controlled environment even after rehab: a place where they can live with others who had been through treatment, where they can find continued support in the outside world before they're ready to go it alone. This place would be one step removed from a halfway house. In a word, it would be a "three-quarter" house.

Together with his friend Larry Bowman, a recovering alcoholic whom he first met at Bethel, Ron opened The Christian Unity Men's Home in Lenoir, North Carolina-a community of recovering addicts where men could find healing and restoration in their lives through worship, discipleship and Christian support. Those who lived at the Home earned their keep by working in the outside world, while finding the structure and support they needed through their fellow residents.

Launching the Home was good for Ron, in that it showcased his exemplary people and organizational skills. Finding the house, restoring it, and getting the project off the ground presented Ron with a series of goals, each with its own challenges. He rose to the occasion every time.

Ron and Larry looked long and hard for a house, searching from sun up until sun down for what seemed like weeks, until they finally found a dilapidated two-story house on Broadway Street in Lenoir. They met with the owner and worked out a rental agreement. One Sunday, Ron invited Brooks and me, along with Larry's mom and aunts, over to Lenoir to share in their excitement and vision.

I must confess, it didn't look like much at first. The house had not been occupied in over five years, though from the looks of things (the weeds and the grass had grown as high as the front windows) it seemed much longer than that. The interior looked impossible to renovate. But the layout was perfect. It was a large two story house with enough bedrooms upstairs to accommodate twelve men. Downstairs, there was a sizeable living room with an adjoining sun room, dining room, and kitchen. There was also a large room suitable for an office, plus a small bedroom and bath suitable for a house manager. The house also had a large lawn out front and a spacious yard out back. With a lot of work and a little imagination, it had the potential to become a beautiful home.

With the help of volunteers from nearby Bethel Colony, Ron and Larry worked all summer to get the house in shape. They started cleanup in the yard, mowing, cleaning up debris and hauling it away. That was a tremendous task in itself. The interior needed painting and new carpeting, along with plumbing repair and other items that were not operating properly. Step by step, though, the house began to take on a new look.

Family and friends donated furniture, as did some of the local churches in the area. Ron had some furniture of his own which he moved there, along with a desk, file cabinet and other things for his office. Lenoir Rhyne College donated all the beds and mattresses. Ron financed everything with his own money. He used some money that Brooks and I had set aside for him, as well as income he was earning from the rent of his barn. He also used money that we had sent him for living expenses.

Larry had a home in nearby Granite Falls. With his two children fully grown and on their own, he was living alone, so he rented out a room to Ron during this time. Ron and Larry made a good team. Larry was quiet and shy, but good with his hands, and was particularly adept at carpentry and painting. Ron was more outgoing and a better organizer. They worked well alongside each other.

I made many trips to Lenoir that summer, volunteering my help in the furnishing and decorating. Ron was very pleased with the progress of the project and it helped to occupy his mind from the grief of all he had lost. Aside from a few material things, about the only thing he had to his name was his six-year-old Norwegian Elkhound, Samantha, which he had raised since she was a puppy. Ron loved that dog like nothing else. No matter what, Samantha was there for him, loving him when it seemed no one else did.

It brought Ron such joy to be productive again, working hard to accomplish his goals. He spoke often of how he felt the hand of God leading him every step of the way, bringing each task to completion. That gave him confidence, and with that confidence he began to dream big. "If this house goes well," he wrote in a journal from 1995, "then I know I can open another one.

Finishing the house up, preparing for the journey ahead, we had our first devotional together on the Christian life of hills and valleys. We reflect back on our deep valleys, but praise God; today we look down from the top of a large mountain seeing how deep the valleys have been. We look back up to Heaven praising God for our life of hills and valleys.

Ron and Larry's hard work culminated in August 1995, when the Christian Unity Men's Home opened its doors for the first time. They began with seven residents, along with a live-in house manager-a recovering addict who had worked at Bethel Colony in a similar capacity. Even though Ron and Larry lived (or perhaps more accurately, *slept*) off site, they worked many long hours at the Home, arriving in the early morning and usually leaving after their night sessions with the men.

After a few weeks of operation, they held an open house on the Sunday before Labor Day, 1995. This was a big day and quite an accomplishment. Parents of the residents, along with many friends and family members, came to support this great success. Paul Ritchie from Bethel Colony took part in the dedication ceremony and festivities of the day. Larry Owens from Bethel Christian Home had also hoped to attend, but was unable to do so at the last minute. He did, however, promise Ron that he'd come up and do some group therapy with the clients.

For Brooks and me, the highlight of the day was Ron's opening remarks, and how he thanked his family and friends over and over for coming to the dedication. It brought tears to my eyes when I looked around and saw what God had done through his and Larry's hard work and obedience. Ron talked openly and honestly, just as he always did, about his past and how excited he was about embarking on this new ministry. He had come to believe that his own struggles in and out of drug treatment had served to prepare him to help the lives of others who struggled with the pain of addiction.

The main thing I see in my life, whether you're a drug addict or an alcoholic, is that you have to get rid of self. Self-centeredness is a sin. When we put self before God, that's idolatry. And God is a jealous God. I put self before God,

I put horses before God; I put a lot of things in my life before God. And yet God has spared me. He has spared my life, and [has helped me grow] through that.

Self-centered people don't know where to draw boundaries. They don't know where they end and others begin.

That's what we try to do here [at the Christian Unity Men's Home]. We try to help the men, through God's Word and His truth, [learn how] to die to self, so that they can get rid of those old resentments of bitterness and anger and hurt and fear and jealousy, all those poisons that cause a man to go back out and definitely drink again.

Another key thing we emphasize here is balance. We are taught in Ecclesiastes about balance: "There's a time to plant and a time to harvest." We try to create a balance between worship, work and play. We encourage a man to find a church where he feels comfortable, where he can receive and nurture and are able to find that balance that God has for all of us in our life. We can neglect our family and church and work and all those areas-we can get them mixed up, and either work too much or be with family too much or even go to church sometimes when we really should be taking care of family. We can really get things out of kilter. And for an addict, balance is crucial. It certainly has been in my life.

You know, it's hard for a parent. They have to remove their hands, so that God can put his hands on us. It's hard for a mother and father to give up . . . and it's a fearful thing, to have to be able to take your hands off us so that God can put his hand on us. And that's the thing we deal with in families up here. We try to help put families back together, marriages back together. Through mine and Larry's experiences, God has prepared us and he will continue to [help us grow] in this ministry.

* * *

Unlike a traditional halfway house, residents had to earn their keep by finding gainful employment and paying a weekly rent. This way, by the time each man was ready to leave the Home, he will have established himself on the outside and learned how to live once again as a functioning member of society. Residents were also expected to make sure that each man pulled his weight and lived up to his end of the bargain. House rules and responsibilities were assigned and posted at the beginning of each week. The house was kept clean and neat, meals cooked, floors vacuumed and mopped every day.

Ron believed this built-in accountability would help the men in their fight to stay clean and sober. But he also knew it would benefit himself. It was exactly the sort of support a recovering addict needed before taking that final step and resuming life on his own.

Ron put a lot of thought into creating a structure for the residents (or "clients") that struck a balance between work, life, and prayer as they transitioned back into society. He arranged for a nearby temp agency to help the clients find jobs. He worked closely with the local churches to find the right environment for the residents to worship in. He also asked Larry Owens from Bethel to help counsel the families of the residents in their efforts to put their lives back together again.

Unfortunately, a number of early snafus would make Ron's

job as director all the more stressful. First, he had to fire his live-in manager a few weeks before the dedication when he discovered the man did not have a driver's license. While this may seem like a minor reason, it's hardly trivial once you realize that one of the manager's primary responsibilities was driving the residents to and from their jobs. Even more discomforting, Ron knew that the man had worked on staff at Bethel Colony for over two years-during which time the man was often entrusted with the responsibility of driving residents around the town in the Bethel van.

Then, slowly, other things began to go wrong. Some of the residents had problems holding jobs or couldn't pay their rent. Yet Ron couldn't bring himself to come down hard on them-he was much too compassionate for his own good. In fact, because he could not find it in his heart to turn anyone down, he allowed some men to reside in the house who were clearly not strong enough to face the challenges of living in a "three-quarter" environment.

One by one, they may have seemed like little things. But once you put them all in a row, they became like a bunch of dominoes. As soon as one toppled, the others tumbled down.

All in all, it proved to be way too soon for Ron to take on all that stress and responsibility. For these reasons and more, he would close down the Christian Unity Men's Home after only a few months of operation. Brooks and I settled affairs with the owner of the house, and arranged to have the furniture kept in storage until Ron had time to think about either reopening another house or donating the items to a suitable place.

Unfortunately, Ron would also have another drug relapse. He spent 30 days in a treatment program in Lexington, and another 30 days in a center in Winston-Salem, before finally enrolling himself at Caring Services, a long-term Christian-based rehabilitation center in High Point, North Carolina.

* * *

The failure of the Christian Unity Men's Home devastated Ron. And yet, even amid his despair, his capacity for helping others continued to shine through. It was not until after Ron's death that we discovered that the seeds sown through all this hard work were not in vain, and continue to be reaped and harvested to this day.

After rehabbing at Caring Services, Ron occasionally volunteered in their office. Through AA, he met a woman named Linda who lived in one of the halfway houses for women. She was a single mother from Chicago who was struggling with alcoholism. When she was ready to leave the halfway house, Ron not only helped Linda find an apartment, he also gave her some of the furniture that was once used at the Christian Unity Men's Home and shared his household items with her. (The rest of the furnishings were donated to Caring Services.) He also drove Linda to work each day, until she could afford to buy a car.

With Ron's help, Linda did indeed get her life back on track. Brooks and I didn't know at the time, but our son's compassion would yield an unexpected dividend for the both of us two years later. . . lifting our spirits and giving us hope in the months following his death.

CHAPTER SIXTEEN

Finding Help in Atlanta

By Christmas 1996, Ron was living in an apartment in North Wilkesboro. When he came home for the holidays that year, he presented Brooks with a bee hive that he had made while working with a friend and his family who made bee hives for sale and also sold honey. Ron loved Christmas, and he felt so good to be able to give his dad a gift that he had made himself. Little did we know that this would be Ron's last Christmas at home. Being an amateur bee keeper, Brooks has taken a lot of pride in the bee hive, and we occasionally enjoy honey from it. We have the bee hive on the back of our property today.

Still, Ron kept struggling with loneliness and despair. I would go up to see him and encourage him whenever I could. Brooks and I knew he was not doing well, but we really had done all that we could do. Even though we never gave up on Ron and Ron never gave up on himself, I honestly felt at that point that we had done all we could possibly do.

I don't say that lightly. As I mentioned before, it's never easy for a mother and father to completely let go and put their trust in God. It's never easy to demonstrate tough love, even when you know it's the right thing to do. We may have made mistakes along the way in learning how to handle Ron's addiction, but we also learned many of the things we would need to do as a result of our experience. It gives me great peace today, and it's easier to live with myself, knowing that we did all we knew to do to find help for him. I have no regrets about that.

If you have a loved one suffering from addiction, our advice would be to seek someone with experience that understands addiction, and get help for yourself that will instruct you on the right steps to take to intervene and find help for the addict. You may be trying to love him through it, but that will not work. Remember that you are not dealing with the real person-you're speaking to the drugs.

* * *

One night in February 1997, I got a call around midnight. It was Ron, saying that he and his dog, Samantha, were "going to die" unless he got some help.

"Ron," I said, "there's nothing else I can do."

"Mom," he said, "will you please come?"

I kept saying, "Ron, there's nothing I can do."

I hung up the phone. A few minutes later, he called back to say that he had just spoken to Larry Owens at the Bethel Christian Home in Atlanta. "Larry says he knows a doctor who can help me," he said. "But I have to fly down there to see him."

I told him that I'd drive up to North Wilkesboro in the morning and help him arrange a flight to Atlanta for that evening. It was just like he said. The place was a mess, and Ron looked even worse. He had been back on cocaine again and had exhausted all avenues of getting more.

He got up, showered, and struggled to get some clothes together. He had nothing clean to pack, so we ended up spending most of the day at a laundry, washing and drying clothes. He was hungry. We got him something to eat, and then stopped by the store to get him toiletries and other things for the trip.

All during the day, he kept begging me to take him to our house to spend the night, and he would leave for Atlanta the next morning. He said, "Mom, let me go home and just sit and watch TV with Dad one more time."

That was one thing he had really come to enjoy. He would say, "Dad and I can sit for hours, and even though we might not be carrying on a conversation, there is that feeling of love between us that's so comforting." He would say, "My Dad is my best friend."

With God's grace, I held firm. "Ron, I'm sorry, but you're going to the airport, and that's that."

But it wasn't quite that simple. As it happened, Larry Owens wouldn't be able to pick up Ron until the following morning, so I had no choice but take him home. He followed through as he had promised by leaving all his clothes in the car, only taking out an overnight bag. It was like a miracle that Ron was able to sit and watch some TV with his Dad, because his cravings were always so intense. We made it through the night and things went as planned, leaving for the airport early the next morning. On the way, we even went by to get a new copy of his driver's license that he had misplaced or lost. It was truly a miracle.

When Ron reached Atlanta, Larry took him to see Dr. Tommy Richardson, a specialist who treated cocaine addicts with medication. After meeting with Ron, Dr. Richardson admitted him into Charter Peachford Hospital and immediately prescribed Zoloft-the first time anyone had ever prescribed drugs to treat Ron's addiction.

Once before, Brooks and I had taken Ron to see a psychiatrist in Charlotte, hoping we might get something prescribed for Ron's depression. That was the first time Ron had ever opened up and told a doctor that he was so depressed that he could hardly function.

Ron made nine visits to this psychiatrist. (He was off cocaine at the time. Had he been on drugs, there was no way he could have followed through with nine visits. Brooks and I knew that far too well.) The doctor asked us to sit in on two of the visits. During those times we confirmed to the doctor that what Ron had told him about his depression was absolutely correct.

We spent a total of $1,500.00 with this doctor. He sat and listened, but beyond that he did nothing-at least, nothing that convinced us that he knew anything about addiction. This truly frustrated us and would make us wary of psychiatrists in the future. The fact that Dr. Richardson prescribed some kind of medication was at least a step in the right direction.

After a short stay at Charter Peachford, Ron moved back into the Bethel Christian Home, all the while remaining in the care of

Dr. Richardson. Ron began treatment with an understanding from Brooks that he could return to his position of vice president of the rebar business at Steelco if he stayed in Atlanta for a year and complete his rehabilitation.

Motivated, Ron quickly adjusted to his new life in Atlanta. After landing an apartment in Atlanta, he rented two of his rooms to a couple of young recovering addicts whom he had been counseling. Ron spent time listening to their problems, sharing things he had learned the hard way, and encouraging them. The parents of one of these young men sent Ron their son's spending money so he could handle it for him. All that knowledge and accountability was back, and he was again nurturing others.

Ron found work as a car salesman for a Cadillac dealership and became involved with his local church. He also became active with the 8111 Club, a local Alcoholics Anonymous group where he would meet a recovering addict named Cathy. . . and an energetic counselor at Bethel named Ketta Guy. Cathy and Ketta would not only become close to Ron, they would each have a significant impact on Brooks and my life in the months following Ron's death.

* * *

Ron liked Atlanta and told us that he felt better than he had in a long time. He made friends with a middle-aged doctor, who was a recovering alcoholic and had come to Atlanta for rehabilitation. Ron drove the man to and from places he needed to go, because he had not gotten his driver's license reinstated. Brooks and I visited back and forth, going to church with him and enjoying various activities. We were building a new home at the time, and Ron would drive me around Atlanta to places like the lighting company where we selected chandeliers for our new home.

In the spring of 1997, Ron met a young lady who was a divorced mother of three. (There are reasons why I don't wish to use this person's real name. So for purposes of this book, let's call her "Betty Anne.") Ron always loved kids, and looked forward to the possibility of having children of his own. He thought Betty Anne was the perfect girl for him.

The romance accelerated to the point where Ron gave her an engagement ring in June and set a wedding date in August. Plans were all made for a small family wedding until suddenly everything stopped. Citing problems with her ex-husband, Betty Anne postponed the wedding.

This crushed Ron to the point where (as he would tell us later on) he felt as if he would have an emotional breakdown. So where did he go to kill the pain? Back to cocaine. By November, he was back at Charter Peachford Hospital, again under the care of Dr. Richardson.

Ron had not been home since a visit for his dad's birthday in June. Dr. Richardson thought that it would be good for Ron if he spent Thanksgiving with us, so he drove up for the weekend along with his roommate, Neil Messenger.

Though he was still despondent over the breakup, Ron had a good visit with us and enjoyed seeing how our new home turned out. He took the opportunity to go by Davis Steel and visit with his brother Rick and some of his co-workers. One night that weekend, we rented the movie *Jingle All the Way* with Arnold Schwarzenegger. I can still hear his chuckles as we all sat and watched it together.

My mother, also known as Ron's "Maw-Maw Ruth," came out to eat Thanksgiving lunch with us. Ron really loved to eat, especially good home cooked meals. It was always a joy to watch how much he enjoyed it. His request for Thanksgiving was always sweet potato pies. It would be several years before I could bring myself to bake more sweet potato pies and when I finally did, I broke down in tears. I could not help but think of him as I prepared them.

Ron's last words to me before returning to Atlanta that Sunday afternoon were, "Mom, don't worry about me. I'm going to be okay. I'm going back to church at Wieuca Baptist." He resumed treatment upon returning to Atlanta, and remained under Dr. Richardson's direct supervision through the early weeks of December.

None of us knew it at the time, but that Thanksgiving visit would be the last time we would ever see Ron alive.

Part Two:

Journey to Justice

CHAPTER SEVENTEEN

Ron is Missing

M y heart raced with hope as I picked up the phone to check messages. *Perhaps there was news*, I thought. *Who knows, perhaps it was even Ron himself.*

It was about 10:00 p.m. on Thursday, January 1, 1998. Brooks and I had just returned home from a night at the movies. The past week had been incredibly stressful, for reasons that had nothing to do with the holidays, and we had both hoped to find a little escape from our constant fear and worry.

Diane had been telling us for weeks how we just had to see *Titanic*, which was the big holiday movie that year. She told us that it really did live up to all the hype, and that it was everything a movie was supposed to be "and more." And had Brooks and I seen it under different circumstances, we probably would have agreed.

As much as we love movies, though, all I could do that night was think of Ron.

It had been five days since we last heard from him. That was the phone conversation we had on Saturday, December 27, 1997, when he called us sounding more despondent than Brooks and I could ever remember. Ron said that his car, which had been missing, was found with a flat tire at a towing company in Atlanta after being towed away a few days before from an illegal parking place. But Ron did not have the money to get the car out of the shop and purchase a new tire. Nor did he have the funds to repay the $50.00

137

he owed to some individual named "Mike."

Brooks and I arranged to wire Ron $250.00, enough to cover the costs of retrieving the car, buying a tire, and repaying the debt to "Mike." We wired the money at about 10:00 a.m.; we learned later on that the funds were picked up at an A&P grocery store around noon that afternoon.

Ron thanked us for helping him out of this bind. But then he made a remark that chilled us both to the bone. *"Mom, Dad, there's something not right,"* he said. *"These people stick together."* He also said something about how fascinated "Mike" was with guns. There was a tone in his voice we'd heard before, but not in a long, long time. Ron was frightened for his life.

Brooks told Ron that we would drive to Atlanta just as soon as we wired the money. He also urged him to get out of there-wherever he was-as soon as he could, and to let us know where we could find him. "We'll be down there late this afternoon," said Brooks. "Call us on your mom's mobile phone, and tell us where to meet you."

"I really appreciate this," said Ron. "Love you, Dad."

"I love you, too, Ron."

Brooks and I were able to wire the money immediately, but we soon discovered that driving down to Atlanta was, unfortunately, not an option. The weather called for snowfall that afternoon-which meant that the earliest we could possibly leave was the following morning. Atlanta, of course, was a good five hours away. While almost everyone dreams of a white Christmas, it's only once in a while that it ever actually snows in Charlotte during the holidays, so this came as quite a surprise.

Unfortunately, we had no way of reaching Ron. He did not have a cell phone at that time-and as he had called us collect that morning, we had no way of knowing what number he was calling from. (Remember, this was 1997, a few years before Caller ID and Call Return became regular features on most telephone systems.) Nor did we have a number for this mysterious figure known only as "Mike." For that matter, we knew of no "Mike" that Ron could have known, in Atlanta or anywhere else.

I looked at Brooks. "What should we do?"

Brooks checked his watch. "Jean, I'm afraid at the moment,

there's not much more we can do," he said. "Look, it's just about noon. Ron should have the money by now. If he doesn't call us right away, he'll call us this evening, and we'll tell him we'll head on down just as soon as the weather clears. It'll be all right."

Only Ron didn't call right away. Nor did we hear from him the rest of Saturday, or the next day, Sunday.

Still, there was no cause for alarm. At least, that's what we kept telling each other. Brooks and I had walked many times with Ron over the years as he struggled to beat his addiction, and the three of us had grown very close along the way. No matter where he lived, he made a point of calling us almost every day.

It wasn't until the phone rang late Sunday night that we began to fear the worst. The call came from Neil Messenger, Ron's roommate in Atlanta, whom we had met when he and Ron visited us for Thanksgiving just a few weeks before. "Jean, this is Neil," he said.

"Neil, I'm so glad you called," I said as Brooks picked up the extension. "Have you heard from Ron?"

"No, ma'am," he said. "That's why I'm calling. I found out that Ron hasn't picked up his car yet, and he hasn't come back for clothes. I know where the car is, Brooks. What should I do about it?"

"Just leave the car where it is, Neil," Brooks replied. "We're coming down there just as soon as we can."

"I know he's been seeing Dr. Richardson," said Neil. "Should I call Charter Peachford Hospital?"

A torrent of emotions suddenly came rushing over me. "No, Neil," I said. "He would have called us if he had checked himself in."

Neil promised to stay in touch, and said that he would check with us over the course of the next few days. In fact, the next day, Monday, December 29, there was a message from Neil on the recorder: *"Hi, Jean, this is Neal. Just calling to see if you've heard from Ron. I have not heard a thing from him. We have until Monday to do something about his car-I got the guy at the garage to keep it for another week. I'm more concerned about Ron. If you hear from him, give me a call, so I'll know he's okay. I guess that's it. 'Bye. Be well."*

Neil was also the one who left the message that was waiting

for us when Brooks and I returned from the movies on Thursday, January 1: *"Jean, this is Neal. I still haven't heard from Ron. Please call me."*

So I picked up the phone and dialed him back, while Brooks listened on the extension.

"I take it, from your message, you didn't find out anything," said Brooks.

"No, sir, I didn't," Neal replied. Then, without hesitation, he said, "Do you think we should check with the sheriff?"

I was in a state of shock, so I said, "Neil, I wouldn't know how to go about it. I don't even know the counties down there. Would you mind doing it for us?"

"Sure, Jean, not at all," he said. "I'll call you right back."

Neil called back a few minutes later. "I just talked with the Forsyth County Sheriff's Department. They told me there was an unidentified body found a couple of days ago-but it couldn't possibly be Ron. This guy had a Harley Davidson tattoo on his upper arm."

When I heard that, I went numb, while a huge lump started forming in my throat. "Neil, Ron had a tattoo, a small Harley Davidson emblem."

Neil went silent for a moment. "I never knew that," he finally said.

"Not too many people knew it, either," I said.

There was a reason for that. Ron was never proud of that tattoo, so consequently he never told anyone about it. It reminded him of a period of time he had come to describe as "a weak point in my life, spiritually." That was when he was 18 and sought refuge from three personal tragedies-the death of his cousin Doug, the death of his girlfriend's mother, and later, his breakup with his girlfriend-by joining a gang of local bikers who, like Ron, had rebelled against their families, their faith, and their community. As part of his rebellion, Ron had a tattoo etched on his upper arm. It was small and modest, as tattoos go-just the Harley Davidson emblem, with little wings sprouting out of the letters. About the only way anyone could see it was if he rolled the sleeve of his T-shirt all the way up. Just the same, once Ron returned to his prayer life, he came to regret that tattoo. In fact, he spoke several times about having it removed.

In the end, Brooks and I were certainly glad that he never got around to doing that. That tattoo proved to be a huge factor in identifying his body after the murder.

* * * * *

Brooks asked Neil for the number to the Forsyth County Sheriff's Office in Atlanta, then we put in a call. The woman we spoke with gave us some more information about the body they had found.

As it happened, she would give us too much information. That was when we found out that the victim's head was missing.

The woman immediately apologized once she said that, as though she realized she had just said something she wasn't supposed to. But by that time it was too late.

As you can imagine, it took a while for everything to sink in. Learning that the victim had a tattoo like Ron's worried me sick, even more than the news of the missing head. *Still,* I tried to assure myself, *that doesn't necessarily mean its Ron. That body could just as easily be someone else.*

"What do you suppose we should do?" I finally asked Brooks.

"Jean, I don't know if there's much we can do at the moment." He looked at his watch. It was just before midnight.

"Look, I got an idea," said Brooks. "Let's lay down and try to get some rest. Might do us some good. Then we'll talk about it in the morning, when we're fresh."

It was a good idea, except that neither of us was really able to rest. As I lay in bed, I couldn't help but think about how lonesome, sad, and scared Ron was when we spoke to him on Saturday-and how strange it was that he never called us when we didn't show up in Atlanta after assuring him that we would. That wasn't like him at all.

Then I kept thinking about the body of that poor man they had found, with the tattoo just like Ron's on his arm, and the horrible thing that had happened to him.

Instantly, I sat up in bed and turned to Brooks. "Brooks," I said, "something tells me it's important that we leave for Atlanta *right now*."

Brooks turned on the light. "All right," he said. "Let's do it."

And that's exactly what we did. At two o'clock in the morning, Brooks and I got up, got dressed, and headed straight for Atlanta.

I sat quietly in our car as we drove into the night. All I could do was think of how far Ron had come over the past 12 years to overcome his addiction. No matter how many times our son stumbled, God had always protected him.

Wherever he was, I surely hoped that he was safe this time.

CHAPTER EIGHTEEN

The Worst Night of Our Lives

The manikin stood there plain as day, its head looking down like a skier ready to start downhill, as we waited in the lobby of the Forsyth County Sheriff's Office in Cumming, Georgia. It was about eight o'clock in the morning on Friday, January 2, 1998. Brooks and I were tired and numb from driving all night.

We had arrived in Atlanta around 7:00 a.m. We made a brief stop at Ron's apartment, spoke briefly with Neil, and got directions to the sheriff's office. Then we headed to Cumming, about 45 minutes away. We were both anxious to meet with Sheriff Denny Hendrix about the unidentified man whose body had been found smoldering in a graveyard five nights before. We were hoping for the best, but couldn't help but think the worst, as we sat in the lobby like zombies as we waited to be called into the sheriff's office.

I looked at the manikin, thinking to myself that it resembled Ron, and that the clothes it was wearing were also like Ron's. But I was so numb, not just from the long drive but also from the stress and worry over not hearing from Ron in nearly a week that I couldn't figure out why it was there.

Because the victim had been burned beyond recognition, there were only fragments of clothing left by the time the police discovered his body. That was one of the first things Sheriff Hendrix told us when he met with us that morning. He had one of the deputies buy clothes similar to what the victim was wearing-an Adidas jacket, a golf shirt, light blue Structure jeans, and a beige Ralph Lauren "Chaps" baseball cap-and put them on the manikin in hopes that might help identify him.

It was strange, seeing that lifeless figure standing before us with its head drooping. Those were exactly the kind of clothes Ron wore. Not only that, I knew that Structure jeans were his favorite brand, and that I had given him a pair that I'd found among some of his things when Ron visited us for Thanksgiving only a few weeks before.

Ron loved to shop-or at least, he liked to browse. Many times when I visited him, we would go to the mall to look around. I remembered buying him a cap just like the manikin was wearing, sometime in the past.

Then we went inside Sheriff Hendrix's office. One of the first things he asked us was to describe the tattoo on Ron's arm to see whether it was similar to the one found on the victim. We told him it was just a small standard Harley Davidson emblem.

Hendrix then held up a small piece of tracing paper that they had traced from the victim's arm. The paper had an image of wings spreading out from either side of the words "Harley Davidson."

"Was it like this?" he asked.

"Yes," we said. "Exactly."

"He had that done when he was 18," I added. "It was on his upper arm, so you couldn't always see it. That's why not too many people know about it. As a matter of fact, Ron has told us many times that he wished he'd had it taken off."

We talked a little about Structure jeans and the other clothes that were worn by the victim. Structure jeans are not a widely known brand of jeans-as a matter of fact, Hendrix told us he had never heard of them before. But they were Ron's favorite.

Then he started asking other kinds of questions: "Did he wear briefs, or did he wear boxers?"

"Boxers," I said.

Well, the more we talked to him, the more it sank in. *That man they found is Ron, and the manikin in the lobby was dressed to look like Ron.*

As we sat there in the office, Hendrix told us they were working on over 20 different missing persons cases that week. At one point, the phone rang. It was a man calling to tell the sheriff he believed the victim was *his* son.

Hendrix spoke with him for a few minutes, asking many of the same questions he had just finished asking us. By the time he hung up, he'd been able to provide enough information so that the father knew that the body was not that of his son.

What a relief, I thought. *At least that father still has hope.*

After talking some more to the sheriff, Brooks and I drove back to the apartment and gathered Ron's personal belongings-everything, that is, except his wardrobe. Because Ron had worked as a car salesman prior to his relapse, he dressed sharp every day. He had good taste in clothes, shoes, and neckties. One of the very first things that Ron always did upon recovering from a fall from sobriety was to work on his appearance. How he looked was always very important to him. If he needed a haircut, he took care of that immediately. If he needed his clothes washed or sent to the laundry to be starched, he'd also take care of that immediately. He always said, "It makes me feel good about myself to look sharp."

We decided to leave his clothes and shoes behind, and decide that if the victim was Ron, we would donate them later on to Bethel Christian Home.

We packed everything in the trunk and drove over to the Fulton County Police Department. There, we met with detectives from the Major Case Division, as well as Special Agent Wayne White from the Georgia Bureau of Investigation in Gainsville, Georgia. We could not believe how quickly Agent White arrived. Special Agent Jeff Branyon was also involved in the investigation.

Because many details of the crime were still sketchy at that point, there wasn't much the G.B.I. could tell us. They did say that the victim had been dismembered, transported to a cemetery near Hopewell United Methodist Church, and partially burned. The upper arm where the tattoo was located, however, had not been burned. That turned out to be a crucial factor in finally identifying the body.

As you might imagine, all kind of things were going on in my mind. *If that was Ron,* I thought, *it had to be more than one person that did this to him.* As strong as he was, and with all his skills in the martial arts, there was no way he would have let one single assailant attack him. Ron could have easily disarmed him in one move. This had to be the work of a gang.

The G.B.I. added that they did not believe this to be a drug-related killing. In most drug-related homicides, the victim is simply shot to death. There usually isn't any of the gruesome mutilation of the body that characterized this case. For that reason, the investigators first speculated that it might be a crime of passion, like a love triangle gone badly. They even asked us if Ron had been seeing anyone lately.

We told them that he had been engaged, but that the girl had broken it off a few months before and that he had not been in contact with her since.

At one point, I offered to send the G.B.I. his dental records. "That'll help you identify him, wouldn't it?"

All they would tell us, in an abrupt and awkward way, was that "there was no need for that."

Later that evening, when we remembered the phone conversation we had from the night before with the woman from the sheriff's office, it finally dawned on us why the detectives were so awkward whenever I asked about dental records.

The victim's head was missing.

* * *

We spent the rest of Friday answering questions with various agents. The G.B.I. asked us to spend the night, so we got a motel room in the area and waited for them to contact us.

That night was one of the worst nights in our lives. As raw and as numb as we were, all we could do was cry out to God, *"Please help us."*

We then turned on the TV, curious to know what the media was saying. That was a mistake. On every newscast, on every channel, we kept seeing the images of the graveyard and the body smoldering on the snowy ground. Newscasters kept talking about the "unidentified body." And although we didn't know for certain who the victim was at the time, in our hearts we had come to believe that it was in fact Ron.

At some point, it occurred to me to call Dr. Richardson, the doctor who had been treating Ron at Charter-Peachford Hospital in Atlanta. I told him that we were in town because we believed Ron may have been the victim whose body was found in the graveyard, and that we might need to run lab tests of Ron's blood and the victim's in order to identify him. Could he get them for us?

"Yes, Jean, that is possible," he said. "But I must warn you, sometimes these tests can be complicated. It may be a while before we get any conclusive results."

"I understand," I said. "Just keep us posted."

By Saturday, January 3, Brooks and I had come to a decision. Even though the victim had still not been identified, we went to the Roswell Funeral Home in Roswell, Georgia and met with the director. "We'd like to speak to you in confidence," we said. "We have reason to believe the unidentified body that was found last week is our son's. We live in Charlotte. If that is our son, we're going to need the body shipped back to Charlotte. We would like to make arrangements for that right now in the event he is the victim. Could you please help us?"

"Yes, Mr. and Mrs. Davis," said the director. "I'll keep this in my vault. All you need to do is call us."

Looking back, I have no idea how we were able to think of all those things while in such a state of mind. . . but we even picked out a casket and made all of the necessary arrangements. Had we not done all that, someone would have had to make a trip back down there and take care of all that.

Once again, God had provided what we needed at the right time. He gave us the strength to handle all those things, totally alone without a single family member or anyone. It was just Brooks, the Lord, and me.

* * *

By Saturday evening, there was not much more Brooks and I could do until the results of the blood tests came in-and as Dr. Richardson had said, there was no telling how long that would take.

So we decided to drive back to Charlotte.

Before we left, we decided to call the family. Up to this point we hadn't told anyone what happened-other than a brief call to Rick, and that was only to say that Ron was missing and that we had come down to Atlanta to investigate. We knew we couldn't say anything beyond that until the body was officially identified. And we certainly didn't want to get the news media involved, for fear that the murderers might catch wind of the story and try to slip out of town.

I called Diane at her home in Fayetteville, two hours south of Charlotte. I had hoped to reach her so that she might be able to head up to Charlotte in order to be with our elderly mother when we broke the news. Unfortunately, Diane was out of town that weekend and I did not have a number to reach her.

Brooks, however, was able to reach Rick. "Have you found him, Dad?" asked Rick.

"No," said Brooks. "We've done about all we can for now. We're ready to head on back home."

Brooks only said those few words, not allowing Rick much opportunity for questions.

"Would you and Dana come up to the house about 12:00 noon tomorrow," Brooks then said, "and we'll tell you all about it." We planned it this way in order to break the news to Rick, before anyone else arrived.

Then we left for home, arriving in Charlotte around two in the morning. By this time, we had gone nearly three full days without sleep. Fatigue and illness were beginning to set in. We were both getting flu-like symptoms. Brooks, in fact, had started burning with fever during the drive home from Atlanta.

On Sunday morning, January 4, Brooks called his sister Carolyn, who lives in the same subdivision as we do. He asked her to pick up my mother and bring her to the house after church, as well as to call Brooks' younger sister Doris and her husband, Don. He also asked if she could get the ministers at Mount Harmony Baptist Church to come by the house after services. "Ron has been missing," he said. "We'd like to gather everyone and tell them all at once."

That's all we told her. As run down and exhausted as we both were from the events of the past three days, we felt that was the only way to do it. We simply did not have the strength to go through the story over and over again.

Everyone gathered in the living room around noon: Rick, Dana, Mother, Carolyn, Don, Doris, our friends Nonia and Jimmy Polk, and the two pastors from Mount Harmony Baptist Church. (I had called Nonia that morning. She asked no questions, but came right over, as we requested. I also managed to reach Diane that morning. She and her husband Tommy would arrive later that afternoon, after we had met with everyone.)

We told them all what happened, that we were almost positive that the body in Atlanta was Ron's, but that we couldn't put the word out until we knew for sure.

Everyone was in total shock. It was too much to absorb at one time. I remember my mother became terribly upset. She couldn't understand why we made all those preparations with the funeral home when the only thing we knew for sure was that Ron was missing.

"What do you want us to say at church?" asked one of the pastors.

"Just tell them Ron is missing," said Brooks, "and to please pray for us."

CHAPTER NINETEEN

God's Peace in
the Middle of the Storm

O n the evening of Monday, January 5, 1998, Brooks and I received a phone call from the Georgia Bureau of Investigation with the news no parent ever wants to hear. The G.B.I. had finally confirmed that the murder victim was our son, Ronnie Allen Davis.

Anyone who has ever lost a child or loved one knows just how overwhelming that feeling can be. Suddenly your world has been turned upside down, and it takes all the strength you have to get through the difficult days ahead. That's hard enough for anyone. It becomes even harder when you're literally flat on your back with flu and high fever, as Brooks and I both were.

As you can imagine, people poured into our home to offer prayer, food, and comfort. There had only been one murder in our church and community that anyone could remember, and that victim was an elder member of the community who unfortunately walked into a robbery in his home. The fact that Ron was so young made his death that much more of a shock. Naturally, everyone felt that they wanted or needed to see us. As much as Brooks and I appreciated their support, it was difficult for us to accommodate each and every one of them, especially those first few days. For one, given how sick we were, we did not want to expose anyone, and secondly, we just weren't physically strong enough for visits-although for obvious reasons, we did make exceptions for any visitors who came by from out of town. One such person was my long time friend Shirley Putnam, who I've known since the fifth grade. She was one of the first to see us, as well as our longtime traveling companions, Bill and Moneta Merry from Nashville, Tennessee. Roses were the first to come to our home from long time friend and prayer partner Jackie Brown, who had moved to Raleigh, North Carolina.

Because of our illness, we would have to delay the funeral one extra day (the service would be on January 9, instead of the 8th, as originally scheduled) in order for Brooks and I to be able to make it for family visitation. Even so, we had to sit in chairs while the rest of the people filed through to pay their respects. The funeral parlor would be so packed that night; some people couldn't even get inside the parking lot.

Because of the circumstances of Ron's death, the phone rang constantly with calls from the media. The Charlotte stations were very compassionate and understanding, and did a very good job of reporting the story. We had to refuse any TV interviews until after the funeral, although in the meantime reporters did get comments from the pastor at Mount Harmony Baptist Church, as well as Richard Cochran (the shop superintendent at Davis Steel). They both did a fine job answering questions for the local TV stations.

And then, there were the arrangements for the funeral. The body needed to be transported from Atlanta. An obituary needed to be written. The service had to be planned. There were so many things to do.

Fortunately, by this time, Diane and her husband, Tommy, had arrived from Fayetteville. Had it not been for Diane, I don't know how we would have made it through the week. Friends and other family members helped in whatever way they could, but it was Diane who took over the house and helped coordinate their efforts, staying with us for eight days. With Brooks and I still sick in bed, we planned the funeral from our bedside with our church pastor, while Diane wrote the obituary. This was important to Diane in many ways, as she explains below:

All my life, Brooks and Jean were the ones who took care of me. But that was the first time that I ever really felt needed.

In every crisis of my life, they were there for me, but I never had the chance to do for them what they had always done for me. And that helped me get my focus off me-because I think we're always at our best when we're helping others. We love that feeling of being needed.

To this day, it amazes me how strong they both were throughout that entire time, especially to people who might have just totally fallen apart. [People could hardly believe] how they could sit and talk about it. I think some people were apprehensive about approaching them, not wanting to upset them or bring up anything that was painful. But they were just so incredibly strong.

For whatever reason, God did bless Brooks and me both with incredible strength, especially throughout this time. As numb as we were from the loss of our son, I think because of all of the experiences we had gone through with Ron throughout his journey with addiction, somehow that strengthened us for the days ahead. Having walked with Ron through so many dark hours, and so many deep valleys, you might say that in some way that prepared us for the tremendous pain, anguish, and loss we were feeling immediately after his death.

Still, when I look back on it now, sometimes I wonder just how we managed to get through that week as methodically as we did. I don't think I even had a chance to cry. It wasn't until after the funeral, when the rush of activity began to slow down, that the severity of our loss began to sink in.

* * *

On January 9, 1998, Ron's life was celebrated before a gathering of family and friends at Mount Harmony Baptist Church. Many who knew him and worked with him spoke lovingly of his compassion and his dedication to helping others achieve the victory that he himself fought so hard to attain. Having lived chemical-free for nearly four years before his death, Ron was dedicated to helping others overcome their addiction because he himself knew that victory was possible.

With our hearts breaking from the beginning of the service to the end of that day, there was a peace from God that all was carried out according to His will. Many years prior to this, we had made a promise to God that no matter what the outcome of Ron's life, we would let the true story of his addiction be told as a testimony to help others. The entire service gave us such peace, strength, and comfort that we cannot adequately explain.

The service began with Squire Parsons' "Oh, What a Moment, When We See Jesus," sung by Beverly Entz. Ron had chosen Beverly to sing that same song in September 1995, at the dedication of the Christian Unity Men's Home. Another favorite of Ron's that Lynton Ellisor sang at the Shoulder (as well as during the two concerts he gave at Mount Harmony Baptist Church) was "That's My Desire, To Be Like Jesus." With Ron's death being so sudden and circumstances as they were, we were unable to arrange for Lynton to be there, so the minister of music, Stephen Rector at Mount Harmony graciously honored our request.

Larry Owens and his wife, Sharon, traveled from Bethel Christian Home in Atlanta to pay honor and tribute to Ron. Larry spoke of Ron's compassion and helpfulness, as well as how exceptionally close friends they were to each other. Ron's death came as a devastating blow to Larry. Brooks and I would learn later on that Larry fought with depression for a long time after learning of Ron's death. Among the Scripture readings that day was Luke 10: 25-37, the parable of the Good Samaritan, delivered by Dr. Buddy Pigg. For those who may not be familiar with this passage, a lawyer asks, "Master, what shall I do to inherit eternal life?" Knowing that the man is a lawyer, Jesus asks him to recite what the law says. The man replies, "You shall love your Lord God with all your heart, and with all your soul, and with all your strength, and with all your mind, and you shall love your neighbor as yourself." Jesus tells the man, "You have answered correctly. Do this and you will live."

But when the man asks Jesus, "Who is my neighbor?" Jesus answers by telling the story of a man on a journey. The man is maliciously beaten by thieves and left for dead. Many people pass by the man on their travels, but do nothing to help him. Then a stranger from Samaria comes upon the man and looks at him with compassion. Without hesitation, the Good Samaritan treats the man's wounds and brings him to a nearby inn so that he can rest until he fully recovers.

The moral, of course, is that we are all each other's neighbors. We should always reach out to each other in compassion-even people we don't necessarily know.

Ron was very fortunate because God put a lot of Good Samaritans in his life, people who stopped and went the extra mile for him when others may have given up. And though he struggled with addiction until the day he died, he never forgot the hands of compassion that were shown him by those people. Two people that Ron spoke about often, and who never gave up on him, were his good friends Wayne Hartis and Richard Cochran of Davis Steel. Ron appreciated the help that was given him over the years, and he tried his best to reach out to others.

But as I've mentioned before, sometimes Ron was his own worst enemy. Sometimes despite his best efforts, he couldn't keep himself from falling.

Another person who spoke at the funeral was Reverend Paul Ritchie, executive director of the Bethel Colony of Mercy in Lenoir, where Ron had rehabbed on two occasions. Paul likened Ron to the apostle Peter, one of the first leaders of Christianity and an important figure in the writings of the New Testament. "Peter was a strong headed man with great expectations," said Paul that day:

Peter was the one who stepped out in the water to walk with Jesus, only to stumble once he took his eyes off the Lord and began sinking in the water, to the point where he had to cry out for help. Then again, as our Lord was approaching the cross, Peter said, "I'll die for you." And yet, in his own strength, he failed again.

That reminds me of myself, and Ron-and it probably reminds us of each other, doesn't it, when we depend upon our own strength, only to stumble occasionally.

Ron was a very talented, very able person. And maybe that was his downfall. Because when we're as able as he was, we sometimes try to do so much and often fall short of our own expectations.

Ron was always an asset to us at Bethel Colony. When he was there, he went out of his way to help us in any way that he could. But again, like Peter, [Ron found] when you take your eyes off Jesus, things just don't go as well. But there is no doubt that he is with the Lord this day.

A beautiful tribute came from Nonia Polk, a close friend of our family, and a founding member of the prayer group that helped sustain me when Brooks and I first began to cope with Ron's condition. In some ways, Nonia knew Ron better than anyone else, and her eulogy reflects that. She gave a complete picture of who he was: the Ron who was lost in an addiction to cocaine, and the Ron who found himself with the help of the Lord.

I treasure Nonia's eulogy and think it is beautiful. Many times over the years, when I'm overwhelmed with grief or if I'm simply having a really bad day, I find myself going back to this eulogy and reading it for comfort. Each time I read it, my spirits are lifted and I'm able to carry on.

For this reason and more, I'd like to share these words with you in their entirety:

A joyful celebration-I believe that is what Ron would want this day.

A day to celebrate not only his life, but especially his home-going. For he has obtained the lasting victory he sought and fought for on this earth, but was simply not able to grasp. The battle is over, all victories now won.

Ron is at home in heaven with our Lord and Savior, Jesus Christ. And he is now free from all the struggles that plagued his life. No more pain, sufferings, nor sorrows. No more heartaches no more disappointments. There is no discouragement or depression. No more tears, no more loneliness, no more rejection, no more failures, no more struggles with the ever increasing demands of his flesh for more, more, more.

He is out of bondage and slavery to the flesh, and he is *free*. Free to live in Heaven, a place prepared for him and you and me by our Lord and is filled with indescribable beauty and splendor.

This one who sought peace so diligently on earth now is in peace for he lives with the Prince of Peace. He has only light with no darkness for he lives with the light of the world. Ron is forever safe in heaven, no more fears for his life and no more dangers. He will live in the presence of God always, forever with Him throughout eternity.

And Ron is also with other loved ones, his grandfather Barney, whom he admired and desired to fashion his life by, and his aunt Nancy, who would have welcomed him home with open heart and arms embracing him joyfully, ready to show him around his new home in glory.

How joyful I am for Ron as I remember a young man who sought for his place in his family, his church, and his community with vigor and desire for acceptance and respectability. A desire for a position of honor and a place of stability, to be like his grandfather Barney, his father, Brooks, and his brother, Rick. A desire to serve the Lord and to live in contentment of heart, mind, soul, and body-to give back to the Lord with his life, works, and accomplishments.

However, as his struggles intensified and these desires and goals became dimmer with each passing failure to measure up by his own self-inflicted standard, and in making wrong choices and decisions, his guilt became unbearable when he looked at his parents and family members and saw the depth of heartbreak and suffering he caused them and it became the heaviest cross of all to bear. Because he could never erase the consequence of his actions and the obvious destructive toil it had on them, he fought harder to be attentive, kind, and loving when things were stable and right in his life.

Ron was a complex individual, handsome, with a beautiful smile and winsome personality. But so often the Ron many people saw was the Ron out of control, when drugs raged in his body and he was ruled by this force with over-whelming destruction in his last years.

But Ron had many wonderful years prior to his drug addiction, and even in between the falls. Times he spent as a loving son and grandson and family member and a child of God. He attended church, served the Lord in various ways, studied God's word daily, and prayed always for God's blessings and provision in his life.

Many times I was privileged to meet with him and others in his life at the time and counsel him, share God's holy word with him, and pray with him as he sought God's guidance and wisdom. Many times I marveled at the insight he had as God gave him understanding of His holy word. And how excitedly Ron embraced the totality of God's word.

Ron loved to praise and worship the Lord with energy and exuberance and a joyful heart. He always felt the Lord was a *living* God and should be worshipped joyfully-lively, not as though he was dead.

Ron always reached out to others who suffered in like weaknesses of the flesh and its ultimate desires-as he did. He wanted to help them to find a way to overcome these horrible addictive and destructive habits. And sometimes at his own expense, physically, spiritually, and financially he tried to carry other weaker brothers struggling in like manner to obtain the ever eluding victory. My son Tripp was one Ron reached out to with acceptance, sensitivity, encouragement, compassion, understanding and love. Not many people were willing to give to these young men in this way. Ron always wanted to help others like this-*always*-and did, whenever he could. And the joy was simply evident in Ron when he could give out instead of receiving. And that's what prompted Ron to establish the Christian Unity Men's Home in Lenoir in 1995, a home for men who had already been through rehabilitation but needed a place to live, get a job, and learn to live in the world once again without falling to the temptation of using drugs again and in an encouraging and understanding atmosphere. Ron thought of this home as a three-quarter house, going a little beyond a halfway house.

Ron and I established a special relationship, one that grew over the years and in those years as I embraced this young man always with loving compassion, understanding, encouragement, hope, and acceptance, we built a relationship that withstood many torrential storms in his life and remained steadfast and sure because it was established in the love and acceptance of Christ.

I walked with his parents through years of heartbreaking experiences and joined with them in and through prayer always keeping Ron covered. There were times they could not even pray and I held them before the Lord for His mercy, grace and strength to endure. But never in all of these times did I witness anything from them for their son except unconditional love, immediate forgiveness, and encouragement in hope for a better tomorrow. They exemplified Christlike characteristics which God developed deeper and more completely with each situation. They stood by him when he was down. . . and stood with him when he was well.

While Ron and I had many special times of praying together, I will always remember one particular time above all others. Ron had fallen and had been out in the world with every conflict and problem that could have assaulted his body and the consequences of using drugs had all but destroyed his ability to function. I had gone to visit with him and to pray with him and Brooks and Jean. Ron came into the den in his pajamas, which was very unusual for him-because no matter what, Ron always insisted on dressing for the occasion. But he was so beaten, so exhausted, so completely worn out and destroyed; he could barely walk to the chair. He literally collapsed and sat totally motionless. Usually we would kneel and pray, but Ron could not even do this.

So with Brooks and Jean on the sofa, I knelt at his feet and held his hands in mine and began to share with Ron about God's marvelous grace, his forgiveness, his power to heal and to restore our broken lives, and the vastness of his unconditional love. And then, I prayed for Ron.

And then Ron prayed, so weak it was like a whisper. . . but God could hear. Never had I witnessed such a complete and total brokenness in a human being, such a complete surrender and submission to the Lord to do whatever was needed to touch his life and deliver and heal him from the torrents of the pain inflicted from the life-destroying drugs-even if that meant taking him home to be with Him. He did not want to continue living if it meant coping with the addiction to drugs and its ability to annihilate every ounce of productive and meaningful existence in his life.

I knew I had just witnessed something very profound and powerful in the life of Ron and I knew as he cried out for forgiveness of his sins and for deliverance and help from those parasitical substances eating away at his ability to live and breathe as God had meant for him, that God being a merciful and forgiving Father would embrace that heart cry from his child for help and one day he would answer that prayer-not in part, but completely.

Ron did not want to live if he had to live controlled by outside powers bringing the constant and continuous, insatiable craving for a substance that had no mercy. He wanted freedom from the slavery and bondage of this prison his real self, the real Ron, was in and he wanted to be free to live for the Lord with peace and joy.

And that prayer not only was heard by a loving Father but on this day we know it has been answered in full-for Ron is finally free and is out of the prison of unrest and lives forever in the presence of our Holy God. . . and in peace.

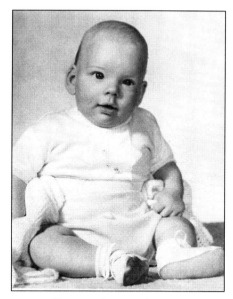

Ron at 3 months old

Our son Rick, 6 years older than Ron

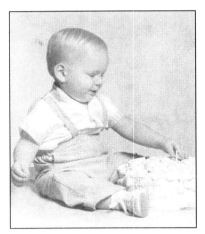

Ron's early years.

Steve Sigmon, with Ron
He was a lifelong friend

Ron's childhood days at the beach

Ron during grammar grade years

Ron's High School graduation
1976

Pop Warner Football Days

Ron's Aikido Class

Ron receiving black belt in Aikido

Ron, Instructor at his Aikido School

Ron loved his dog Samantha and raised him from a puppy, 1997

Homecoming Day at Bethel Colony of Mercy, Lenoir, N. C.
Ron at podium speaking.

The old smokehouse at Ron's grandparent's homeplace,
where Ron lived. He remodeled it into a barn.

A new barn was built and he enjoyed his quarter horses.

Ron, Melissa, and Danny Sigmon.

Ron and Steve Sigmon at a horse show in Columbus, Ohio

Ron and his horse, C50

Melissa's horse with their new colt.

Ron loved Christmas with his family. These were fun times for him

Buying gifts for everyone at Christmas was such a joy for Ron

Ron and his Maw Maw Ruth. His last Christmas home.

Richard Cochran and Ron
presenting him with a Christmas
gift from company employees

Paw Paw Barney frying flounder
at the beach house.

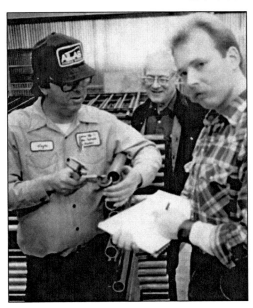

Wayne Hartis, Dr. George Stern and Ron
working on rail testing for National Ornamental
& Miscellaneous Metals Association

Christian Unity Men's Home, Lenoir, N.C. Established 1995

Open House in September 1995. Ron speaking to guests

Ron moved his church membership to Sentell Baptist Church,
Atlanta 1997

Thanksgiving at Ron's home. Tommy, Diane, Maw Maw Ruth,
Jean, Brooks, Ron, Corey & Collin

My sister, Nancy, who was a special aunt to our boys.
She died in 1980.

Jean & Diane in Homestead, VA. My first writing of this
book was started while Diane was in meetings. 2002

Brooks & Jean viewing plaque in memory of Ron in
the church gym. Church where he grew up.

Brooks & Jean
Our 50th Wedding Anniversary,
three years after Ron's death

Brooks & Jean 2008
Life goes on, after the dark cloud of
eight years is lifted

Ron & his Dad, Brooks, admiring Ron's new red Blazer

Jean & Ron during the same
visit home

Ron, June, 1997 on a visit home
for his Dad's birthday.

The location was a few yards back where
the road circle's left, within sight driving in.

Hopewell Untied Methodist Church and the cemetery
where Ron's body was dumped and burned.

Ron's cemetery marker, with his favorite scripture

Prosecution Team: Fred Hall, Investigator Jeff Branyon, GBI Agent Paul Howard, Fulton Country DA Jean, Brooks, Clinton Rucker, Asst. DA Brett Pinion, Asst. DA. GG Carawan, Investigator Theresa Strozier, Victim Witness Assistance Program

My prayer partners, Glend Furr, Margie Price, Jean,
Jackie Brown and Nonia Polk. Late 1980's

Ketta Guy, Ron's counselor in Atlanta, GA.

New friends, since Ron's death, along with my sister and two sisters'-
in law. Back row: Diane Grooms, Dru Quarles, Barbara Brown, Jean,
Carolyn Wilkes. Front row: Linda Combs, Doris Cunningham, Shirley
Currie, Sharon Green & Linda Terhaar.

CHAPTER TWENTY

Nuggets of Gold

The news of Ron's disappearance set off a whirlwind of activity that lasted several weeks. Between meeting with authorities in Atlanta, preparing for the funeral, and fighting off illness and fatigue, Brooks and I found ourselves too numb to breathe, let alone grieve properly for our son. It was not until after the funeral, when the initial shock slowly gave way to feelings of devastating loss, that the enormity of his death began to hit home.

Brooks and I had been through deep waters many times in the 12 years Ron struggled with cocaine, but we never once gave in to despair. We knew in our hearts that no matter how many times Ron stumbled, he was never really alone. Somehow God was always there to help carry our son through his darkest hours, just as He helped the man on the beach in the famous story "Footprints in the Sand." Knowing that, we could always count on one of us being strong even when the other wasn't.

Then, too, there was comfort in the fact that Ron had learned never to fear death. Having nearly died from overdosing before, Ron knew that God had given him a new lease on life, and he was determined to make the most of it. He talked very openly about this with Brooks and I on many occasions, especially during the years of his long-term sobriety. He enjoyed his life on earth, but through his faith he also looked forward to the fact that someday he would experience the place of sweet and quiet peace that awaits us all in the life to come.

But this time was different. As much as we tried to find comfort in the fact that Ron was finally free from his addiction and at peace with the Lord, the savage nature of his murder was simply too much to bear. We could not fathom why anyone would want to harm him. We could not understand how anyone could be so brutal.

For the first time that we could remember, we were both so overwhelmed with despair that neither one of us was capable of giving strength to the other. While we knew that God never gives any of us more than we are capable of handling, after all we had gone through together, our emotional resolve was spent. After watching Ron work so hard to regain control of his life, only to have him taken away from us in so horrible a manner, Brooks and I couldn't help but feel as though we'd finally reached our limits. We never lost our faith and trust in God, but we were both physically and spiritually drained.

And yet, once again, God provided us with the strength and hope to carry on just when we needed it most.

In the days following the funeral, God made His presence known through a remarkable series of occurrences that continued through the weeks and months to come. These events, which Brooks and I have come to know as "nuggets of gold," would lift us above the circumstances in ways we could never have imagined. Not only would they help us cope with the loss of our son, collectively they would show us how God was using Ron's life and death to help others who were struggling with addiction.

After the funeral, for example, our mailbox was flooded every day with sympathy cards. Many of these cards were from friends and family, but quite a few were from perfect strangers-people who Brooks and I did not know personally, but who had known Ron and wanted to tell us about the impact he had on their lives. (Some of these stories, as you will see, are nothing short of miraculous.)

Brooks was never one to care much about the mail before. I mean, I usually brought in the mail every day, and almost always opened everything before he got home. But when it came to those cards, knowing how much they lifted our hearts and kept our spirits up, he couldn't wait for the next one to arrive. He'd go to the mailbox every day so that he could read them first. All in all, we received over 300 cards and letters.

* * *

As Brooks and I began to feel better, we began looking for a way of thanking everyone for thinking of us with their words of kindness, comfort, and encouragement. We wanted it to be special, a card we could create ourselves. Ron's picture would be on the front of the acknowledgment. Brooks chose one that he especially liked of Ron sitting in a chair with his dog, Samantha, between his legs. All we needed now was the right verse that would express our thanks and appreciation.

One day I went to the mailbox and there was a card from Kelly Snipes, the daughter of our longtime friends Bill and Kathy Bramhall. Bill is Vice President of Davis Steel & Iron. The verse was from the Book of Isaiah (Ron's favorite scripture comes from Isaiah) and accompanied one of the most beautiful poems I'd ever read:

"I will uphold you with my righteous right hand."
Isaiah 41:13

When I can't see the way for the tears that dim my eyes
And my world has been turned upside down
I remember the One who has walked this path,
and His love and His grace does abound.
He takes me through the storm that is tearing me apart
to a place of quiet and sweet peace.
Though the tempest may rage, with my hand in His,
I find that my worries cease.
At times there are questions as to what lies ahead,
But in knowing that He holds my hand,
I can face tomorrow with joy in my heart,
For I know He'll not let go of my hand.
Let me praise Him in song and tell of His love,
As on this great promise I stand.
And no matter what the future may bring,
I'll keep holding on to His hand.

There was no author given, so I have no idea who wrote this poem. But once I read it, I just knew this was exactly what we needed at the moment.

Brooks and I then wrote the following on the inside of the card and on the left was the poem.

We acknowledge with grateful appreciation your expressions of love, kindness, sympathy, and especially your prayers, during our tragic loss.

To all those who reached out to Ron in so many ways during his lifetime, thank you from the depths of our hearts. It was such an encouragement to him.

The Family of Ronnie Davis

* * *

One week after the funeral, I was going through Ron's personal things that I had brought back from Atlanta. In his shaving kit was the small black pocket size New Testament Bible that he asked me to send him when he was in Houston, Texas 15 years before. Ron always managed to hold onto that Bible, no matter where he went or how many things he lost. Inside the Bible were several items, including a card with a small picture of Jesus that reads, "If we meet and you forget me, you have lost nothing; but if you meet Jesus Christ and forget Him you have lost everything." I treasure that Bible and carried it with me every time we traveled to Atlanta to attend court proceedings.

Around this time, we also received a letter from Brooks' niece Donna that included a number of touching anecdotes about how Ron touched her life and the lives of the other members of her family. Speaking as a mother, few things in life are more encouraging than reading something positive about your child.

Dear Brooks & Jean,

On the day of our wedding, we received a letter from you in which you gave us advice on how to have a happy marriage. Your letter meant a lot to both of us. It is our wish that this letter will hold equal value in your hearts.

It is our desire to share with you some of our memories of Ronnie. We thought you might like to know how we will always remember him.

Many of my early memories center around your place at that lake. One of the earliest was an argument between Doug McCray (a.k.a. "Big Doug") and Ronnie which took place in the house there.

Doug McCray was Carolyn's son. He was the cousin with cystic fibrosis who died when Ron was 18. Doug and Ron were about the same age, and as I said before, Doug's death had a devastating effect on Ron.

I can vividly recall the argument because it was over my brother, "Little Doug." Big Doug was telling Ronnie how important it was that little Doug shared his name. Ronnie was saying that the most important thing was that someone looks like you. Ronnie kept saying everyone thought Little Doug looked like him because of his hair and eye color. After consulting several adults as to which was the "most" important, the adults declared both to be of equal importance and promptly sent the boys outside. Speaking as the sister of the interested party, it was quite baffling that he was worth fighting over in the first place.

Ron was always the one who could hold his breath under water the longest, ski the best, etc. To this day, I have never personally witnessed anyone else barefoot water ski.

Many years later, when I was 12 and Ronnie was 16, he asked me to stay with him at the house while everyone except us and Maw-Maw went out on the boat.

He said he just wanted to talk with me for a while.

Maw-Maw sat rocking and reading behind us while we sat on the top step and talked for at least an hour. I would like to say some profound things were discussed and solved that day, however, I can recall very little. The one thing I do remember is how grown up and important it made me feel that he a "big teenager" would want me around. This was a trait, making others feel important, which stayed with him into adulthood. Jeff would be the first to attest to this fact.

Jeff was Donna's husband. He worked in our shop for many years.

Jeff and Ronnie shared with each other many conversations, some funny, some serious. Ron once asked Jeff what he thought of him. Jeff replied that he liked Ronnie very much and added that Ronnie was one of the ones who really made him feel like family. Ron grinned, put his arm around Jeff's shoulder and said, "Well, buddy, how else you would expect me to treat you? You are family."

Jeff respected Ronnie and enjoyed being with him. He loved working with and for him. Jeff has always said he felt like he could talk with Ronnie about anything. Ron would always maintain eye contact to let you know you were being listened to.

One day Ron asked Jeff if he would crawl under his house and check some pipes. He told Jeff he was too big to get under there himself. Later when Jeff was finished and had come inside the house to get something to drink, Ron burst out laughing. Jeff asked what was so funny. Ron said that he really wasn't too big to get under the house. He said that he was scared of snakes and really thought there might have been some under there.

My parents told Jeff the other night they wished he would have known Barney. Jeff had been expanding on Ron's many virtues. They told him how everyone who knew Barney liked him. They spoke of how humble he was, how friendly he was, and how people just loved to be around him. There was a reflective pause in the conversation and then almost in unison they replied, "Well, Jeff, you knew Ronnie, and to know Ronnie was like knowing Barney." (Ronnie was more like Barney than he ever gave himself credit for.)

Jeff said upon seeing Ron's cowboy picture on your table, which was the Ronnie he would always remember.

Addiction was a part of Ronnie's life; however, there was so, so, so much more to him than that. We all have our share of problems and no one should feel they are worthy of standing in judgment or of casting stones. I know I certainly can't.

The Ronnie I will always remember is the one with the quick laugh, slow grin, great sense of humor, humble heart, super talent, wonderful listener, lover of life and people. I feel honored to call him cousin and friend.

The first time I ever saw a young man cry was at Carolyn's house on her screen porch. All of the adults were inside with Carolyn because Doug had just died.

Steve, Janet, Lori, and I were outside. Steve was trying to hide the fact he had been crying from us. Ronnie came out just in time to hear me ask Steve if he was crying. Ronnie with tears in his eyes, too, looked at us and said, "So what if he is? I've been crying and I don't care what anybody says about it. Come over here, Steve." Looking back at us he continued, "Someone we loved just died and it hurts and it's okay for us to cry about that." Soon after his speech, we all just sat in silence and cried.

I know I'm not the first and I won't be the last to tell you this, but when I found out about Ronnie, I cried. I did not cry on just one occasion but many, many times. As a great man once said, though, it was okay for me to cry because someone I loved just died and it's okay to cry about that.

We loved him greatly and will miss him just as greatly. Our prayers are with you daily. We share your grief and do not attempt to be so vain as to say we fully understand what you are going through because we know it's not possible.

We simply share it and love you.

Love,
Donna & Jeff

This letter gives you a pretty good picture of Ron from a family perspective. Donna brought up memories of him that I would have never dreamed of. And for her to share them with us at that time gave Brooks and me a lift like you would not believe.

Some of these things may seem small or personal to the outside world. But they were important to us, and their timing was significant. Collectively, they gave us strength that sustained us for the roller coaster ride that was about to begin.

* * * * *

I mentioned before how Brooks and I had come to love the music of Bill and Gloria Gaither. We have collected every one of their "Homecoming" videotapes and have played them many times over the years. The personal testimonies of faith shared by the many artists who have joined the Gaither's in prayer and song have never failed to lift us. This was especially true in the weeks after Ron's funeral, when our spirits were at their lowest ebb.

Around this time a new video called "Singin' in my Soul" came out and featured Jeannie Johnson in the beginning of the program. Several years prior to Ron's death, Bob and Jeannie Johnson gave a concert at one of our Davis Steel Christmas parties. They still live only a few miles from us. I would lay and listen to the tapes playing softly, especially on my worst days, when I could not read or even pray.

One day, I felt led to write Bob and Jeannie and tell them how Jeannie's song blessed me, and also how much the videos had meant to Brooks, Ron, and me over the years. I also shared the details of Ron's brutal death. Bob and Jeannie not only passed on the letter and our story to Bill and Gloria Gaither, they've stayed in touch with us over the years, calling either to ask about court proceedings in Atlanta, or simply to check up on us.

Some time later, I was going through the mail when I came across a handwritten note from Bill Gaither. We had never met the Gaither's before, and yet Bill took the time to send us a beautiful handwritten note offering their prayers for our loss:

Bob and Jeannie passed your letter along to us. I can't imagine the pain you are and have gone through. Our love and prayers are with you.
    We seem so helpless, but at least we can do that.

In His Love,
Bill Gaither

"This is like a nugget of gold!" I exclaimed. I could not wait to show it to Brooks. This was not just words on a piece of paper-for someone as busy and famous as Bill Gaither to take the time to write us a note, which was truly love in action.

As Brooks and I began to reflect back, it seemed like each time we were about to sink back into despair, another "nugget of gold" would come along to lift us just above the circumstances and enable us to carry on.

Who says God doesn't move in mysterious ways!

CHAPTER TWENTY-ONE

The Roller Coaster Ride Begins

Meanwhile, detectives from the Georgia Bureau of Investigation and the Fulton County Police Department continued to probe Ron's murder. Soon they would close in on two suspects: Michael Benjamin LeJeune, 20, and Rekha "Kelly" Anand, 19, both from Roswell, Georgia. LeJeune was a small-time drug dealer determined to make a name for himself in the local drug world. Anand was his longtime girlfriend.

Brooks and I had never heard of these people, nor were we aware of any connection they could have had with Ron. But soon it became clear that LeJeune was the "Mike" who Ron was talking about when we spoke to him around 10:00 a.m. on December 27, 1997. As it happened, Ron called us that morning from LeJeune's apartment (our telephone bill would later reflect a call of 23 minutes from the number listed under Michael LeJeune). Apparently, Ron had been dropped off there in the early morning hours by his roommate, Neil.

As we hung up the phone that Saturday morning, we had no idea just how close Ron was to losing his life. "Love you, Dad" were his final words to us. Within two hours, he would be dead.

According to witnesses, Michael LeJeune purchased a saw at a hardware store near his apartment building sometime after 12 noon on Saturday, December 28. Several hours later, LeJeune and Anand were then spotted carrying large black garbage bags out of their apartment and putting the bags inside the trunk of a 1990 Toyota Corolla registered to LeJeune's mother. It would later come out that the tires on LeJeune's car were an exact match of the tire tracks found the next day at the cemetery where Ron's body was discovered. LeJeune and Anand were also seen that Saturday evening at a service station, where they bought gas.

Of course, this was all circumstantial evidence. The Georgia Bureau of Investigation needed something much more substantial to establish probable cause and obtain a warrant for LeJeune and Anand's arrest. Yet at the same time, it was enough information to give us hope. How many times have we read or seen news stories about homicides where the police have no leads whatsoever to go on? As difficult as it was to cope with Ron's murder, at least Brooks and I could take comfort in knowing the authorities were building a case against the people responsible for this horrible crime. The G.B.I. was not only confident they were tracking the right suspects, they were certain that it was only a matter of time before they brought them into custody.

In the meantime, Brooks and I continued to help in whatever way we could. Through the G.B.I., we established a $10,000 reward for any information leading to the arrest and conviction of Ron's murderer. More than anything else, though, we constantly kept in touch with the authorities, passing along any information we could think of that could possibly help the investigation. When the telephone bill arrived, we sent the G.B.I. a copy of it. As it happened, one of the items we gave them before we left from Atlanta would result in a significant break in the case.

Back on January 2, when Brooks and I drove down to Atlanta after hearing about the unidentified body, we provided detectives with the name, address, and telephone number of Kenneth Vaughn in Jasper, Georgia, a onetime associate of Michael LeJeune who Ron had come in contact with in the last months of his life. Brooks and I had never met Vaughn, and in fact had only spoken to him once before-and that was by the grace of God.

Around the middle of December, we had reason to believe that Ron was still struggling after coming out of Charter Peachford Hospital the first part of the month. According to Western Union records, Ron called us on December 18, 1997 while on his way to Jasper, Georgia. He had relapsed again and was begging for money. For Brooks and me, it was back to tough love. I told Ron emphatically that we would not be sending him any more money until he found some facility or hospital to check himself in to. All Ron said was, "I'll call you when I get there"-*there*, meaning Jasper.

Some time later that afternoon, Ron called again, saying "I'm in Jasper, Georgia," while still begging desperately for money. We went back and forth a few times before he finally said that he would be checking into a halfway house there.

At that point, I demanded the phone number from where he was calling-without realizing that in doing so, I was about to paint Ron into a corner.

Of course, in many ways Ron's behavior was nothing new. But at the same time, he had never given me a telephone number like this whenever he used drugs. Nevertheless, I kept insisting until he finally gave me that number.

Everything sounded strange to me, so I told Ron I wanted to know the facility and the person in charge of it, and that I wouldn't send him anything unless he gave me that information. I told him I would wire it to the facility. At that point, Ron handed the phone over to Kenneth Vaughn.

Vaughn and I talked for several minutes. He told me he was running a halfway house-he even made up some name for it on the spot. (In all likelihood, Ron owed Vaughn some money.) None of the details, however, would become known to us until the next day.

I took down Vaughn's address and phone number and arranged to have the money wired to him. (I still have that same piece of paper with all the information on it.) Then I told him I wanted to speak to Ron. Since I was still under the impression that Ron would be checking himself into a legitimate facility, I made Ron promise before he hung up the phone that he would call us just as soon as he was settled. He had always done that before, just as soon as he became accountable.

When Ron hadn't called us by the following morning, I telephoned Vaughn. Vaughn's girlfriend, Doris, whom he would soon marry, answered the phone. She was not aware of my conversation with Vaughn from the previous day. When I told her what had happened, she sounded absolutely terrified. I was furious, venting on her and explaining our son's relapse and illness. Doris insisted that she knew nothing about drugs, but said that she would have Kenneth return my call. Though Doris seemed very sincere in her response, Vaughn unfortunately never called back.

Suddenly it became clear to me why Ron had been so secretive: he must have been calling from the home of a drug dealer. Knowing how much the drug world operates in shadows, he knew he couldn't give out his location over the phone. Not if he wanted to get out of there alive.

It alarms me to think of the position I had put Ron in. And yet at the same time, when I look back at it now, I can only thank God that I did. Because if I hadn't pushed Ron, he would not have given me Kenneth Vaughn's phone number-and I, in turn, would not have been able to give that number to the G.B.I. And had that been the case, it's entirely possible that Ron's murderer may never have been captured.

Kenneth Vaughn, as you're about to see, played a major role in the arrest of Michael LeJeune.

* * *

G.B.I. detectives located Vaughn in Jasper and questioned him. Vaughn cooperated with the authorities and later told the G.B.I. about a meeting he had with LeJeune and Anand at a Waffle House restaurant outside Atlanta within a few days of the murder. During this time LeJeune admitted to Vaughn that he "did the Ron thing," then proceeded to boast about the shooting in graphic detail.

According to authorities, Ron was killed at approximately 12 noon on Saturday, December 27, shortly after picking up the money Brooks and I had wired him less than two hours before. He was seated upright on a sofa in LeJeune's apartment, his head tilted slightly back as though he was resting. He was shot once in the back of the head. He died instantly, never knowing what had hit him.

Vaughn informed authorities that LeJeune told him that he thought Ron "would never shut up." Exactly, what they were arguing over remains unclear. What is known, however, is that LeJeune took the entire $250.00 we had wired Ron.

According to Vaughn, LeJeune and Anand then dragged Ron's body upstairs in order to dismember it in the bath tub. (This was made necessary by the fact that Ron was a big man-6 feet 2 inches, weighing over 200 pounds-while LeJeune and Anand were both small in stature. Neither was capable of lifting the body.) At first they tried using knives to cut up the body. When that didn't work, LeJeune left the apartment to purchase a saw. When he returned, he and Anand sawed off Ron's limbs.

"He described the sound that it made when bone was being sawed," Vaughn would later testify in court. "He told me the head was bouncing down the stairs."

Vaughn told the G.B.I. that after they severed Ron's limbs, LeJeune and Anand put the body parts inside trash bags. They then filled the rest of the bags with dirty laundry, put them in the trunk of LeJeune's car, and drove out to the cemetery, where they doused the remains with gasoline and set them on fire. They severed the head at the cemetery, which still had the bullet in it.

Vaughn then explained LeJeune's next move, as LeJeune had relayed it to him. LeJeune knew that because the murder weapon was registered to him, he would have to hide Ron's head apart from the body. That way, even if the police were to locate the gun used to kill Ron, they would not be able to find the bullet that killed Ron. (Because LeJeune had ambitions of moving up in the local drug scene, there is some speculation that he wanted to keep the head as a sort of trophy before finally disposing of it several days later.) According to Vaughn, though LeJeune told him at the Waffle House that he did in fact hide Ron's head, he did not disclose where it was hidden. That information would not come out until later in the investigation.

After telling the G.B.I. about his meeting with LeJeune at the Waffle House, Vaughn agreed to place a controlled telephone call to LeJeune's apartment, with G.B.I. agents Wayne White and Jeff Branyon listening in. The transcript of this phone conversation is part of the court record.

According to the transcript, Rekha Anand answered the phone.

At the time Vaughn called, Anand and LeJeune were still trying to remove the blood stains from their carpet. Apparently they tried using carpet cleaner or some other chemical solution, but "that just turned it purple," Anand said to Vaughn.

Vaughn said, "You got to get rid of that carpet then."

"Uh huh," said Anand.

"What did Mike want to talk to me about?" asked Vaughn.

"I don't know," said Anand. "He talked to Donna about it. He didn't really tell me too much, because I was too busy eating."

"It was a thing about the cut off thing?" asked Vaughn. (Though it is not exactly clear what Vaughn meant by the "cut off thing," from the context of the conversation he appears to have been referring to some other drug transaction involving LeJeune.)

"Yeah," said Anand. "I don't know. I think he wants to talk to you some more."

Vaughn then asked Anand to put LeJeune on the phone. As it happened, there was a report in that day's news about another body that had found near the cemetery where LeJeune and Anand had disposed of Ron's remains. Vaughn used this item to try to extract more details from LeJeune about Ron's murder. "That was the same place that you guys put him," he said.

However, this time LeJeune played coy. "I don't know," he said. "I didn't put him anywhere."

"Oh, no, you know what I mean," said Vaughn. "The cemetery out there?"

"Yeah, the same place he was," said LeJeune.

"Okay," said Vaughn.

"And you know what they said?" said LeJeune. "They said that they told him that whoever did it, like burned [him] in fire, and then after it burned, cut him all up."

"So maybe they'll think that whoever did the kid... you know," said Vaughn.

"Huh?" said LeJeune.

"Maybe they think it's the same person," said Vaughn.

"That's what they were thinking," said LeJeune. "They were looking at Jose a little bit, because he had some kind of book. Over by Adam's and them, they found some two bullets, and then they found some book, and the book had... had a bunch of dragons, like Dungeons and Dragons [the popular role-playing fantasy game]. And like all over the book, it was talking about, like, dismembering people and burning them, and all kind of wacky [stuff]."

Vaughn tried his best to elicit more information, but that was the extent to which LeJeune would discuss the matter over the phone. The call ended a few minutes later.

Still, the details about the blood-stained carpet, coupled with Vaughn's account of what LeJeune had told him that night at the Waffle House, gave authorities probable cause to conduct their surveillance of LeJeune's apartment until they obtained a search warrant. A few days later, on January 21, 1998, G.B.I. agents made the arrest. LeJeune and Anand were formally charged with Ron's murder.

G.B.I. agent Wayne White called us just before they made the arrest. "We've got the warrant signed," he said. "We have reason to believe LeJeune might try to skip town, so we're gonna go out and get him now."

"That's great," said Brooks. "We really appreciate your keeping us up to date. But could you do us just one more favor?"

"Sure, Mr. Davis, What do you need?"

"Call us back the moment you bring them in," said Brooks. "No matter how late it is."

They did just that. I remember getting the call at something like four or five in the morning. And I remember the relief we both felt once we knew it was official. Despite our grief, we knew that we could take comfort in the knowledge that the prime suspect in Ron's murder was finally apprehended.

Shortly after the arrest of LeJeune and Anand, Vaughn's lawyer, Jerry Froelich, called us concerning the $10,000.00 reward. Brooks and I confirmed that it would be paid to Vaughn upon the conviction and sentencing of Ron's killer. The money was held in escrow until after the trial.

* * * * * * * *

Whenever Brooks and I speak to people or a group about Ron's life, one question we are often asked is, "Which moment was the worst for you?"

That question has never been easy to answer, because the enormity of the grief is so hard to measure. In many ways, as I mentioned before, the worst came after the funeral was over, when all the people were gone. That's when it hit us the hardest and we really had to grasp for strength.

For me, another difficult time was a combination of sitting in the sheriff's office on the morning of January 2, 1998, looking at the manikin that was dressed like Ron, and answering questions about Ron without knowing whether he was dead or alive. That, plus the phone call we received three nights later, confirming that the victim was Ron, was the hardest moment of all.

For both of us together, the morning of May 18, 1998, when we saw LeJeune and Anand in person for the first time. . . that was especially difficult. That was the day of their arraignment hearing.

I can now understand why some people try to jump over the bench whenever a defendant is led into the courtroom.

During the 30 plus trips to Atlanta and in the course of the entire trial, there has never been one ounce of remorse on Michael LeJeune's face.

It would be one thing if someone had just shot Ron, and we had seen his body, and later buried him. That would be no less painful, mind you, but in a way I could almost live with it Almost.

But when I think about what happened to Ron, I see his desecrated body smoldering in the snow, and I start to wonder once again why anyone could possibly do that to him. When I think about what happened, I find myself constantly fighting off all the horrible images that I wish I could cast from my mind.

That's when it becomes a bit too much. That's when I especially find myself asking God for the strength to get me through it.

I still remember breaking down into tears the first time Brooks and I laid eyes on the man who took Ron's life. We were both overwhelmed with emotion, yet somehow Brooks managed to hold himself together while comforting me. LeJeune sat there with his hair slicked back, all prim and proper, as if he were going to church- a far cry from the scruffy, unkempt soulless figure whose picture we'd seen in the paper. "Like I said, not even the slightest remorse." Like his lawyer, Brian Steel-an ambitious young man who would become a thorn in our side for the next eight years-LeJeune acted as though this was all just a big mistake. How anyone could possibly do that, in the face of all that evidence against him, is beyond my comprehension.

Rekha Anand, on the other hand, was shaky, weepy, and obviously very nervous. Part of the time, she sat there biting her fingernails. Unlike LeJeune, whose parents were from Atlanta and attended the hearing, the only person Anand had to support her was, Fulton County public defender Gary Guichard. Apparently Anand's parents were from New York and did not have the financial means to attend any of the hearings. With one exception, she would remain alone at every court hearing, without any family or friends to support her, over the course of the next five years.

* * * * * * * *

May 18, 1998 was also the day that Kenneth Vaughn, as well G.B.I. agent Jeff Branyon, were called to the stand by the defense and asked to recount the gruesome details of the murder as they knew them. Though Brooks and I had heard much of those details before, it was still very chilling to hear them described in person.

I'll never forget the exchange between Brooks and LeJeune's parents shortly after the hearing. We were standing close to each other in the hallway outside the courtroom when Brooks turned and extended his hand to LeJeune's father.

"I'm sorry about your son," said Brooks.

"I can't believe Michael did this," said Mr. LeJeune. His wife stood silently beside him, tears streaming from her eyes.

That was all they said. There was nothing more either of them could say.

I remember looking at Diane-she had driven us down for the hearing, along with Brooks' sister Carolyn. The three of us were stunned and amazed that Brooks could even do that. Here he was, at the arraignment of the man who had murdered his son, and yet he still reached out in compassion to LeJeune's parents as a father.

Brooks and I have always said that we would rather be in our shoes than theirs. I guess that was his way of showing it.

* * * * * * * *

Still, I'll admit that in some way, the sight of LeJeune in court seemed like another "nugget of gold," a clear-cut sign that the man responsible for Ron's ghastly demise would soon be brought to justice.

We had no idea how wrong we would be. What seemed at first to be a "cut and dried" case against LeJeune gradually began to disintegrate for reasons you would not believe.

Brooks and I didn't know it, but we were about to get a first-hand education on how the judicial system really works. It was a roller coaster ride that would test our resolve again and again over the course of the next seven years.

Chapter Twenty-Two

"Your Son's Death Saved my Life"

I mentioned before that many years before Ron's death, when Brooks and I finally learned to let go of our pride and trust completely in God, we put Ron's life in God's hands and made Him a promise. We promised God that whatever He allowed to happen, we would not be bitter; instead, we would use it to glorify Him. From that moment on, we put our trust in God, and as we did, He lifted the heavy load . . . as He continues to do today.

I'd like to tell you that it has always been that easy, but truth be told, it hasn't. When you lose a child or loved one, especially in a way as brutal and inexplicable as Ron's murder, it tears you apart. It leaves a void in your life that can never be filled.

And yet, with our trust in God, Brooks and I also know that we are never lost, even in our deepest valleys. With God's help, our love for Ron grew deeper, and our bond as a family became stronger than ever, especially in the last ten years of his life. With God's help, Ron also rediscovered his spiritual life. The more he learned to trust in God again, the more his love for God grew-and the more he showed God's presence in his life by sharing His goodness, and helping others who struggled with addiction.

Ron's funeral reminded us of the many lives our son had touched while he was alive. With God's help, Ron would also save the life of a young woman even after his death. That story is without question the most remarkable "nugget of gold" Brooks and I have ever been blessed with.

A few days after the funeral, I received a telephone call from a young man who said that he and his wife knew Ron from Atlanta. By that time, Diane had gone home, and Brooks was still sick in bed, so I had to handle all the telephone calls. We had never met these people before, and for reasons of safety, I cannot reveal their real names.

This young couple, you see, were both friends of Michael LeJeune and Rekha Anand. In fact, the husband-let's call him "Johnny"-went on to tell me that he was at LeJeune's apartment on the afternoon of Ron's murder. He drove over to pick up some tools he had left behind when he noticed LeJeune and Anand carrying large black garbage bags out of the apartment. Not only that, there were more bags inside-and they even asked him to help carry them out!

Johnny told me that he and his wife knew Ron from the 8111 Club, the AA group whose meetings Ron attended regularly several times a week while he was in Atlanta. He had just heard about the body that was found near the Hopewell Church cemetery. When he learned the victim was Ron, he felt compelled to call.

"Mrs. Davis," he said, "I want to tell you that I come from a Christian family, just like Ron did-and I've had some problems with addiction in the past. But I'm on my feet now, and I'm back at work. I just wanted you to know that."

I was so shocked by the call that I wanted to be careful to say the right thing. So I asked Johnny for his telephone number, and also asked him if I could call agent Wayne White at the Georgia Bureau of Investigation and tell him exactly what he had just told me.

Johnny told me that he was trying to get his life back on track in order to try and restore his marriage, and that he did not want to do anything that would get him in trouble. When I assured him that I would explain all that to Agent White, he agreed to give me his work number. Agent White told me later that he had called Johnny and spoke to him.

I also told Johnny how much I appreciated his call. We talked about Ron for a long while. He told me that he and his wife were separated, and that she knew Ron better than he did, but they both cared for him very much.

At some point, I asked Johnny if he'd like a tape of the funeral. (As I mentioned before, it was the practice of Mount Harmony Baptist Church to make an audio recording of every service.) He said yes, and asked me to send it to the home of his parents.

There's no question that Johnny passed along that tape to his wife-for purposes of this book, let's call her "Cathy"-and Brooks and I are so grateful that he did. About a month later, we received a letter from Cathy. In that letter she shared with us a story so inspiring; it can only be described as a miracle:

My name is Cathy. You've talked with my husband, Johnny. I just wanted to write and thank you so much for the letter and tape of Ron's funeral. He was very special to me and his death has made an incredible impact on my recovery. It is amazing to me how someone with the kind of pain you must have can still reach out to people you don't even know-and people who were associated with Ron's negative side.

I, too, have been struggling with crack addiction for about 13 years. I also come from a very strong Christian family. Maybe these things were what attracted me to Ron. The first night I met him, he seemed so "real" and straightforward. You don't meet many addicts like that. Although he knew what he was doing was wrong, he never quit talking about gaining control of his addiction or about his love for his family. I think maybe he was more open with me due to the situation I was in.

My husband and I have been separated for about a year. Early in December, my Mom took my two children, two and five years old, away from me and told me to get help. I weighed 95 pounds and am 5 ft., 7 inches. I hadn't slept or eaten in days. I was devastated and had definitely hit "bottom." I enrolled in the Northside Recovery Center for the second time, a bitter and angry person, determined to get my kids back and nothing else. I wasn't living anywhere at the time and had two days left to go into their halfway house. Ron let me stay with him those two days. He seemed so excited about my going into recovery and said he wished he could go, too. I teased him and said he could go, but he said he had already tried that. I only understand now, after your letters, how truly happy he was for me.

That final day, December 21, 1997, I told him I was backing out. I just couldn't go through with it. He told me he would carry me if he had to. When I left he hugged me and kissed me on the top of my head and said that everything was gonna turn out just fine. December 22nd, I came into recovery. I hated everyone, but mostly myself.

I had been there a week when they discovered him. I knew that tattoo, but thought, "Surely, millions must have them. It couldn't be Ron."

The day he was identified was the day my life changed. You see, up until then, all I wanted was to get my kids back by finishing this program anyway I had to. That day was one of raging emotions: shock, fear, terror, repulsion, you name it, I felt it. The cocaine had always numbed my emotions and this day, with about two weeks clean, they all came flooding back. How could anyone do this to him? Did I know these people? I couldn't sleep, couldn't turn off my lights and was afraid to be left alone. My mind was racing so hard I couldn't think straight.

Two days later I did what I had to do. I got on my knees and prayed harder than I had in a long time, and God brought me peace. Suddenly I realized that I truly wanted to be free from this disease. I could see all the destruction it had caused and how that could just have easily been me-either with Ron or by myself.

I wanted to be a good mother to my children and the child God had created me to be. Many people at 8111 AA Group talked about Ron from seeing him in and out of there. One night, I was asked to chair a meeting, not even 30 days clean. I shared about the Ron I knew and loved and his insights on addiction that he talked so well, but couldn't seem to grasp him- self. The more I shared, the more the pain seemed not to be so intolerable. At this point, I just wanted to catch the _____ who did this.

The morning of my 30 days clean came shock number two. Two people who were very close to me, people I called friends-people who I trusted to watch my children-were accused of this. How could this be, God? Is my judgment so bad that I couldn't even fathom them doing this? Would Mike have done this to me or my children? After all, we were supposedly friends.

I went to my CA Group and cried, ranted, raved and then picked up my 30-day chip. Thank the Lord for a wonderful sponsor and supportive group. They couldn't believe I hadn't used over all this and all I could think was, *how could I use???* I think Ron would have been extremely disappointed.

Besides, with each disaster, God was making me stronger and stronger. God showed me a vision of myself in the middle of chaos and this HUGE hand, reaching down and picking me up right out of the middle. It was so overwhelming, I realized it truly was HIS footprints in the sand and He was carrying me through.

Last week, I found out I had Lupus, just as I got 60 days clean. I don't know why God is choosing all my landmark days to bear bad news, but who am I to ask? Today, I can live with this. This program has taught me to turn my life over to God and truly, He does a much better job of handling it than I do. I've started my steps. Step 1 taught me gratefulness and when I look on these last two months, I can't be anything but grateful. Step 2 has taught me hope. I know in my heart God wouldn't have brought me this far to drop me now.

Your son and my friend's death opened my heart and eyes so God could show me these things. I often wondered why something so horrible had to happen until I read your letters. I now see that Ron has been taken home and is TRULY FINALLY FREE. Jesus cured Ron of his addiction and in the meantime changed many lives for the better and that's the best form of recovery I can think of.

Sometimes I wonder whether Jesus isn't letting Ron hold my hand, because I swear, sometimes I can hear his voice and see him smiling down at me in approval.

You are a blessed family and I know Ron loved ya'll so much. I hope you don't mind my writing this, but I thought it might ease a little pain to know some good has come out of Ron's death. It has been a real life saver for me.

Much love, and God Bless,
Cathy

I cannot tell you how uplifting it was, for Brooks and me both, to get that letter. Ron was as down as we had ever heard him, struggling to cope that week of Christmas 1997-and yet, even in the depths of despair, he continued to reach out to Cathy. Remember, the last time we saw Ron was during the Thanksgiving holiday, one month before the murder. I can imagine him calling on his grandfather's favorite phrase as he continued to encourage her: *"Keep on keeping on."*

That letter reminded us once again how the God of the good times is also our God in the bad times. And as much as we grieved the loss of our son, we are never without hope, because God is always with us.

CHAPTER TWENTY-THREE

A Scholarship in Ron's Memory

A lot of people probably gave up on Ron, but Brooks and I never lost hope. No matter how many times he relapsed, it became like a stepping stone that would help him to the next spiritual level. As much as it broke our hearts to witness the pain and consequences he brought on himself whenever he used drugs, it lifts our spirits to hear stories like Cathy's-to know how many lives Ron touched along the way, and that his own life was not in vain.

Our faith in Ron would be affirmed once again three months after his death. That's when Brooks and I met Brian Brown, another former addict who also turned his life around with the help of our son. Brian's story is yet another miraculous "nugget of gold" that continues to give us peace today.

A short time after Ron's funeral, I received a letter from Becky Yates, the executive director of Caring Services, the Christian-based halfway house in High Point, North Carolina where Ron briefly rehabbed in 1996.

Ron liked the people at Caring Services so much, he not only did volunteer work occasionally in their offices, but continued to reach out to other clients who struggled to recover from their addiction. And as I mentioned before, he donated many of the items and furnishings from his Christian Unity Men's Home that was kept in storage to Caring Services. In his short time there, he had made his presence felt in more ways than one-so the news of his murder hit especially close to home. In fact, he was the first client of that facility ever to have died.

Becky wrote us with a special request. Because of the tremendous impact Ron had had on the program, the Board of Directors at Caring Services wanted our permission to start a scholarship in Ron's name that would fund a relapse prevention program. All funds would be specially earmarked for extra counseling, resources, and supportive services to Caring Services residents who are either chronic relapsers or who pose a high risk for relapse. It would be a tribute to Ron that would also carry on the work he had started at Christian Unity Men's home, reaching out to those who lack the healthy recovery system they need to overcome their addiction. Even though the Christian Unity Men's Home had long since closed down, Ron would be so happy to know that his efforts were not in vain-that the seeds he had planted would carry on in helping others who were chronic relapsers.

I cannot tell you how much that news meant to us, coming as it did at a time when Brooks and I were still coping with the shock of Ron's murder. It just lifted our hearts to know that somehow God had seen that some good might come from this horrible, senseless act of evil.

A few weeks later, in April 1998, the Board of Directors formally announced the establishment of the Ronnie A. Davis Memorial Scholarship Fund at their annual banquet dinner. Becky invited Brooks and me as guests of honor. After dinner, she asked us to stand and say a few words about Ron. Though we were both still struggling emotionally, God gave us the strength to do just that.

I no longer have the notes of the speech we gave that night, but I remember sharing how much Ron thought of everyone at Caring Services, and how touched he would be about the Memorial Scholarship in his memory. We talked of how he ended up in Atlanta later on under the care of Dr. Tommy Richardson-the first person to ever offer medical attention for his addiction. We also shared the statement Ron made to us six months prior to his death: that he felt in his soul that someday God would give him a word for his church and community-but that "it wouldn't be from Ron, but from God. For now, I'll just walk the walk." Little did he know that the word from God would come through his life as well as his death.

After we spoke, a young man named Brian Brown came up to the podium to speak. Brian was a graduate of the Caring Services program who briefly rehabbed with Ron in 1996. Like Ron, Brian had also managed a recovery center while struggling to overcome his own addiction. Like Cathy, his life was also changed by Ron, and he decided to use his friend's death as a reminder to make the most of his time before it was too late.

As Brian spoke, it soon became clear that while he only knew Ron for a short time, he cared for him deeply and had grown to understand him as few people did. Brooks and I were so moved by his heartfelt testimony; we asked if he would agree to type up his story so that we might someday share it with others. Brian not only agreed, he also graciously gave me his consent when I asked if I could share his story in this book.

A few months after the banquet, Brian sent me his story along with a short note. "Thank you for allowing me to share my story with the world," he wrote. "I would like to say that it was difficult to just share about me. My spirit went in another direction. This entry is more about my relationship with your son and my relationship with God today. It was a pleasure and it filled my heart."

Every time I read Brian's story about how much his relationship with Ron meant to him, my heart just beams with joy. I hope it touches your heart, as well.

It was March of 1996 when I first met Ron. We bonded instantly. Looking back I can see how God put us together at the same time for a reason. I had been clean for 14 months and I also managed a recovery house in the area. I was really hurting bad and all around me were addicts who knew little to nothing about recovery. Then there was Ron, who not only knew of recovery but who had previously owned a recovery house. We spent hours talking about how sweet recovery had been to us. We shared the pain of the guilt, remorse and shame that had landed us in the same place that was so familiar to us. The empty hole that haunted our spirit grew with each passing day. We had each other and through all the insanity that led to us meeting at that moment little did I know that Ron was going to make a major impact on my life and God would send us on this journey together.

I left Ron and arrived in High Point, North Carolina at a recovery environment called Caring Services. This came to be the place where my recovery began to transform into something exciting and new. To my surprise, Ron was sent to the same place a week later. God had answered a prayer for me, my buddy was with me and all was right in the world. I soon learned that what I wanted out of recovery was different than that of my trusted friend. Sure, we both wanted to enjoy life and live drug free but I had the understanding of patience in my heart and soul. I tried the best I could to tell Ron to slow down, but he wanted to do things his way, and I supported his every effort. (This was another example of Ron's short interest span and impatience.) He was always loving and supportive of me and we really stood by each other. As time went on, Ron withdrew from me because I continued to live in the halfway house and he, on the other hand, moved into his own place. From that point on all I could do was pray for my friend. . . and pray I did.

After several months, Ron started using again. I still tried to be there for him as much as I could but I had to be careful because now I was dealing with someone I did not know. Everything about him was different. I knew he was empty on the inside, so I tried to give him something to hold on to-me. I remember him coming to my job one night, and it was quite uncomfortable for him. He was not himself, and as I tried to calm him we both cried. I feel he cried about what he had become and I cried because I had not one clue as to how to help my friend. [Soon after that time] Ron moved away and I never heard from him again.

It was tragic news when I received the information of his brutal death. As I cried, I reflected back on the laughter and the many times we hugged each other for strength. And it would be that strength that would continue to guide me. He encouraged me when I was afraid many times, and now it was time to face myself, knowing that my friend would always be a part of whom I am and who I am learning to be.

With each passing day as I face this life with a belief in God and a belief in self, I hold on daily to the spirit of my friend because he taught me that I was worthy of love. He taught me that my dreams could be reality no matter how far out of reach they seem. The death of my friend made a great impact on my life. It was one of the many things that directed me to be where I am in life today. I had finally started to do something productive and then this notion to try and go to college would not let go. It was scary for me to quit a full-time job with benefits. I never made good grades in school, so where was this coming from, I wondered. My thoughts were: I am 38 years old, it is too late, drugs have fried my brain, what could I possibly want to go to school for, but as ridiculous as the idea sounded in my head, it felt right in my heart.

Today, I am a full-time college student and most days I am still afraid of so many things. Money is more than tight. I have no room for error. It's down to the bare necessities. I had to give up my dental and health insurance to go back to school. My car is not the newest model, so I'm always doing one thing or another to it. I rarely see a movie without the kindness of a friend and I only work part-time because 100% of self goes into my studies. I have been blessed to work at a drug and alcohol treatment center so I get to keep the disease of addiction close and up front-after all, I plan to be a substance abuse counselor with God's grace. My last semester, I received the honor of being on the President's list with a 4.0 grade point average. God has walked with me all the way. The support of friends and loved ones make it all worthwhile. I am grateful for what I do have so the few things I don't have are just - things.

With each passing day, I try and live in that day. I am able to face things that I never thought I would be able to stand up to-living life on life's terms, not Brian's. I accept that life has its ups and downs and I may not agree with it, but I'm learning to adapt to what it is in front of me. I spend a lot of time sharing who I am with others, so that their hope may one day be freedom. . . that same freedom Ron and I spent hours and hours sharing about now today belongs to me.

Loving and Respectfully Submitted,
Brian Brown

Brian Brown sent me these words in 1999. Brooks and I kept in contact with him for several years, and we occasionally sent him some spending money to help him with his studies. We are happy to report that he graduated from Guilford Technical College, near Greensboro with a 4.0 average and a goal to become a substance abuse counselor some day. That dream has since become a reality. Today he is on staff at Caring Services in the capacity of service coordinator.

I'd like to think that somewhere up in Heaven, Ron is also filled with joy, knowing that God continues to work through him even after his death. Ron may have struggled with his own self esteem, but he could surely bring it out in others.

CHAPTER TWENTY-FOUR

"Remember, We're in This for the Long Haul"

I mentioned before how Brooks and I have occasionally had the opportunity to speak to groups about our story. If there's one idea we always try to get across, it's this: no matter how dark things seem, or how low you feel, God is always there for us if we're willing to let Him in.

That has been certainly true for us. There is no way we could have sustained ourselves throughout the roller coaster of emotions we've experienced, first through our journey through Ron's addiction, then our journey through the judicial system, without the help of God.

As devastating as Ron's murder was, Brooks and I continue to believe in the wisdom of God and the knowledge that He will make His purpose known to us when He is ready for us to understand it.

I mean, we can't help but think we're ready all the time-otherwise, we wouldn't be human. But just because we think we're ready to know God's purpose doesn't always mean we actually are. Only God knows when that moment is for sure. Hard as it can be, though, sometimes we just need to be patient, have faith, and remember that God will provide us with what we need at precisely the right moment.

There have been many examples of this throughout these pages, particularly the series of little miracles following Ron's death that

I've described as "nuggets of gold." One thing for which Brooks and I will always be grateful is the introduction of three special people who have graced our lives in the years since Ron's death. These people have since become close friends who have constantly shown us love, comfort, and moral support as we continue to walk through our journey.

Of all the miracles that God blessed us with over the past nine years, in many ways our friendships with these people are the most precious "nuggets" of all. I'd like to take a moment and introduce you to them now:

Sharon Green

Sharon and her husband Tom were the first residents of the new housing subdivision that Brooks and I joined shortly before Ron's death. We moved into our home not long after they moved into theirs.

Immediately after Ron's murder, Sharon made a point of calling me almost every day just to check on us and see how we were doing. They also made themselves available to stay at our home while we were at the funeral home for visitation. Since Tom is retired from a military career, both he and Sharon work part time at a local funeral home. They have a real gift for comforting and assisting others.

As time went by, Sharon and I came to discover how much we had in common, and have since become very close friends. Among other things, we love shopping, decorating our homes, and going out to lunch. Sharon is a very upbeat person and has a laugh that can lift you out of your sad moments. I am so grateful for her friendship and especially for living so close to us.

Once again, God filled my needs at just the right moment-this time, with a neighbor who became a close friend.

During the depressing winter months after Ron's death, Sharon would come regularly and walk the treadmill at our house, so that we had even more time to talk. It was during this time that we planned a trip to New York City for the four of us. At the time we had no idea when the very first hearing in Atlanta would be scheduled. We made arrangements to fly out on Friday, May 15, 1998-four months after Michael LeJeune and Rekha Anand were apprehended and charged with Ron's murder.

As it happened, just as we were about to leave for New York early Friday morning, we received word that a bond hearing for LeJeune and Anand was scheduled for first thing Monday morning, May 18-the day after we were scheduled to return. That meant that for Brooks and I to make the hearing, we'd have to jump in the car as soon as we arrived in Charlotte on Sunday night and immediately make that long five-hour drive down to Atlanta.

As much as we looked forward to our weekend trip to the Big Apple, it hardly seemed worth the hassle. On the scale of things, being in Atlanta for Monday's hearing was far more important. Yet at the same time, Brooks and I knew that the time away would be good for us, and besides, we didn't want to disappoint Tom and Sharon.

Fortunately, we were able to arrange for Diane, Nonia, and Brooks' sister Carolyn to meet us at the Charlotte airport as soon as we arrived on Sunday night. They would drive us down to Atlanta. That way, we could rest up for the hearing without the strain and worry about driving all night.

Still, as wonderful as it was to enjoy the sights of New York that weekend, you can imagine how tense Brooks and I were. After all, that hearing in Atlanta marked the first time we would see LeJeune and Anand in person. I mentioned before how painful it was to see them in the courtroom that day.

And yet, as difficult as that experience was, our anxiety in the days just before that hearing was allayed, thanks to the presence of Tom and Sharon Green.

* * *

Dru Quarles

Dru was my physician in the years prior to Ron's death. One of the nurses at the clinic where she practiced was a friend of mine named Mildred Fisher. Mildred and I have known each other for ages, and it was she who recommended Dru as my new doctor after my previous doctor left the clinic. Over the ensuing years, the relationship between Dru and I would gradually change from "doctor to patient" to "friend to friend."

One day, not long after Ron's murder, I was sitting around the house feeling very depressed when suddenly the phone rang. It was Dru. "Jean," she said, "I was just thinking about you. I'm throwing a surprise party for my parents this Saturday evening-it's their 40th wedding anniversary. I wondered if you and Brooks might like to join us."

Isn't it amazing how God's timing is always so perfect?

Brooks and I went to the party that night and were greeted by Dru's entire family. Little did I know that this would be the start of yet another special friendship.

'Not long afterward, Dru left her practice to stay home and be a fulltime mom to her daughter Anabelle, who was 18 months old at the time. (Dru and her husband, Bob, have since had another child, a beautiful boy named Sam.) Soon we began to meet for lunch from time to time and our friendship continued to grow. Brooks and I celebrate Christmas Eve with Dru and her family every year. Not only that, we were honored when Dru and Bob asked us to be godparents to their children.

Though Dru is much younger than me (she was 37 when we first became friends), the difference in our ages has never been a barrier for either of us. She is very intelligent and wise beyond her years, with a big heart and a sense of humor that makes her a joy to be around. I have known her to take an elderly woman, who was also one of her patients, into her home and provide her with a place to live while she was making a housing transition. Then another time, when that same lady fell and broke her arm, Dru again took her in and took care of her. She is such a loving and caring person, always thinking of others.

One day during the summer of 2003, at a time when it looked like the case against LeJeune might finally come to trial, Dru contacted seven of my friends and asked them each for an old piece of gold jewelry. She then took the pieces and had them made into a gold nugget pendant for me and a tie pin for Brooks. Her idea was for Brooks and I each to have a "nugget of gold" that we could wear throughout the trial as a reminder that we are loved and prayed for-and that those of our friends who couldn't be there in person, would still be there in spirit. It was one of the most touching things anyone has ever done for us.

Dru and I have grown so close, and yet it took a while before I could finally bring myself to call her just "Dru." Even when we first became friends, she was still "Dr. Quarles" to me. Then one day, while we were at the beach, "You know, it sounds kind of silly for me to keep calling you 'Dr. Quarles.'"

We laughed and she agreed. Now she is "just Dru."

* * *

Ketta Guy

About two years after Ron's death, I was home having a particularly rough day when once again, the phone rang. I picked up the phone and I found myself talking to a woman named Ketta Guy. Ketta said she was not only from Atlanta, she was also one of Ron's counselors when he rehabbed at Bethel Christian Home.

Ketta had just recently heard about the tragedy and wanted to extend her condolences. She said that she felt as though she knew us already because Ron was always talking about his family, his grandfather Barney, and especially his parents.

"Ron really loved his family," she said.

Ketta talked about how each time she met with his group, she'd always look at Ron and think to herself how totally different he was from everyone else. He didn't look like, act like, or dress like any other addict she knew, and she was always amazed by his honesty and generosity. She talked about the insights Ron had about addiction and his knowledge of the Bible, and how he always spoke openly about his experience in order to help others.

"When Ronnie got leveled out after a relapse," Ketta said, "he had compassion, love, a sense of brokenness about himself, and a desire to be better and do better all of the time. His life has truly impacted mine forever. Every time I see an addict or homeless person, I think of Ron. He has given me a deeper compassion and love for the homeless and the addicts than I ever would have imagined.

"In spite of what has happened, as long as I live and have breath in my body, I will bear witness to the lost and to those who are challenged with addictions, and share Ron's story with them."

These are the things that have brought Brooks and I the most comfort: hearing from people who knew Ron and had been a part of his life. When you suddenly lose a loved one, your own memories and the memories of those who knew him are really the only things you have to hold onto. Somehow you need to talk about the loved one and mention his name whenever you feel like bringing those memories into a conversation.

I mentioned before how difficult it was for Brooks and I not to be able to see Ron's body after the murder, as though he had simply disappeared. That's why it's so comforting just to talk about him, especially with people who knew him... people such as Ketta Guy.

Ketta and I bonded instantly. Before long we began talking about the possibility of meeting in the future. About three months after that first phone call, I invited Ketta up for the weekend. I'll never forget what she said to Brooks and me when she left at the end of the weekend. She said, "Just remember, we're in this for the long haul."

How true that has been. Ever since that time, Ketta has not only been a faithful friend and encourager who regularly calls just to check in on me, she has been our constant companion at many hearings in Atlanta. It seemed that every time we got our hopes up thinking that the trial would finally begin, discouragement and stress would inevitably sink in with every setback. I can't tell you the number of times we have feared that the criminals might go free because of technicalities. Being a Christian Certified Counselor, Ketta has always been quick to console me whenever I sink into despair.

* * * * *

Brooks and I are so blessed to have many long time friends who have loved and supported us. Some are mentioned in this book, but it would be impossible to mention everyone for fear of leaving someone out. These friends are to never be forgotten.

I always think of the scripture *"A true friend sticks closer than a brother."* Proverbs 18:24. A true friend is there in the good times, as well as the bad. A true friend will say to you without hesitation, "We're in this for the long haul."

216

Chapter Twenty-Five

Our Hearts Will Not Be Quashed

Even without setbacks, a death penalty murder case is a roller coaster ride that can grind your emotions to a nub. It's like treating a horrible wound: you know it's going to be painful, and you know no matter how long it takes, it will never completely heal. There will be always be a scar to remind you of the loss your family has suffered.

When Michael LeJeune and Kelly Anand were charged with Ron's murder in January 1998, Brooks and I were led to believe it was only a matter of time before justice would be done. The agents from the Georgia Bureau of Investigation were confident they had apprehended the man responsible for this heinous crime, and that the trial should begin "within two years' time at most." Not only that, the physical evidence gathered against LeJeune was so overwhelming, it seemed like just a matter of time before the prosecution got a conviction.

And yet, due entirely to a string of legal technicalities and other delay tactics instigated by LeJeune's lawyer, Brian Steel-it would be nearly eight years before the case ever went to trial. Every time we got hopes up, and we appeared close to a trial date, Steel would pull the rug out from under us and convince the court to further delay the proceedings on even more obscure and inane grounds. Not only that, with each delay the once airtight case began falling apart, piece by piece, before our very eyes.

217

These tactics served to inflict even more pain on our already drained emotions. With each delay, the emotional scars I spoke of before opened up all over again.

Brian Steel, of course, insisted that these delays were all in the name of justice.

I realize my bias in saying this, but these delays had nothing remotely to do with justice. Rather, they were designed to shift the focus entirely away from Michael LeJeune and increasingly onto Ron. The more the case got pushed aside on yet another technicality, the more Ron's life was diminished. Brian Steel consistently characterized Ron as "just another drug addict," as though his life did not matter at all.

That's why Brooks and I never missed a single scheduled hearing, traveling to Atlanta over 30 times between January 1998 and November 2005. In a case that has turned repeatedly on arcane points of law, our presence was important because it sent a simple message. It reminded the court that at the end of the day, the case is still about a horrible crime that was committed on the morning of December 27, 1997… and that the victim of that crime-*our son*-was a man who was loved and cared about by friends and family.

That may not have the eloquence of Christopher Darden, or the flash and verve of Johnnie Cochran, but it's still a powerful statement to make.

* * *

Here's a recap of the major developments of the case:

After arresting LeJeune in January 1998, law enforcement agents seized his mother's 1990 Toyota Corolla, which was parked in front of his apartment on the day of the murder. They had the car towed to G.B.I. headquarters in DeKalb County, then obtained a warrant to search the car (as well as a warrant to search LeJeune's apartment) from a Fulton County magistrate.

Police soon found traces of Ron's blood and skin tissue in both the apartment and inside the car. The Georgia Bureau of Investigation later determined that the tire tracks found near the graveyard where Ron's body was found matched the tires of LeJeune's car.

Meanwhile, G.B.I. agents also obtained eyewitness accounts of LeJeune purchasing several items on the afternoon of the murder (December 27), including a handsaw, a bag of cement, and a container of gasoline, as well as accounts of LeJeune and Anand carrying large garbage bags out of LeJeune's apartment within hours of the murder.

Plus, as I mentioned before, the G.B.I. also had the testimony of onetime LeJeune associate Kenneth Vaughn that resulted directly to the arrest of LeJeune. Vaughn told authorities that he had met with LeJeune at a Waffle House restaurant a few days after the murder—and that during this meeting LeJeune bragged openly about shooting Ron.

All of this evidence was presented to the Fulton County grand jury within days of LeJeune's arrest. Two months later, on March 17, 1998, the grand jury issued a true bill of indictment against LeJeune and Anand on charges of malice murder, felony murder, aggravated assault, and concealing the death of another person.

Everything about the case seemed so clear-cut. There was no doubt as to what happened and who had committed the crime. Again, it seemed inevitable that justice would be rendered.

Little did we know that from that point on, everything would slowly unravel.

* * *

I mentioned before that the bond hearing took place in Atlanta on May 18, 1998. Not only was that the first time we saw LeJeune and Steel in the courtroom, it also marked our introduction to Fulton County District Attorney Paul Howard and the prosecutors assigned to the case: Assistant District Attorneys Clinton Rucker, Peggy Katz, and Anna Greene. (Several years later, Assistant D.A. Brett Pinion would replace Peggy Katz.) Brooks and I had spoken to Clinton Rucker several times over the phone in the months after LeJeune's arrest, but the bond hearing was our first chance to place a face with the name.

Upon our arrival we were greeted by Niki Berger, the director of the Atlanta Victim Witness Assistance Program. As I stated earlier,

Paul Howard started this program in 1984 as a vehicle for survivors of homicide, as well as victims, witnesses, and family members impacted by domestic violence, child abuse, and other serious crimes. The program has grown tremendously since its inception, providing a wide range of counseling and services to help people cope with problems of personal injury, property loss, and psychological trauma.

Being from out of town, Brooks and I found it especially helpful and comforting to have someone assist us by escorting us around, as well as actually staying with us the entire time we were in the courtroom. Another benefit of the Victim Witness Assistance Program was that until 2003, their budget provided lodging and mileage expenses for people such as Brooks and me who come from out of town, as well as other members of the victim's families. (Due to budget cuts, the program now covers lodging and mileage costs for out-of-town victims' parents or immediate family only.) They also pay the expenses for each out-of-town witness who is called to testify for the trial. A few months later, when Niki Berger went on maternity leave, Theresa Strozier replaced her as our contact. Each time we arrived in town for a hearing, Theresa would meet us in the lobby of the D.A.'s office and usher us upstairs, where Clinton Rucker would update us on the case and answer any questions we might have. Theresa has always kept in touch with us over the years, calling periodically to either give us information or just to see how we were doing.

(Niki's first child, by the way, was born on December 27, 1998, the one-year anniversary of Ron's death. He is in school now, and Niki has since had another child.)

The bond hearing on May 18, 1998 was also our introduction to the presiding judge, the Honorable Constance Russell of the Fulton County Superior Court. From the very beginning, Judge Russell struck us both as a straight-shooting, "no-nonsense" kind of arbiter. She was cool, calm, and ultimately fair, demanding respect and punctuality from both the defense and the prosecution.

We didn't know it at the time, but our case was Russell's first death penalty case as a judge. Not only that, Russell was relatively new to the bench, having only been a judge about a year when she was assigned our case in January 1998. In many respects, she was still learning her way as a judge, still learning how to manage a courtroom. Given those circumstances, she did a remarkable job handling a case that would challenge her in ways she could never thought possible.

Brooks and I didn't always agree with Judge Russell. There were times, particularly in regard to some of her rulings on evidentiary matters, when she only added to our level of frustration. But at the end of the day, she proved herself to be a person of great integrity, and for that she earned our gratitude and respect.

* * *

LeJeune was denied bond that morning, but that didn't stop Brian Steel from filing a motion to quash the indictment.

Soon after the grand jury issued a true bill of indictment, Steel learned from a private investigator that one of the members of the grand jury that indicted LeJeune was technically not a resident of Fulton County. Apparently the man in question had recently been separated from his wife, causing him to leave his home in Cobb County in February 1998 and move in temporarily with his parents in Atlanta. But as the prosecution argued in its opposition to the motion to quash, while the juror may have lived in Cobb County, he was not registered to vote there-instead, he was registered to vote in Fulton County. Since the voting registrar is the list from which grand jurors are chosen in Fulton County, the juror's eligibility should not be held to question and the indictment should therefore stand.

Unfortunately, Judge Russell did not see it that way. Fifteen months later, on May 13, 1999, she issued a ruling in favor of the defense.

As hard as that was to accept, it appeared as though the setback would only be temporary. Not only did the prosecution assure us they'd appeal the judge's ruling, they told us they would seek another indictment as soon as possible. Sure enough, on May 14, the very next day, the prosecutors took the case to another grand jury, which promptly returned a second true bill of indictment against LeJeune.

Brian Steel, however, cried foul, claiming that once the prosecution appealed the ruling on the first indictment, the Fulton County

Superior Court had no authority to issue a second because, technically speaking, the jurisdiction of the case was in the hands of the Georgia Court of Appeals pending its decision. Therefore, he contended, the second indictment is illegal and should be also quashed.

Steel further complained that the second indictment was returned before he could arrange a preliminary hearing for his client before a magistrate judge. The second indictment caused the magistrate to rule that he had no power to hold such a hearing, since a grand jury had already determined probable cause against LeJeune.

While it is technically correct that a murder suspect is statutorily entitled to a preliminary hearing, it is also not uncommon for prosecutors to seek indictments right away by going straight to the grand jury.

Brian Steel is not a stupid man. Surely he knew this to be true. This struck us as yet another blatant attempt on his part to delay the inevitable.

That's why it angers me to think about attorneys who know beyond a shadow of doubt their client is guilty but defend them anyway. They know people like Michael LeJeune are brutal murderers, yet they deliberately manipulate the system to try to set them free.

Steel is married with children of his own. I cannot imagine how he and other defense attorneys sleep at night, knowing how many criminals are walking the streets today-people whose release they are entirely responsible for-who end up killing again and again and again.

* * *

As a precaution, the prosecution withdrew its appeal on the ruling to quash the first indictment. But there was still a risk involved. Under Georgia state law, a second quashed indictment has the equivalent effect of double jeopardy: it prevents the prosecution of a defendant on the crimes for which he is charged. That meant if Steel succeeded in throwing out the second indictment, Ron's killer would be free to walk!

Rather than risk that, the prosecution filed a motion to *nolle prosse* (i.e., no longer prosecute) the second indictment and instead seek a third indictment against LeJeune. Judge Russell granted the motion. On this occasion, the third time was indeed the charm. The prosecution obtained a third grand jury indictment, and the charges against LeJeune remained.

Brian Steel, however, had only begun to fight. One year later, in July 2000, the defense sought to suppress key evidence against LeJeune (including the samples of Ron's blood and skin tissue found in LeJeune's apartment and car) on the grounds that the search warrants for both the apartment and car were illegally obtained.

As I explained earlier, once the G.B.I. arrested LeJeune, they immediately seized his car and had it towed from his apartment. They knew from the information obtained from Kenneth Vaughn that the car contained evidence vital to the case and did not want it tampered with in any way. So they loaded the car on a flatbed truck and had it transported to G.B.I. headquarters in Gainesville. Three days later, a Fulton County magistrate issued a warrant to search the car.

Steel, however, argued that while the crime was committed in Fulton County, the car at the time the search warrant was issued was actually in another county: DeKalb County, where Gainesville is located. Therefore, technically speaking, the judge who issued the search warrant did not have jurisdiction to do so. The G.B.I. should have instead obtained a warrant from a judge in DeKalb County. For that reason, he argued, the search warrant was invalid and any evidence found in the car should not be admissible in court.

Fortunately for us, that argument didn't fly with Judge Russell. She ruled in favor of the prosecution and upheld the evidence from the car. But when it came to the evidence found in the apartment, her ruling was much less favorable.

LeJeune and Anand were arrested in the early morning hours of January 21, 1998. Several hours before that, G.B.I. agents were scrambling to find a Fulton County judge who could sign a warrant to search LeJeune's apartment. Sometime around eight or nine o'clock on the night of January 20, they located a judge who was dining at a nearby restaurant and got him to sign the warrant.

As it happens, this judge was an older man who was semi-retired.

While he was serving a temporary term on the Fulton County bench at the time, he had not been sworn in as a practicing judge for over 12 years. Technically speaking, Steel argued, that made the warrant for the search of the apartment invalid.

Furthermore, in obtaining the search warrant, the G.B.I. presented this judge with an affidavit from Kenneth Vaughn recounting how LeJeune boasted about shooting Ron during the meeting at the Waffle House restaurant. The judge read the affidavit and signed the warrant on the strength of Vaughn's testimony. (While I am no lawyer, I'd like to believe that most people, knowing an affidavit to be a sworn statement, would have done the same thing.) And yet Steel had the gall to argue that the judge "had no information from which he could access the veracity" of Vaughan's statement, as well as "no evidence that the police had corroborated Vaughan's story." Therefore, Steel argued, the judge did not have probable cause to issue the warrant, and the evidence found in the apartment on the basis of that warrant should consequently be suppressed.

The prosecution, however, argued that the G.B.I. did not present Vaughn as a confidential informant (which would have required the judge to verify his testimony), but in fact as "a witness with direct knowledge of the suspect's statements." They urged the court to use that standard in rendering its decision on the evidence.

Unfortunately, this time Judge Russell sided with the defense. On December 7, 2001-nearly four years to the date of Ron's murder-she issued a ruling that invalidated the search warrant and suppressed the evidence found in the apartment.

While the prosecution was quick to file an appeal, and District Attorney Howard spoke optimistically about his hope "for a quick and favorable resolution in the appellate courts," this was clearly a devastating blow.

It was bad enough that our son was murdered. But his body was also desecrated to the point where Brooks and I were deprived of the right to see him. It was if he just disappeared. In that sense, there can never be any closure.

That's why it was so important to us that this case went to trial. Brooks and I are not vengeful people in any way, but we wanted to see justice done.

Still, when you endure all these delays and see most of the evidence supporting your case gutted before your eyes, it becomes just a bit too much to take. I'll confess, there were times when we couldn't help but wonder whether a dark cloud was hanging over us.

Those were the moments when our faith in God has especially carried us through.

* * *

As Christians, we believe that God promises to never give us more than we can bear and we continually reminded ourselves of this.

God gives us all the ability to handle adversity, but in His wisdom He also knows that some of us are more capable than others. Not to sound boastful, but when I look back at everything Brooks and I went through along Ron's journey through addiction, I feel that God entrusted us with him because He knew that we could handle it. In that sense, our experiences with Ron throughout his struggle with cocaine gave us the strength to cope with the agonizing delays and setbacks that faced us in the eight years since the case against his murderers began. It made us stronger, and it made our faith in God stronger, because it reminds us that so much in life is beyond our control.

People walk through grief differently. Brooks has told me there were many times, especially early on, when he would find himself becoming very angry at the person responsible for Ron's murder, only to stop himself and say, *"Dear God, please forgive me and help me."* Instead of becoming consumed with anger about Ron's death, he would ask God to help him think about the many positive memories we have from when Ron was alive. That's a simple yet effective way in which prayer has helped him cope.

Some people need to go through stages of anger or bitterness before finally coming to acceptance-and I think God understands that.

We've chosen not to do that. We've chosen to accept what happened, to live with the knowledge that one day God will reunite us with Ron in Heaven.

That doesn't mean we don't miss him. Indeed, we miss him every day. It's just a decision we've made together that comes from our faith as Christians.

That faith has also helped us cope with the ups and downs of the case against Ron's killer. Every day we asked for God's help to accept whatever course the case took, no matter how painful it may have been. Our faith reminds us that whatever the outcome is on earth, the person responsible for Ron's murder still faces a final judgment. And that judgment lies entirely in God's hands.

CHAPTER TWENTY-SIX

Our Voices are Finally Heard

B y the middle of 2001, with the case against LeJeune well into its fourth year without any sign of resolution, Brooks and I decided to hire our own private counsel. This was not in any way a reflection on the District Attorney's Office-indeed, we have always appreciated the long hours and tireless dedication of Paul Howard and his staff have put into the prosecution of Ron's killer. As often as we had to travel to Atlanta for hearings over the years, it is probably quite unusual for a D.A.'s office to form as close a bond as they have with our family.

"I have encountered many families who have been devastated by tragedy," Assistant District Attorney Peggy Katz told me in a letter. "But I have never met anyone like you both, after all you have been through. More than anything we have sought in our office, we want justice for Ron, and continue to work toward that end. Despite the terrible circumstances which have brought us together, I am grateful for the privilege of knowing you."

Brooks and I are grateful not only for their continued efforts on our behalf, but also for the genuine concern the D.A.'s office always showed us.

It's just that being out of state, we felt it might help to have a third party who was "closer to the action," so to speak: someone who could consult with the prosecution periodically on our behalf and explain aspects about the case to us that we did not understand. We ended up hiring the firm of Rogers and Howard, LLC, of Decatur, Georgia. Andy Rogers and Cliff Howard (no relation to D.A. Paul Howard) were both attorneys who specialized in the field of victim's issues.

It was also around this time that someone suggested that Brooks and I write a letter to Judge Russell explaining the pain, stress, and grief we continued to experience because of the delays in the case, and that we'd appreciate it if she could set aside a trial date on her calendar as soon as possible. (Nearly a year had passed since the evidentiary hearings took place in July 2000, and Judge Russell still had not ruled on any of the motions, saying only that she would "rule on everything at one time.")

As it happens, not long after we first got this notion, Brooks and I met a federal judge from the Charlotte area at a luncheon. We got to chatting with this judge, and in the course of conversation we apprised him of our situation.

This judge offered to meet us for lunch so that we could talk about the case at length. We took him up on his offer, and during that lunch we asked this judge what he thought about our writing Judge Russell a letter expressing our concerns about the delays and asking for a trial date. He not only said it was not uncommon in homicide cases for the family of the victim to make such a request, he told us that he had received many such letters himself.

So with the help of our attorney Andy Rogers, we sent Judge Russell the following letter:

Dear Judge Russell:

Please be advised that this firm has been retained by Jean and Brooks Davis, parents of the December 1997 murder victim, Ronnie Allen Davis. As you may recall, the defendants named above are currently awaiting trial on this case, which is assigned to your honor.

You are no doubt aware of the fact that Mr. and Mrs. Davis have been hoping for the resolution of this case for some time. They have made numerous trips to Atlanta for various hearings and meetings over the past 3 years. They have been and continue to be frustrated and disheartened by the many delays of the trial of this case. In the earlier part of this year they contacted an attorney friend of theirs in the D.A.'s office in North Carolina where they live. He was asked to review this case to help the Davis' understand the reasons for the numerous delays of the prosecution. They were then advised that, being from out of state, it may be helpful to take the somewhat unusual step of hiring private counsel to inquire into the situation.

We have reviewed the details of the posture of this case and made inquiries of the D.A.'s office. We have been advised that your honor intends to rule on all of the currently pending motions at one time. We have also learned that the D.A.'s office is ready for trial and is awaiting the court's ruling on pending motions and the scheduling of a trial date, but has no indication as to when this may occur.

Previous to our writing this letter to you, we contacted your law clerk, Ms. Anderson, to inquire into whether your honor may be taking action on this case in the near future and were told that she has no information in this regard. As a result, we are contacting you directly to inquire into whether the court intends to place this case on a trial calendar in the near future and, if so, when that may occur.

As quoted from a letter the Davis' received from their family doctor with whom they have counseled since the death of their son: "There is a horrible wound, which will always leave a huge, ugly scar. With each trip to Atlanta and all the unsettled issues, the wound is torn open and irritated over and over. It seems that the longer things go on, the less outraged people become over the brutal and horrific crime these murderers committed." While the Davis' clearly understand and appreciate the fact that the defendants are presumed innocent unless and until proven guilty, they are anxious for the State to have the opportunity to present this case to a jury. We are hopeful that your honor appreciates the tremendous pain and stress the Davis' continue to suffer as this case remains pending.

Please contact us with any information you have that we can pass along to the Davis'. Also, we hope your honor will let us know whether there is anything our firm can do to assist the court.

Sincerely,
ROGERS & HOWARD, L.L.C.

Andrew T. Rogers

We provided copies of this letter to the District Attorney's Office, Brian Steel, and Gary Guichard, the lawyer for Rekha Anand. It was a strong yet friendly inquiry on our part, firm yet still very respectful. If nothing else, it was a chance for our family to be heard for the first time.

Unfortunately, Judge Russell didn't see it that way. As soon as she received the letter, she called a hearing to inform both the prosecution and the defense that she had received a letter from the victim's family, but that she "would not read the letter" and that upon conclusion of the hearing she would promptly "tear it up and put it in the trash."

I'll admit, it angered and disappointed me to hear that Judge Russell had reacted that way. It was our belief going into this case that justice was to be blind and impartial, yet Russell's reaction hardly seemed impartial at all. It was not until some time had passed that I came to understand her decision. To render a truly fair and unbiased judgment on any matter in our case, she had to weigh the facts clearly and precisely, and not allow herself to be swayed in any way by emotion or sentiment. That's difficult for anyone to do, especially a judge in a court of law. In the case of our letter, I imagine Judge Russell felt that had she read the letter, it may have compromised her ability to decide on our case without showing any prejudice. So regardless of what she may have felt personally, it was in her best interest, as well as our best interest, not to read the letter at all.

As I say, I came to understand Judge Russell's decision. But that doesn't mean I liked it!

* * *

Meanwhile, while the prosecution appealed Judge Russell's December 2001 ruling that threw out the evidence found in LeJeune's apartment, Brian Steel countered by appealing the decision that upheld the evidence found in the car. The matter eventually made its way up to the Georgia Supreme Court. Oral arguments were set for October 22, 2002.

That would prove to be a day we will never forget, but for all the wrong reasons.

The hearing commenced at approximately nine o'clock. There were a few other cases before ours on that morning's docket, so we sat with our lawyers and waited patiently for a couple of hours before our case, *The People of the State of Georgia v. Michael LeJeune*, finally came up.

The defense was allowed to argue first. Steel, of course, was thorough as usual. The seven justices on the Georgia Supreme Court-Chief Justice Norman S. Fletcher and Justices Leah Ward Sears, Robert Benham, Carol W. Hunstein, George H. Carley, Hugh P. Thompson, and P. Harris Hines-all listened attentively to his argument and asked several questions.

Then it was the prosecution's turn. Peggy Katz did an excellent job on our behalf, and the justices also asked her questions. She was about two-thirds of the way into her presentation when suddenly all seven justices rose from their chairs and announced that it was "Twelve o'clock, lunch time!" and that "the time allocated for this case was over."

Brooks and I were dumbfounded. Considering that we had waited all these months for this hearing, and sat through all those other cases all throughout the morning, you would think the Supreme Court would have the decency to wait until our side was finished making its argument before adjourning for lunch.

The prosecution lobbied valiantly for more time. After a few minutes of commotion, one of the judges finally came out and told Peggy, "We'll give you five more minutes. If you can't wrap it up in five minutes, then give us the balance of your argument in writing. Those are your choices. What do you want to do?"

Knowing how much was at stake; Peggy wisely chose not to rush through the rest of her presentation. Sometime later, after filing a motion for an extension of time, she delivered a brief that concluded her argument in writing.

Still, given how the morning ended, that did not bode well for our side. Unfortunately, things would get worse.

The Georgia Supreme Court, in a unanimous ruling issued on February 13, 2003, not only upheld the decision to disregard the evidence found in LeJeune's apartment, but reversed the decision to uphold the evidence found in the car on the grounds that that search warrant was also illegal. That meant that most of the hard evidence that linked LeJeune to the murder of our son-the samples of Ron's blood and skin tissue found in both the apartment and the car-was suddenly invalid.

And yet, amazingly enough, and as hard as that was to swallow, there was still a ray of hope.

Shortly before the Supreme Court rendered its decision, the prosecution struck a deal with LeJeune's accomplice, Rekha Anand. Anand agreed to testify against LeJeune and reveal the location of Ron's missing head in exchange for her release from prison. She provided this information in February 2003 as part of a videotaped statement.

On this videotape, Anand told prosecutors that LeJeune killed Ron on December 27, 1997, and that she was in the kitchen of LeJeune's apartment when he shot Ron in the back of the head. Anand further testified that LeJeune severed Ron's head so that he could extract the bullet to prevent any link with the gun.

After helping LeJeune dispose of Ron's dismembered body at the graveyard, Anand said that they removed the head with the bullet in it, poured gas on the rest of the body, and set it afire. Sometime later she and LeJeune put Ron's head in a bucket and took it to the home of LeJeune's parents in Hall County, near Lake Lanier. (LeJeune's parents were not home at the time.) She said that LeJeune went inside the family workshop, where he placed the head inside a vise and tried to remove the bullet. When that wasn't successful, they went out and bought cement, poured it into the bucket on top of Ron's head, and waited a day for the cement to dry. Anand then said that she and LeJeune took his father's canoe and rowed out to the deepest part of Lake Lanier, where they dumped the bucket and the saw before rowing back to shore.

Based on information Anand provided in her videotaped statement, G.B.I. investigators obtained a warrant from a magistrate to search the home of LeJeune's parents, as well as the area of Lake Lanier outside their home. The G.B.I. then transported Anand out to the lake, where she showed them the vicinity of where she and LeJeune disposed of the head and the saw. A team of divers then searched the lake in late February and early March 2003. Their efforts, however, were unsuccessful because the water was 160 feet deep with a lot of silt and debris-not to mention, bitterly cold on account of the late winter temperatures. (Amazingly enough, despite the diving activity that went on around the lake over the course of this period, no word of the G.B.I. investigation was ever leaked to the Atlanta media until several weeks later, when reporters contacted us through our attorney Cliff Howard to make a few statements.)

On June 2, 2003, Rekha Anand pled guilty to one count of concealing the death of another. She received a commuted 10-year prison sentence in exchange for her testimony against LeJeune at the time of trial. As part of the plea bargain, the first five years were commuted to time served, with the remaining five years to be served on probation. That term, however, was to be suspended if Anand successfully completed one year of probation. She was released from prison the following day in the custody of an aunt. It was the first time in the then-six-year history of the case that a member of Anand's family ever attended one of the hearings.

Anand was remarkably composed in court that day-a far cry from the shaky, weepy figure Brooks and I first saw on the morning of the arraignment hearing five years before. She never once hesitated as she answered question after question from attorneys, remaining very matter of fact as she described all the gruesome details.

I studied Anand closely as I watched her being questioned by Brian Steel. You could tell from the specificity with which she answered every question that she was recounting a true life experience and not fabricating anything. Yet sometimes I wonder whether she was relieved for getting things off her chest or if she really was that coldhearted. I don't imagine I'll ever know. Nevertheless, she did finally do the right thing, and for that I am glad.

Meanwhile, on the strength of the warrant issued by the magistrate in February 2003, the G.B.I. secured samples of Ron's blood found in the workshop of the home of LeJeune's parents. They also seized the vise that LeJeune used to try to remove the bullet from Ron's head. That same magistrate also granted new warrants to search both LeJeune's apartment and his mother's 1990 Toyota Corolla (which had since been sold after it was originally searched in 1998).

Unfortunately, Steel got Judge Russell to invalidate the new search warrants-as well as any evidence uncovered as a result of them-on the basis of yet another technicality. This time, he convinced the judge that Anand's testimony about the vise was "too stale."

"In reviewing a search warrant, time is a relevant variable," Judge Russell ruled in August 2003. While Anand established that the vise was in the home at the time of the murder, she had no way of knowing whether that same vise would still be there six years later. Therefore, the defense argued, it was up to the G.B.I. to verify to the judge who signed the warrant that the vice was still the same. Since the G.B.I. did not do that, the search warrant should be invalidated and the evidence from the parents' home should be suppressed.

The defense also convinced Russell to throw out the new search warrants for LeJeune's apartment and car. Steel argued that the G.B.I. tracked down the car through its VIN number, which it had obtained through the original search warrant in 1998. But since the original search warrant was since ruled to be illegal, that meant that technically, the car was also located through "illegally obtained evidence." Therefore, the new search warrant for the car should also be considered invalid.

As for the new warrant to search LeJeune's apartment, Judge Russell ruled that the state failed to provide proper consent to search the premises, despite the fact that the apartment manager allowed investigators inside. "No evidence was presented regarding the manager's authority to consent, the status of the apartment at the time that the search occurred, whether it was occupied, or whether it was abandoned," she said in her ruling of July 28, 2003.

As if that weren't enough, Judge Russell also ruled that the magistrate who issued the warrant for the apartment "had no authority to do so." She said that once a case is assigned to a particular judge, "no other judge has the authority to address issues associated with that particular case." Therefore, in her opinion, that rendered the warrant invalid.

Needless to say, the prosecution felt that Russell made a bad ruling all the way around and elected to appeal. Oral arguments were made before the Georgia Supreme Court on January 20, 2004. The Court issued its ruling on March 29, 2004. I'll tell you how they ruled in just a bit.

First, though, I want to say that June 2, 2003 marked another turning point in the case against Ron's murderer. That was also the day Brooks and I, as many friends and other members of our family, were allowed to present our impact statements and enter them into the record. An "impact statement" is a brief comment delivered in court which explains how the brutal taking of Ron's life affected our lives.

Brooks and I spoke first, followed by Rick, Dana, and Diane (who had accompanied us on all but two of the 21 trips we made to Atlanta up to that point). Also speaking in court that day were Ketta Guy, Larry Owens, and Brooks' sister Carolyn Wilkes. Also in attendance with us was Nonia Polk, Brooks' brother Cliff Davis and his wife, Dorothy, and John Miller, a doctor friend of Ron's from Atlanta.

As you can imagine, a lot of emotion was felt throughout the courtroom that day. Even Judge Russell was affected. For the first time ever, she actually showed compassion to our family, allowing us all as much time as we needed to deliver our statements. She even paused to offer Rick a glass of water after he struggled with emotions as he began to speak.

Following the proceedings, Brooks and I were touched when Anand's attorneys, led by Gary Guichard, came over and expressed their sympathy. They even apologized for the length it had taken to get to this point.

Brian Steel, on the other hand, kept his distance.

I cannot tell you what a release it was. After more than six years of heartbreak and frustration over setbacks, delays, and legal technicalities, our voices were finally heard.

There were, however, two impact statements that were entered into the record but not given orally because the persons making the statements were unable to attend the hearing. One of these was the statement of our dear friend and faithful supporter Dru Quarles.

As Ron's parents, Brooks and I were somewhat restricted by court guidelines in terms of what we could include in our impact statements. But since the court considered Dru a third party, she was given a little more latitude in terms of what she could say. For this reason, I'd like to share her statement with you. In many ways Dru's comments capture what Brooks and I feel in our hearts more eloquently than we ever could:

> I do not understand the loss of a child, but I have worked with many parents who have, and the grief and pain experienced is beyond comprehension. It is the worst thing a person can endure. No infection, no cancer causes as much as suffering and excruciating pain. It is as a large part of you has died and you are left alive, just waiting for the rest of you to die and wishing that you would.
>
> I have been trying to write an impact statement for over a week now. Every time I start to compose it, I get angry. I am angry at the thoughtless taking of the life of a wonderful, compassionate man. I am especially angry with the problems Jean and Brooks have had in seeing the young man responsible for this horrible crime brought to trial.
>
> All of this said, how do I write a victim impact statement for the brutal murder of your child? What a ridiculous request. It is like trying to write a short paragraph about the suffering at Auschwitz.
>
> For those of you reading this that have children, you know the depth of love you have for them-whether they are three minutes old or 39 years old. I thought I understood this before I had children. After having them, I realize all I knew was just the 10% of the iceberg that you see above the water,

and not the 90% that floats below to the great depths of the ocean.

I cannot imagine what it feels like to have to bury your child. What does it feel like to know that your child's life was ended in such a brutal fashion, to wonder if he suffered, to wonder if in his last breath he knew how deeply you love him, how gladly you would give everything you have to be on that couch in the millisecond before that gun was fired?

I cannot imagine. I really, physically cannot imagine this. It is too horrific. My mind will not let me travel there. It is any parent's worst nightmare.

As a physician and a Christian, my whole way of thinking is one of healing and making whole, complete, well. To learn of someone who so flippantly takes the life of another goes against everything I believe and stand for. It is the ultimate crime. You are not only murdering Ron Davis, but part of his mother, his father, his brother, his nieces and nephew, his friends and destroying the possibility of all of the good things he would contribute to those around him with the rest of his life.

Beyond this, the gruesome nature of the actions of Mr. LeJeune is unthinkable. How do you sit in judgment of someone like this? How can you compare someone who behaves like this to the rest of the human race? I have a hard time accepting the two species.

As I write this, I look up at the face of my daughter as she dances around the room in her yellow dress, getting ready to leave for church, or think of my son smiling as he bounced out of bed this morning. I would be affected for the rest of my life if I knew they had spent five minutes with a person who was capable of committing such a crime. How much more so if that person took them away from me, especially in such a way as Ron Davis was taken from his parents?

Impact statement, indeed, it can't be written. It can only be experienced. And my prayer is that you and I never do.

* * *

237

On March 29, 2004, the Georgia Supreme Court issued its decision on whether to uphold Judge Russell's ruling from August 2003 that threw out the physical evidence obtained in February 2003 on the grounds that the new search warrants were invalid. To our great relief, the Court resoundingly overturned Judge Russell by a unanimous, 7-0 decree.

A few days after the decision, Brooks and I received the following letter from our attorney Cliff Howard. "I think it is interesting that the decision was unanimous," he wrote.

> Not one of the justices felt that Judge Russell's decision which held that the G.B.I. was required to ask her for the search warrants they obtained to seize the evidence the second time was a correct ruling. While it is of very little importance relative to the ordeal the two of you have been through combined with the delay in bringing this case to trial, this decision will be of great help to law enforcement and prosecutors throughout the state. It will limit the arguments that defense attorneys can make on behalf of their clients relative to any search warrant in any case.
>
> The clarity by this decision will make it less likely that families of another victim will suffer the same type of delays you have had to endure as this issue had been decided with very little room for argument. The fact that there is no dissenting opinion means that a trial judge faced with the same issue in the future will be very unlikely to rule with the defense.
>
> I certainly recognize that this information in no way relieves the stress and/or pain of having to wait for the decision and the resolution of the case. I just thought you would like to know that there will be potential benefits for families who are similarly situated in the future.

Needless to say, Brooks and I were ecstatic. After enduring so many legal setbacks, we were so relieved to have such an important decision go our way. By upholding the validity of the search warrants (and by extension, the physical evidence gathered as a result of those warrants), the Georgia Supreme Court's ruling meant that we were inching ever closer to a trial date.

Brian Steel, of course, announced that he would take the matter all the way to the U.S. Supreme Court. As we understand the process, once an appeal is filed, the Court has 95 days from the date of the appeal to consider whether it will decide on the matter, or uphold the decision of the Georgia Supreme Court.

In September 2004, the U.S. Supreme Court informed Steel that it had rejected his appeal. The final obstacle to a trial had been lifted. After seven long years of waiting, Brooks and I were about to have our day in court.

CHAPTER TWENTY-SEVEN

A Blessing in Disguise

With the U.S. Supreme Court ruling in September 2004, Brooks and I had hoped it would be possible to have a court date scheduled before the end of the year. Unfortunately, that was not to be. Jury selection began in January 2005, seven years after the murder. Notices were sent to 350 people; as part of their instructions, prospective jurors were also asked to complete a questionnaire, which they were to bring with them on the day they reported to court. Attorneys for the prosecution and defense went through these responses and notified 150 prospective jurors to report for *voir dire*-additional questioning before attorneys from both sides, as well as Judge Russell. This pool of jurors was questioned in groups of 12 at a time, with some being dismissed for hardships and other reasons.

For those who have never witnessed this aspect of our legal system, I can tell you that it went very slowly. Some days, only one or two jurors were selected from a single group. All in all, it took four weeks to narrow the pool down from 150 to 62, then again from 62 to the final selection of 12 jurors and four alternates. (By comparison, it took only three days to select the jury for the Michael Jackson child molestation trial of 2005.) Upon their selection, Judge Russell informed the jurors that they would be sequestered at a nearby hotel, and that the trial was expected to last anywhere from four to six weeks.

Brooks and I moved into a hotel suite two blocks from the court-

241

house. We ended up staying in Atlanta for the entire length of the jury selection and trial. This proved to be the best thing for us, especially since it took five hours to travel from Charlotte to Atlanta. This way, we could keep our minds focused on what was happening with the trial without the additional stress of driving back and forth each week from home. Diane stayed with us in a connecting suite for the entire time we were in Atlanta.

The trial began on Tuesday, March 8, 2005-yet another entry of the amazing litany of eights. Rick was with us throughout the entire first week. Ketta Guy and our attorney, Cliff Howard, also joined us for the first day.

The first day started off on an alarming note. Judge Russell had barely finished addressing the jury when the defense filed a motion to put Ron on trial, in order to prove that he was a violent person. It was yet another tactic by Brian Steel to try and free Michael LeJeune. Fortunately, Judge Russell overruled this motion, but Steel had another trick up his sleeve. This time, he announced that he would prove that Kenneth Vaughn was the murderer. Kenneth Vaughn, of course, is the informant due the reward of $10,000.00 for the conviction and sentencing of Ron's killer.

Then it was time for both sides to deliver their opening statements. Assistant D.A. Brett Pinion presented the case on behalf of the prosecution. We understand it was very compelling. I say "We understand" because Brooks and I were not allowed to hear it. Even though the defendant was on trial for the murder of our son, Brian Steel used yet another technicality to keep us out of the courtroom. Here's how that went down.

The defense informed the prosecution before the trial began that LeJeune's father would be a witness for the defense. Strictly speaking, that prevented Mr. LeJeune from being in the courtroom until the time he was called to testify-even though, like Brooks and I, he was the parent of one in the principal figures in the trial. Naturally, Brian Steel insisted that "if Mr. LeJeune cannot be in the courtroom, then the Davis' cannot be, either." As a result, Brooks and I also had to wait outside until we were called to the stand, which prevented us from hearing opening statements. That's why our lead prosecutor, Assistant D.A. Clinton Rucker saw to it that we were the first two witnesses for the prosecution. He wanted us inside that courtroom as soon as he possibly could.

We also understand that Brian Steel's opening argument was also compelling-so much so, some family members told us, tongue in cheek, that he made them question who murdered Ron. But, of course, Steel's argument had nothing to do with reality. If it did, then why would he try so long and hard to plea bargain for his client?

Many times, Steel tried to broker a deal, despite the fact that he knew the only deal the state would accept was life imprisonment, without parole-a point that D.A. Paul Howard had made clear from the moment LeJeune was arrested. However, in December 2003, with the Georgia Supreme Court still deliberating the appeal of Judge Russell's ruling from August 2003 on the search of LeJeune's apartment from February 2003, and in light of the previous other court rulings that had compromised the strength of the prosecution's case, Assistant D.A. Clinton Rucker called and asked Brooks and I if we would consider offering LeJeune a deal of 20 years in prison, with the possibility of parole. We told Rucker no, but that we would be open to *40* years, with the possibility of parole.

It was a difficult decision, one that we spent many hours praying over and discussing with family. But in the end, we agreed to extend the offer. Remember, by that point we were closing in on the sixth anniversary of Ron's murder. Our thinking was, LeJeune was already in jail; while it would break our hearts to offer him a deal, because we badly wanted a conviction, at the same time a guilty plea would at least provide us with the closure for which we had waited so long. That gave us a feeling of God's peace in the storm, that we could somehow turn the page on this horrible chapter and move on with our lives.

That hope was quickly dashed, however, when Steel informed Rucker that LeJeune had spurned our offer. It was yet another devastating blow, which caused us to have yet another stressful Christmas that year.

Still, I can see how Steel's opening statement might have swayed someone on the jury who did not follow the case closely-someone, for example, who may not have been aware of the lengths Steel went, all the way up to the U.S. Supreme Court, to try to get all of the hard evidence against LeJeune thrown out of the case. Why on earth would he go to all that trouble, if he thought all along that Kenneth Vaughn was the real killer?

* * *

Brooks and I were to be the first witnesses called after opening statements. Testifying in court was something I had dreaded for a long time. But when I was called to be sworn in, I could not believe how calm and at ease I was. It was by no means a normal day, and yet I felt no differently than I had any other day. Clearly, this was God's presence at work, the strength that comes from answered prayer. No other explanation is possible.

I took the stand. The prosecution asked me questions about Ron's background, his accomplishments, his last telephone call to us on the morning of December 27, 1997, and other information that would be helpful to the case. Unlike some witnesses, we were not briefed in advance on how to answer certain questions, because the prosecution did not want us to sound rehearsed. Besides, we had kept so close in touch with the D.A.'s office, as far as they were concerned, no preparation was necessary. As Clinton Rucker told us, "Without you knowing it, I've been interviewing you for over seven years."

I answered every question as clearly and as honestly as I could-even with Brian Steel objecting constantly, which easily could have rattled me. When the time came for cross examination, I explained that Ron was absolutely not a violent person. I said that his skill in aikido was an art of defense, not offense. I also stated that the reason an addict exhibits irrational behavior while using is his morals, the people he chooses to be around, and the decisions he makes while under the influence to be far removed from what he really believes and the way in which he was raised.

I must have been on the witness stand for at least two hours. I'm sure Brooks nearly wore out the soles of his shoes from walking the hall with anxiety.

The court adjourned for lunch, and then it was Brooks' turn to testify. He did well, and even managed to crack a joke or two each time he started to recount something Ron said to us, only to be stopped in mid-sentence by Judge Russell.

For those who may not be familiar with the proceedings of a criminal trial, as witnesses we could not testify about anything that Ron said to us during the phone conversation we had with him just two hours before his murder. That was considered hearsay, and was therefore not admissible. So we could only tell the jury what we said to Ron, or explain something we said for clarification.

After a few "hearsay" admonitions from Judge Russell, Brooks finally looked at her and said, "Judge, is this kind of like the game show *Jeopardy*, where you have to answer every question with a question?"

Judge Russell got a kick out of that. "Go ahead, Mr. Davis," she said with a smile. "You're doing all right." Even some of the jurors smiled or chuckled at the judge's response, which put Brooks even more at ease.

* * *

We were four days into the trial when the most tragic and alarming thing happened in another courtroom at the Fulton County Courthouse. Rekha Anand had just taken the stand in our case on the morning of Friday, March 11, 2005, when we saw a deputy whisper something to Judge Russell before hurriedly escorting her back to her chamber. An instant later, the jury was also taken out of the courtroom. Immediately after that, there was a flurry of cell phone calls with the news that *Judge Rowland Barnes has been shot, Judge Barnes is dead.* There was also word that a court reporter, Julie Brandau, had also been shot and killed in her attempt to help Judge Barnes. A little later on, we were told that both the judge and the court reporter had been killed by an inmate named Brian Nichols, who was on trial for the rape of his girlfriend. A female deputy, Cynthia Hall, was escorting Nichols to a holding cell where inmates change from prison clothes to civilian clothes, when Nichols overpowered the deputy by beating her in the face, which left her horribly disfigured. Nichols then confiscated the woman's keys and removed her gun from the black box where it was stored. Apparently, there was supposed to be two deputies escorting Nichols to court, but for some reason one was absent. Nichols then shot and killed Deputy

Hoyt Teasley outside the courthouse as he fled the building.

We spent the next three hours locked in our courtroom. Little did we know that outside the building, the entire world was watching this drama unfold. The search for Nichols was a major story that day in Atlanta-and as I'm sure many of you recall, it was all over cable television, especially on CNN, whose headquarters are in Atlanta.

Meanwhile, as we waited inside the courtroom, Assistant D.A. Clinton Rucker asked G.G. Carawan, an investigator who had been with the police department homicide division prior to joining the D.A.'s office, to get her gun. Carawan then escorted us to the rest-room, while we were in lockup. It was an emotional time for every-one in that courtroom: the attorneys, deputies, and especially Brooks and I, as we witnessed this horrible turn of events play out right before our eyes. We sat there helpless as some of the lawyers stood motionless in disbelief. I'll never forget the sight of Assistant D.A. Brett Pinion standing alone against a wall, praying because he was so distraught. Brett had worked many cases before in Judge Barnes courtroom over the previous five years, and could just have easily been in that courtroom had he not been assigned to our case. Brooks waited a few moments before walking over to join Brett in prayer. We heard many wonderful stories told about Judge Barnes and the way he treated those that worked for him.

Finally, once the courthouse had been cleared, Judge Russell emerged from her chambers and had the jurors brought back into the courtroom. The only thing they knew was a report overheard from a deputy's radio that a judge had been shot. They knew no other details. At that time, Russell informed the jury that there had been an incident in the courthouse, but that it had nothing to do with our case. She also instructed them that they would be taken back to their hotel and would not be allowed to have family visitation that weekend. She informed them that she would be personally calling their family members immediately to let them know that they were safe and unharmed.

When we were finally released from the courthouse that day, we had never witnessed a scene like the one around the Fulton County Courthouse. All areas near the courthouse were roped off with yellow tape, while cameras and police were everywhere. I was approached by a reporter and asked if we were in the same courtroom. Meanwhile, the criminal, Brian Nichols, had fled to the parking deck across the street where he pistol whipped a man who was with the *Atlanta Journal-Constitution* and took his car, a green Honda. Throughout the rest of Friday and continuing into Saturday, the police and all divisions of law enforcement searched for that Honda. What they failed to do, however, was check the parking deck. Apparently, Nichols had driven down to another level left the car, walking out a side entrance and up the street to the Marta transportation, whose entrance was directly across the street from our hotel.

We will never forget that day, that weekend, and the days that followed. Like so many across the country, Brooks, Diane, and I stayed glued to the TV throughout the weekend.

The next morning, Saturday, March 12, we were lounging in our pajamas, having been completely exhausted from the previous day's events, when an announcement came over the hotel speakers: *Evacuate the building. Evacuate the building immediately.* We were on the 14th floor, and so we ran down 28 flights of stairs to the street to learn that it was a fire in the restaurant adjoining the hotel. Everyone's emotions were so high, since the criminal had not been caught at that time

Meanwhile, after escaping the courthouse on Friday, Brian Nichols shot and killed customs agent David Wilhelm, who was working on his new home. Nichols confiscated Wilhelm's truck and fled. That night, around 2:00 a.m., Nichols pulled into an apartment complex, where he forced a young woman named Ashley Smith into her apartment, as she was getting out of her car. Apparently, Smith had just moved into her apartment two days before; she was still unpacking and had decided to run out for cigarettes when Nichols took her by surprise. He held her hostage all night. It was quite a story how she gained his trust by sharing her life adversities with drugs, how she was trying to get on her feet to get custody of her little girl, and how she read to him passages from Rick Warren's book, *The Purpose Driven Life.* (At one point, Nichols even told her he thought she was "an angel sent from God.") The next morning Nichols agreed to let Smith leave the apartment to pick up her little girl. It was then that she was able to call the police, and shortly afterwards, he surrendered, peacefully. I believe that this was divine intervention.

Ashley Smith has since written a book about her life and struggle with drugs, as well as the story about that horrible night when Nichols held her hostage. She has appeared on many national TV shows, and continues a speaking tour that I am sure will affect many lives. It is my hope and my prayer that this book, like Ashley Smith's book, will also minister to a lot of hurting people who need encouragement and strength.

* * *

On Monday morning, March 14, Brooks and I returned to court at the usual time. Judge Russell had the jurors brought in and again mentioned the incident, but still did not give them any details. Remember, the jury had been sequestered the entire weekend without having any access to a TV, newspaper, or any communication with the outside world. I can only imagine the anxiety they must have gone through. One juror said that he thought they had been treated like children. Still, when questioned individually, they all said they could continue.

Once the jury was brought back in, Rekha Anand was called back to the witness stand. No sooner had the trial resumed than Brian Steel began asking for a mistrial, claiming that it was impossible for LeJeune to get a fair trial with emotions running high in Atlanta. Judge Russell overruled that motion, and Anand's testimony continued. However, at noon, before we left for lunch, Steel made a second motion for a mistrial. This time, Judge Russell asked LeJeune to stand and speak his desire directly into the microphone. He said quite plainly, "I'd like to go ahead with the trial." We broke for lunch with our spirits high that the trial would continue.

When the trial resumed that afternoon, Steel continued questioning Anand about a series of letters that she had written LeJeune while she was in jail. This was Anand's fourth day of cross examination, of which approximately three days were spent reading and questioning Anand concerning the 60 plus letters. Steel's motive for this line of questioning was to try and prove that Anand's attorney, Gary Guichard, had actually coerced her into confessing so that she could get out of jail. Meanwhile, Guichard was scheduled to be on the witness stand the following day. He and other witnesses spent hours and days in the hallway, while Steel read letter after letter.

Finally, around 4:30 p.m. on Monday, March 14, Brian Steel asked for a recess, at which time he, LeJeune, and the rest of the defense team adjourned to LeJeune's holding cell for an impromptu meeting. Judge Russell waited beyond the time they asked for before finally telling a deputy to knock on the door and order them back into the courtroom. Upon their return, Steel once again asked the court for a mistrial. Once again, LeJeune was asked to stand and state his desire into the record. Only this time, he said, "Yeah, I'll go for a mistrial."

We were all shocked, disappointed and numb. The jurors were called back in, thanked for their services and told they were released from the case. Judge Russell stated that she would bring more jurors in the very next week and start over. Before the jurors left, they asked if they could talk with us. Some of them hugged us, telling us how sorry they were and that the majority of them wanted to finish the trial. We and the prosecution were so pleased with the jurors; one man told me that many of them were Christians. I remember hoping that whoever was chosen for the second trial, that they be as professional and intelligent as those who served on the first.

Brooks and I went back to the hotel discouraged and stunned. We couldn't believe what had happened. We received a call from the D.A.'s office two days later informing us that there had been a status hearing, and that the trial had been rescheduled for early September.

There are no words to describe our feelings: anger, disappointment, you name it, that's how we felt. We had to return to Atlanta, driving five hours both ways to move all our belongings back home.

Two weeks later, Brooks and I were getting reconciled and making plans to take a trip to Florida to rest our bodies and emotions, when I received another call from the D.A.'s office. A hearing had been set for Wednesday of the following week to reschedule the trial as soon as possible. Once again, it appeared our lives would be put on hold. It was impossible to make any kind of plans with all this hanging over us.

We also learned that another meeting had been called after Steel filed a motion for an "out of time speedy trial." How absurd. Remember, he was the one who was always blocking our case from coming to trial, with appeals and whatever else he could think of to delay the proceedings, in hopes of saving his client's neck. Thank goodness Judge Russell overruled this motion.

Then again, Brooks and I were afraid there might still be a delay to the start of the second trial, if the defense decided to appeal once again to the U.S. Supreme Court to overrule the Georgia Supreme Court's March 2004 decision regarding the validity of the search warrants obtained in February 2003. However, we soon learned that this was not going to happen, because the deadline for the defense to file an appeal had already lapsed. Jury selection for the second trial was scheduled to begin in September 2005.

As devastating as it was to have a mistrial declared, Brooks and I refused to let it destroy us. With God's help, we were determined to continue on, one day at a time, until this horrible nightmare was over. There had to be a purpose in all this, we kept telling each other. There just had to be.

And there was. We just didn't know it at the time.

It would be another eight months-imagine that-before we could look back, see God's wisdom, and realize that the declaration of a mistrial would turn out to be a blessing in disguise.

CHAPTER TWENTY-EIGHT

Momentum Swings Our Way

J ury selection for the second trial began in September 2005 and lasted approximately six weeks-two weeks longer than it took for the first trial. The defense, as it had done for the first trial, hired two consultants for jury selection; the prosecution hired none. Some prospective jurors questioned were adamant about the death penalty, while others did not believe in it at all. As you can imagine, both the prosecution and the defense were looking to compile as balanced and impartial a jury as possible. Therefore, those who showed themselves to be on either extreme of the capital punishment equation were excused immediately.

Brooks and I sat there nearly every day, hour by hour, observing the process. (There were a few hearings we did not attend, as they were scheduled literally at a moment's notice, which did not allow the D.A.'s office time to inform us in advance.) Though the prosecutors said that our presence wasn't necessary for jury selection, they did not discourage us from being there. They knew that Brooks and I wanted to send a message to the defendant that we were not going away until we saw that justice was served. Besides, we really did want to see what kind of jurors would be serving on the trial.

Nevertheless, jury selection was a slow, methodical process. Each juror was asked whether he or she felt unsafe being in the courthouse after the shooting earlier in the year. A few answered yes, and were dismissed for that reason. I'm sure some used any excuse they could think of to avoid being selected. However, Judge

Russell was adamant that it was their civic duty to serve on this trial. She said, "There's going to be a trial, and the courthouse is not going to shut down." As was the case with the first trial, the jury members and the alternates were sequestered.

The second trial began on Monday, October 31, 2005, three weeks before Thanksgiving. After spending over a month in Atlanta for the jury selection alone, Brooks and I were prepared to be there for at least another month. Judge Russell, to her credit, seemed sensitive to that-not to mention the likelihood that unless steps were taken to expedite the trial, the jurors and alternates would have to remain separated from their families during the Thanksgiving holiday weekend. For that reason, she declared that the trial would be held six days a week, including Saturdays, to ensure that it would be completed before Thursday, November 24, Thanksgiving Day.

After everything we went through in the first trial, I was really dreading the second trial. Even though I remembered how God had strengthened me when I testified the first time, I also remembered how shocked and depressed we were over the mistrial being declared. Our lead prosecutor, Clinton Rucker, was a huge help in keeping our spirits up. He kept saying, "Brooks, Jean, please don't be discouraged." He told us to think of the first trial as "a trial run," and that "it was really in our favor" to start over.

It took us a while to see that, but Rucker was absolutely right. In a way, it was as though God had given us a second chance to see that justice was done.

At the same time, however, the experience of reliving all the horrible details of Ron's murder was not something I looked forward to. I felt we needed support this time, even more than we did before. Once the jury was selected for the second trial, we asked several family members to come to Atlanta. Diane flew down from Charlotte, while Carolyn, Doris, and her husband, Don, drove down. They all arrived in time for opening statements. Carolyn, Doris, and Don stayed the entire first week, while Diane remained with us for the second week. Rick had spent a week with us in Atlanta for the first trial; he said he would be there for the second trial later in the month. Other family members also let us know that we could count on their presence, as they were needed.

Having gone through this experience twice now, I can empathize with other families, especially those who have to attend trials out of town. Your life really is put on hold, and in our case, it felt as though we had been robbed of eight years of our lives.

We have since been told that our case set a record of sorts. Michael LeJeune spent more time in jail without a trial than any other inmate in Fulton County history. While I am glad he remained behind bars all those years, I cannot help but feel this case should have gone to trial in less than half that time.

* * *

There were a few changes in the second trial. Though Brett Pinion did a great job delivering the opening statement in the first trial, the decision was made that Clinton Rucker would give the opening statement for the second trial. Rucker also did an excellent job.

Another difference is that unlike the first trial, when Brian Steel had maneuvered to keep us outside the courtroom during opening arguments, Brooks and I were allowed inside from the very moment Judge Russell called the second trial to order. That was because the LeJeune family had insisted on being present for opening statements during the second trial. That development allowed the prosecution to take Steel's rationale for keeping Brooks and I out of the courtroom the first time around and flip it around. If the court could make an exception for the LeJeunes, it could also make one for us.

The prosecution also flipped the order in which they presented witnesses. Though they once again led off with Brooks and me, instead of having Rekha Anand testify immediately after us (as they had done in the first trial), this time they decided to call all of their other witnesses to the stand first, and save Anand's testimony for last. This strategy would prove to be very effective, as we would soon see.

Of course, the defense's strategy was the same as before: to implicate Kenneth Vaughn as Ron's killer. Despite the fact that Judge Russell had thrown out the motion from the first trial to prove Ron a violent person, it was apparent that Brian Steel was going to take every opportunity to discredit our son's reputation, especially given the type of witnesses he intended to question.

Let me reiterate that whenever anything positive was said about Ron, it made the defense squirm. For instance, one day during the jury selection process, a prospective juror revealed during *voir dire* that he happened to have worked with Ron. This revelation, of course, immediately disqualified him as a juror. Before he was dismissed, however, this man said on record that our son was "a nice guy," which was precisely the kind of remark Brian Steel wanted to suppress.

Another prospective juror made a statement that made the defense uncomfortable. Unfortunately, I never had a chance to speak to this man, so I do not know his name... but I will never forget what he said. He identified himself as a defense attorney with a lot of experience trying criminal cases. As you can imagine, he was also sent home right away once he disclosed that about himself. Before he left, however, this man asked the court if he could have a few words. Judge Russell told him yes. He told her how he originally felt about his job when he graduated law school many years before, and how he feels about it now.

"Your honor, I used to think my job was to beat the prosecution, no matter what," the prospective juror said. "I'm not so sure about that anymore. Not when you have a case like this. I just don't feel it's right for anyone to spend so much of the state's money just to free this one criminal-and I say this as a defense lawyer, myself!"

The lawyer also went on to say that he believed that some changes need to be made in our justice system. The moment he said that, I couldn't help but glance over at Brian Steel and everyone else at the defense table. They all had their heads down. They could not bear to hear this man, let alone look him in the eye.

Judge Russell, by contrast, listened keenly and patiently as the lawyer said his piece. Then she formally excused him as a juror. The man had barely left the courtroom when Steel stood up and asked Russell to "hold him here longer." Apparently that was an attempt at humor on Steel's part, but from where we sat, it was more arrogant than funny. Judge Russell wisely ignored him.

Still, I never cease to be dismayed at how often defense attorneys such as Brian Steel try to put the victim on trial. It really does seem as though the criminal has all the rights. I suppose that's why it's called the criminal justice system.

* * *

My testimony began on the afternoon of Monday, October 31, and carried over into Tuesday, November 1. Brooks completed his testimony on Tuesday. We were told that we both did very well-so well, in fact, that Brian Steel later admitted privately to Clinton Rucker that we gave him no help whatsoever in his cross examination.

Kenneth Vaughn was the next witness after Brooks. He testified about the night he met LeJeune and Anand at a Waffle House in Atlanta on Sunday, January 18, 1998, where they related to him with cold precision the details of how LeJeune shot Ron on Saturday, December 27, 1997, and how the two of them desecrated and disposed of his body later that night.

Vaughn told the court of how plainly LeJeune spoke of his reasons for killing Ron: that LeJeune shot Ron because Ron wouldn't repay the $50.00 he still owed LeJeune after LeJeune had fronted Ron nearly $200.00 worth of cocaine the night before, and because Ron had the gall to ask LeJeune to front him another $50.00 worth of cocaine, even though he had not completely repaid LeJeune for the previous night's transaction. Vaughn also said under oath that LeJeune told him that night at the Waffle House about how agitated he was at Ron in the moments before he shot him. LeJeune told Vaughn that Ron was highly strung and that he "wouldn't shut up."

That was LeJeune's entire motivation for killing our son. "That's what he told me," Vaughn said in his testimony.

In our many past experiences with Ron, knowing full well how often he would con and manipulate people whenever he was on drugs, it was our opinion that he was trying to keep enough of the cash we had wired him in order to get his car back. Plus we also knew from our dealings with Ron that one's craving from cocaine is so intense that it's impossible to make rational decisions.

Vaughn then told the court of how LeJeune described the shock and horror on Ron's face in the remaining seconds of his life, just before LeJeune pulled the trigger. He then spoke of how LeJeune told him of his decision to dismember Ron's body, because it was too large for LeJeune and Anand to move. LeJeune told Vaughn that he "went out and bought a saw and came back," Vaughn testified. "He was talking about how he cut up the body, and how it sounds when bone gets cut up."

Vaughn then recalled how queasy he became upon hearing the details of this gruesome story. "I ordered some food, but I couldn't eat it," he told the jury. "I just... I ordered it [but] it sat there. It wasn't really pleasant, what they were talking about."

When it came time for cross-examination, Brian Steel did everything he could to discredit Vaughn's testimony. First, he confronted Vaughn on an inconsistency in Vaughn's statement to the G.B.I. when he testified that LeJeune had told him that night at the Waffle House the location where he had hidden Ron's head. Vaughn told Steel that although LeJeune had told him at the Waffle House of the decision to decapitate Ron, LeJeune never told him where he had disposed of Ron's head. "It was in the paper yesterday," Vaughn explained.

"It was in the paper yesterday," Steel said mockingly. "So you're bringing facts to this jury that you read about in the newspaper?"

"That's where I saw it," Vaughn replied.

"But you told this jury Michael LeJeune told you that," Steel said.

"And I just said I made a mistake," said Vaughn.

Steel then tried to cast Vaughn as an ill-tempered man who argued with Ron in LeJeune's apartment while LeJeune was away, then shot Ron and tried to frame LeJeune for the murder. He kept battering Vaughn with question after question, as if he were Matlock or Perry Mason trying to get a dramatic confession on the witness stand in the last few minutes of an episode.

Despite the histrionics, Brian Steel could not shake Vaughn. No matter what was thrown at him, Vaughn came back with the same answer-the right answer: *"I did not kill Ronnie Davis. Michael LeJeune did."*

But Brian Steel, as you can imagine, did not give up easily. His cross-examination of Vaughn continued well into the fourth day of the trial. That was when he decided to shift gears and try to pick apart the details of the controlled call Vaughn made on behalf of the G.B.I. on January 19, 1998.

Vaughn testified that he sought counsel from attorney Jerry Froelich shortly after LeJeune told him at the Waffle House that he had killed Ron. "No one had ever confessed a murder to me before," Vaughn said to the jury. "I didn't really know what I needed to do. So I thought it was best to get some representation, that I have someone tell me who I need to talk to, "how do I need to go about it."

"But you knew who to talk to," Steel countered during cross-examination. "[The police] told you."

"Yeah," Vaughn replied. "But I didn't want to do it by myself."

Vaughn then testified that he spoke with Froelich on the phone on the night of January 18, 1998, and then later met Froelich at his office. There, Froelich called the police and arranged for Vaughn to meet with the G.B.I. Upon being interviewed by Bureau investigators, Vaughn agreed to make the call to LeJeune.

"Mr. Vaughn," asked Steel, "when you made that phone call to Mr. LeJeune, did you know what he was going to say on the other end?"

"No," said Vaughn.

"Then why did you risk making that phone call?" asked Steel.

"Well, one, they asked if I would do it," replied Vaughn. "And, two, just to see if maybe he would go ahead and tell some people the same things he told me."

At that point, Steel had excerpts of the controlled call read into the record, then tried to use these excerpts to convince the jury that the call in no way linked LeJeune to Ron's murder. First, he pointed out that LeJeune said nothing in the course of the phone conversation with Vaughn that can be construed as a confession to the murder-a point which the prosecution did not dispute. Steel then tried to discredit the call further by telling the jury that Vaughn made no attempt to implicate LeJeune by asking him leading questions-which, again, the prosecution did not dispute.

Nevertheless, Vaughn held firm. "I was doing the best I could to not alert him that I was being recorded and I was trying to pry for information," he told the jury.

"But, sir," said Steel, "that was the whole point of the exercise, wasn't it-to get information?"

"That's the point of the exercise," replied Vaughn. "But again, I'm not trained in that type of procedure, you know. I just called to talk to him in hopes that he would say something."

"You didn't even ask these probing questions, except once Michael LeJeune says it didn't happen," continued Steel. "You got nothing on that controlled call out of Kelly Anand implicating her in the death of Ron Davis, except for cleaning up carpet. Do you realize that?"

"It's not really [up to] me to determine what can be implicated off of that tape," replied Vaughn. "There's a lot of things you could probably implicate off that tape. But I think you-all will decide that yourselves."

That point was certainly true. Steel kept asking Vaughn to interpret what was said on the tape, but the court overruled him. That was a matter for the jury to decide.

More to the point, while it's certainly true that LeJeune told Vaughn nothing that could implicate him in Ron's murder, it's also true that he did nothing to deny it. He never said anything like, "What are you talking about, Ken?"-which is exactly the thing you would expect to hear from someone if indeed they were truly innocent.

* * *

Vaughn's wife, Doris, and his mother, Dorothy Vaughn, were among the other witnesses who testified on the fourth day of the trial.

Dorothy Vaughn is a retired director of alumni relations for Hunter College in New York City; Kenneth is her only son. Mrs. Vaughn told the court that her husband died in November 1997; for that reason, it was especially important that she spend Christmas that year with Kenneth and his family. She testified that she flew down to visit Kenneth and Doris on Wednesday, December 24, 1997, and returned to New York on Sunday, December 28, 1997. She said that while she did not stay at her son's house, she and Kenneth spent a lot of time together throughout the holiday weekend.

Mrs. Vaughn told the court that Kenneth, Doris, and she had dinner with a friend on the night of Friday, December 26. "I remember that," she said, "because we got a ticket [on the way back] for forgetting Travis' seat belt." (Travis is Kenneth Vaughn's stepson; he was seven years old at the time.) She then said that she and Kenneth spent the whole day together, sightseeing and shopping, on Saturday, December 27-the day of Ron's murder-and that Kenneth drove her to the airport for her return flight on Sunday, December 28-the day Ron's body was discovered.

If that didn't poke a hole in the defense's argument-after all, it would have been impossible for Kenneth Vaughn to commit a murder, hide the body, and do away with the evidence on December 27, when he was with his mother the entire day-then surely Mrs. Vaughn's next statement did. Mrs. Vaughn not only told the court that Kenneth received a ticket for illegal parking at the airport (when he went inside the terminal for a few minutes to tell her goodbye), but that she had kept that ticket after all these years. (The ticket was dated and time-stamped, December 28, 1997; the prosecution promptly entered it into the case as an exhibit.) That ticket also turned out to be a blessing in disguise, in that it served to strengthen Vaughn's alibi for December 27 and 28.

Mrs. Vaughn admitted to being a little nervous when she first took the stand, but Clinton Rucker soon made her feel comfortable. She was dignified and professional, and came across as yet another solid witness for our side. Brooks and I did not have a chance to speak to her, but it had to have embarrassed her to know that her only son was involved in selling and distributing cocaine. It is our understanding that Ron's murder helped turned his life around. Kenneth Vaughn is an intelligent man, much more so than Michael LeJeune. I still can't fathom how the two of them ever came to be friends in the first place. It had to have been the drugs.

* * *

Doris Vaughn, Kenneth's wife, was also a good witness, though Steel did manage to rattle her a little during cross-examination. The issue concerned her memory of her husband's whereabouts on the day of Ron's murder. Though she had previously stated in a 1999 deposition that Kenneth was with his mother on the morning and afternoon of December 27, Steel bombarded Doris with questions that were designed to confuse her about her own statement. For a moment, it appeared as though the misdirection had worked. Steel finished cross-examination by again asking Doris where Kenneth was on the morning in question. At that point, all she could say was, "I'm not sure."

Fortunately, Brett Pinion was able to neutralize Steel when he approached Doris for re-direct examination. He pulled out the transcript of her 1999 statement, directed her attention to the pages where she discussed her recollection of the events of December 27, and asked if that refreshed her memory. This time, Doris said yes.

Steel then asked the court for permission to re-direct Doris Vaughn. To his surprise, Judge Russell wouldn't allow it. "Did the prosecution raise a new subject matter?" she asked. "If he did not, the answer is no."

"Well, to me, yes," said Steel.

Russell called Steel, Rucker, and Pinion to the bench so that she could explain her ruling in private. "All [Pinion] did was follow up on the areas you talked about," she told Steel. "At some point, it's got to be over."

This calls to mind one other noticeable difference between the first trial and the second. Remember how Judge Russell always seemed to side with the defense during the early stages of the case? (I'm not suggesting in any way that she was prejudiced against the prosecutors. I'm just saying that, from where we sat, you can't help but feel frustrated when nearly every critical ruling in the pre-trial hearings goes in favor of the other side.) Well, by the time the second trial started, Brooks and I got the impression that she'd had her fill of Brian Steel. We have no idea what brought about the change in her demeanor, if indeed there was any change at all. It just seemed to us that instead of Judge Russell always appearing to favor one side, she had now become very fair to both sides, and had taken control of the case in the process.

We had a feeling that things were going to be different when, at one point early in the second trial, *Judge Russell herself* began objecting to some of the things Brian Steel said! That told us right away that she intended to keep him on a tight leash-although it apparently took a while for Steel to understand that. For example, even though Russell had made herself clear on the matter of further questioning Doris Vaughn, Steel insisted on arguing with her anyway.

"I understand it's got to be over," Steel said to Russell

"I do. And I respect you. I think you're wonderful. But, Judge, witness after witness, the D.A. gets the last word."

"Yeah, that's right," said Judge Russell. "And when you put up witnesses, you will get the last word, too."

"I just want [the jury] to know everything," said Steel.

"And you know what?" said Russell. "The way this works is, they get to put them up, you get to cross. And once you're done, they get to re-direct. And unless they say something new, it will always be tit for tat."

This, of course, is standard court protocol. Because Doris Vaughn was a witness for the state, the state had the right to ask follow-up questions after cross-examination-just as the defense has the right to re-direct any witnesses they introduce as part of their case. In other words, each side has the last say when it comes to questioning their own witnesses. It's up to the judge to make the final determination on when the questioning ends. That's the rule, pure and simple. As Judge Russell explained: "The fact is, at a certain point, it has to be over. Somebody has to have the last word."

Brian Steel knew that to be true, and yet he wouldn't take no for an answer. "Can I just have a continuing objection?" he asked.

"No, sir," said Judge Russell. "You can't have a continuing objection because what I have told you is, if they raise a new subject matter [in the course of re-direct examination of one of their own witnesses], I will allow you further cross-examination. And if it is your position that they raised a new subject matter, you present it to me, and I will rule on it. So, "no."

"But I just said in my opinion-"

"Okay," interrupted Judge Russell. "I disagree with you. I get to do that. But that means you don't get to have a continuing objection. You get to tell me the situation, and then I get to decide about it. Because, I have not said in any way that you are barred from recrossing."

"So far you have," sniped Steel.

"So far I've been right," replied the judge, "until somebody says otherwise."

"Well, *I* say otherwise," retorted Steel.

Judge Russell tugged the shoulder of her robe. "When you get one of these," she said, "you win. The way this works is, I always win Round One."

The jury was not in the courtroom at the time-the judge had called a 15-minute recess after dismissing Doris Vaughn from the stand-but everyone else got a good laugh at poor Brian Steel's expense. Judge Russell really cut him down to size.

* * *

Later in the fourth day, the jury heard testimony from Tim Brooks, the G.B.I. crime scene investigator who investigated the cemetery where the remains of Ron's body were found on the morning on December 28, 1997. As part of his testimony, C.S.I. Brooks described photographs of one of Ron's burned feet while it was still inside a sock; Ron's severed neck area and torso; parts of Ron's severed arms, including the bicep of his left arm, where he had the tattoo of the Harley Davidson emblem; and other physical evidence recovered from the crime scene, including burned remnants of Ron's clothes, and remnants of burned blue plastic (which was later determined to be part of a blue tarp that LeJeune and Anand used to transport Ron's body). At one point, C.S.I. Brooks told the jury that in the course of investigating hundreds of crime scenes throughout his long career, he had never come across a crime scene as heinous as what he saw at the cemetery that morning.

Tim Brooks was also a good witness, but his testimony was one we did not hear in person. At our own request, Brooks and I stepped out of the courtroom while he was on the witness stand. To this day, we have never examined the crime scene photos. We made the decision long ago never to look at them. We know every detail of Ron's murder. Even without seeing the actual photos, it's been impossible to cast from our minds the images of his horrible demise, no matter how hard we try. Just reading about them in the court transcript later on was almost more than I could bear. No parent should have to lose a child in such a brutal and heinous way.

Other witnesses from the fourth day included Tracy Ehman, a nursing student who was jailed overnight on January 21, 1998 following an argument with her leasing officer; and Lt. Karen O'Hagen of the Fulton County Police Department, the officer who arrested Ehman as a result of an unfortunate incident.

I say "unfortunate" because, prior to her arrest on January 21, Tracy Ehman had no police record whatsoever, not even a traffic ticket or a moving violation. But upon learning that night that the lease on her apartment was not going to be renewed (despite the fact that she was not only a good tenant, but one who had never missed a payment), Ehman went to the leasing office, where she proceeded to discuss her situation with the woman on duty. In the course of their conversation, Ehman noticed her payment record in plain sight on the woman's desk. Ehman asked to see the report, but the leasing officer inexplicably refused. Frustrated, and understandably upset, Ehman reached across the desk and tried to pick up the report. In so doing, however, she inadvertently brushed up against the woman's shoulder. The woman overreacted, the police were summoned, and as a result, Ehman was arrested on charges of robbery by snatch and simple battery. She spent the night in a holding cell.

It was one of those terrible misunderstandings. Fortunately for Ehman, the charges were dropped the following morning and expunged from her record.

Fortunately for Brooks and me, however, because of her fateful arrest, Tracy Ehman was in a position to witness a conversation that proved vital to the case against LeJeune.

Ehman told the jury that she was handcuffed next to Rekha Anand inside the jail transport van during the trip to the courthouse on the morning of January 22. Also inside the van, seated across from Ehman and Anand, was Michael LeJeune, handcuffed next to another man. Ehman told the court that LeJeune and Anand "were kissing and talking" during the trip, and that they were discussing "some things they had done regarding a murder."

Ehman further testified that at one point LeJeune said that "they would've gotten away with everything if somebody named Ken hadn't come into the apartment and seen the head. I can recall them discussing some things that I guess the G.B.I. had said to them, but some things that they were talking about they had done or hadn't done... They were discussing that they hadn't changed their shoes, that they left tracks in the cemetery. They were discussing something about a blue tarp, that they had a blue tarp. They discussed two guns, one that they thought was silver.

"I believe that they were [also] discussing saws, a saw or saws," Ehman continued to tell the jury. "They said that the G.B.I. came to me and said that they found the saws at this place, and [Anand] said, 'Well, what I was supposed to say, [the saw wasn't] there.

"I also remember them discussing-I don't know which one said it, but discussing if they found blood in the apartment, they would say it was from a litter of kittens that they had had." This statement, by the way, is consistent with information that Kenneth Vaughn was able to ascertain from the controlled call to LeJeune's apartment.

Needless to say, Ehman testified that she was "caught off guard" by the casual way in which LeJeune and Anand spoke to each other about the details of the crime. She said that they also talked about it as they continued to kiss and say things like "I love you" and "I'm sorry I got you into this."

Ehman further testified that LeJeune tried to intimidate her into remaining silent. "He said, 'I know where you live,'" she told the jury. "We had small talk on the way to the court... and [he] said, "Yeah, I know where you live now, and my brother is going to be coming down to check out business." That's what he said to me. It was like, 'Keep your mouth shut.'

"When I got to the courthouse, I started hyper-ventilating," Ehman continued. "I was shaking, and I felt like I was going to throw up everywhere. They brought us [into the courtroom] and the marshal looked at me and said, 'Are you okay,' and I said no. And so they took me back to the judge's chambers, and I told the marshal what I had heard."

When it came time to cross-examine Ehman, Brian Steel tried to convince the jury that the conversation she had overheard in the van concerned information LeJeune and Anand had learned from the G.B.I. agents investigating the case-not details they had handled themselves. In other words, Steel claimed that LeJeune and Anand only knew about the saw and the blood in their apartment because the G.B.I. told them about those details in the course of interrogating them.

That's a plausible enough explanation. But if that were really the case, then what was the point of threatening Ehman? Why would LeJeune care whether she told anyone what she heard, unless he had something to hide?

Steel further asked Ehman about a detail she had mentioned before in a deposition-specifically, the fact that Ehman had previously testified that, at one point during their conversation that morning inside the jail van, she heard LeJeune and Anand say that there were two guns, and that she believed she heard LeJeune and Anand say that one of these guns "was Kenneth's gun." Steel, of course, had hoped to use this part of Ehman's testimony as part of his attempt to cast Kenneth Vaughn as Ron's murderer. Steel asked Ehman just a few more questions before dismissing her from the witness stand.

The jury then heard from Lt. O'Hagen, Ehman's arresting officer. O'Hagen was present at the courthouse when Ehman and the other passengers arrived on the morning of January 22. She testified that at some point, she was summoned by one of the marshals to come to the restroom in the judge's chambers. Upon arrival, O'Hagen saw Tracy Ehman inside the restroom, where "she was shaking, she was crying, and she was beginning to hyperventilate." At that point, O'Hagan was apprised of the death threat LeJeune made against Ehman only moments before, on the way over to the courthouse.

O'Hagen further testified that while she was not the officer who drove Ehman, LeJeune, Anand and the other inmate to the courthouse on the morning of January 22, she had transported prisoners many times before in that same police van. She described the vehicle as a 15-passenger Ford Econoline van, with a driver seat up front, and three rows of seats in back, for the prisoners. A partition with a wire screen separates the prisoners from the driver. There are various police radios in the front compartment, as well as a music radio. For that reason, Lt. O'Hagen testified that, unless the prisoners yelled or banged on the partition, it would be difficult for the driver of the van to overhear any conversation that went on in the back.

* * *

Rekha Anand then took the stand late in the day. She told the court that Ron came by the one-bedroom loft apartment she and LeJeune shared on the morning of Saturday, December 27, 1997, and wanted to buy cocaine. Apparently Ron tried to pay for the drugs with a check, but when Anand called the bank to verify the funds, she learned there was not enough money in Ron's account to cover the check. At this point, Anand testified, LeJeune became increasingly angry at Ron. Ron kept asking LeJeune for more cocaine, even though it was obvious that he didn't have any money.

It was around this time that Ron called Brooks and me to ask if we would wire him money to retrieve his car that had been towed and to purchase a tire. We told him we would do that. That was the conversation that took place around ten o'clock on Saturday, December 27-the last time we would ever speak to him.

Anand then told the jury that she, LeJeune, and Ron drove to an A&P store to pick up the money we had wired him, and then went back to the apartment. Upon their return, LeJeune sent Anand into the kitchen so that she could retrieve the cocaine, which she had kept hidden inside her clothes. She was removing the drugs from her bra when she heard a loud popping sound, which she likened to a firecracker. She raced back into the hallway, just as LeJeune was rushing toward her. He had a gun in his hand, and was pointing in the direction of the living room. "I thought he'd never shut up," he said.

Anand then testified that when she walked back into the living room, she saw Ron slumped on the couch. At first she thought he was just sleeping, but when she looked closely, she saw a bullet hole on the left side of his forehead and blood trickling down his face. She said she stood there in shock for several minutes before deciding to clean the area where Ron had been shot. "It just kicked in that I gotta start cleaning up," she said under oath. "At this point, I'm still using drugs, and I'm still high... and cocaine makes you want to do things. I was thinking about the carpet and furniture and not getting blood on any of those things."

Anand then told the jury that she and LeJeune dragged Ron's

body from the sofa and "stuffed" it into the downstairs half-bath. Apparently, they were expecting company coming by any minute-customers who wanted to buy cocaine from LeJeune. "Michael started going through Ronnie's wallet, and took the remainder of his money," she said. "I was straightening up the coffee table, just basically cleaning. Every cleaning product that I had underneath the counter I grabbed, including bleach, and I tried to get up the bloodstains [from the carpet]."

A while later, after completing a deal with LeJeune's customers, Anand and LeJeune decided to move Ron's body to the upstairs master bathroom so that the blood from Ron's head would drain into the tub instead of onto the floor. During this time, Anand told the jury, she and LeJeune tried to figure out what to do with the body. That was the point when LeJeune decided to dismember it. "Michael had a Bowie knife and was trying to cut one of Ronnie's limbs off," she explained. "Then I suggested, when I saw that the Bowie knife wasn't working because it didn't have a serrated edge, that Michael go out and get a saw."

At this point, Assistant D.A. Rucker interrupted Anand's testimony to show the jury a replica of the saw that she and LeJeune purchased from a Home Depot for the purpose of cutting up Ron's body. Judge Russell then called for a brief recess when a female juror became upset upon seeing the saw.

When court resumed, Anand told the jury that while she did not witness LeJeune cutting off Ron's arms and legs, she could hear it from the kitchen. She described it as sounding "ten times more horrific" than the sound of a saw through chicken bone. Anand said that they put the body parts into black garbage bags, then into laundry baskets and tossed dirty clothes on top. That way, should neighbors see them walking by, it would appear as if she and LeJeune were heading out to do their laundry.

Anand then testified that later that evening, she and LeJeune drove to the house near Lake Lanier owned by LeJeune's parents. (LeJeune's parents, as mentioned before, were out of town for the Christmas holidays.) The plan was to dispose of Ron's body parts somewhere along the way and burn them.

Sometime between 3:00 a.m. and 6:00 a.m. on Sunday, December

28, Anand and LeJeune stopped at a service station, filled up the car's tank as well as a small red gas can, and drove around looking for a dark, secluded place. Upon discovering the Hopewell Church cemetery in Forsyth County, they doused the remains of Ron's body and lit them on fire. It was at that point, Anand testified, that LeJeune decided to decapitate Ron's torso. As she explained to the jury, "Michael told me he didn't want the fragments [of the bullet] that were in Ronnie's head to be traced back to him and to the gun he had."

They abandoned the body, and then proceeded to the lake house. Ron's head was still inside the car. Upon arrival, LeJeune went into his father's workshop while Anand washed clothes and took a nap. She told the jury that when she woke up, she learned that LeJeune had placed Ron's head in a vise to try to extract the bullet fragments from his skull. When that didn't work, he put Ron's head in a tin bucket, covered it with leaves and twigs, and decided to burn it. That didn't work, so she and LeJeune drove to a nearby hardware store, bought some cement, which they mixed and poured into the bucket over Ron's head. Anand then told the jury that after hiding the bucket in a closet for a couple of days, they rowed out to the middle of Lake Lanier and threw it and the saw into the water.

* * *

Listening to Anand's testimony that day was overwhelming for Brooks and me. Reliving the events of Ron's murder unleashed a torrent of emotions, opening up wounds that had never quite healed.

Yet at the same time, it was different. I felt the same strength I'd felt the day I testified in the first trial, the strength that comes from answered prayer. And as I watched each witness take the stand-their collective testimony backing Steel and the defense team further and further into a corner-I felt the confidence that comes from God's love. After so many twists and turns in this case, I began to feel for the first time as though momentum had swung our way.

Once again, God was providing us with the strength we needed at precisely the right moment. And believe me, Brooks and I would need every ounce of that strength to deal with the shocking revelation that was about to hit the courtroom.

Chapter Twenty-Nine

Divine Intervention

Court was not held on Friday, November 4 because of a judges meeting. Carolyn, Doris, and Don went touring in Atlanta, while Brooks, Diane and I spent the day resting. As pleased as we were with how well the first week of the trial was going, between jury selection and especially the events of Wednesday and Thursday, the previous six weeks, as you can imagine, were also incredibly draining. Most afternoons, I found myself so exhausted physically and emotionally after attending court that all I could do once we got back to the hotel was head straight for bed. Needless to say, we both welcomed the opportunity to recharge our batteries. The trial resumed with the continuation of Rehka Anand's testimony on Saturday, November 5.

In the meantime, Assistant D.A. Brett Pinion worked late Thursday night and early Friday morning poring over files that had been supplied to the prosecution eight days before, on October 27, 2005, by Gary Guichard, the Fulton County public defender who represented Rekha Anand from her arrest in January 1998 until her plea bargain deal in June 2003. Guichard, of course, negotiated the deal that gave Anand immunity in exchange for her cooperation with the state. The files provided by Guichard contained, among other things, over 50 pages of notes made by Guichard and other lawyers and social workers assigned to Anand's case. The information in these notes-not to mention, the events that led the state to obtain Guichard's files in the first place-set off a host of fireworks that would dramatically change the course of the trial.

Like nearly every other aspect of this case, however, it's a complicated story. Therefore, a little background is in order.

I mentioned before that during the first trial, Rekha Anand was on the witness stand at the time of the courthouse shootings on Friday, March 11, 2005-the horrific event that eventually led Judge Russell to declare a mistrial on Monday, March 14. Before the mistrial was declared, however, Brian Steel spent the better part of two days impeaching Anand's testimony, arguing that Anand's memory of the details of Ron's murder was often contradicted by the physical evidence and the testimony of other witnesses. To make his case, Steel introduced into evidence over five dozen letters that Anand had supposedly written to LeJeune while she was an inmate at the Fulton County jail. According to Steel, Anand professed her innocence repeatedly throughout these letters, despite the fact she had already confessed to being an accomplice in Ron's murder as part of the videotaped statement she provided to the prosecution in February 2003. According to Steel, Anand told LeJeune in these letters that the only reason she confessed was that she had been coerced into doing so by her attorney, Gary Guichard, whom she allegedly denounced in her letters as a "public pretender" who never returned her phone calls. Also according to Steel, Anand wrote LeJeune that she only agreed to cooperate with the state for fear that the prosecutors "would send her to death row" because they "wanted only to win a conviction."

The prosecution was blindsided-they knew nothing of the existence of these letters until Steel revealed them in open court. Anand, of course, was the state's star witness. Though our prosecutors tried to stem the tide by pointing out that Anand was still very much in love with LeJeune at the time she confessed in 2003 (therefore, anything she wrote in those letters may have been said simply in order to placate him), there is no question that the impeachment of her testimony was a damaging blow to our case. In fact, after Judge Russell declared the first trial to be a mistrial, Steel boasted to a reporter that he was told by several jurors that the jury did not like Anand. Assuming that to be true, who knows what would have happened had the first trial been allowed to continue?

But, of course, it didn't continue. And as angry and frustrated as Brooks and I were at the time, in a strange way-as God's ways often are-having the first trial end as a mistrial ended up in our favor. As I mentioned earlier, it allowed the prosecutors to rearrange the order of witnesses for the second trial, saving Rehka Anand as one of the last witnesses to testify in their case, instead of making one of their first. This way, by playing to the strength of their witnesses, and parading them out one after another, the state was able to overcome a major disadvantage-remember, the defense had succeeded in getting all of the hard evidence against LeJeune thrown out of the case-and still present a powerful, very convincing case. As I say, by the time Anand took the stand on Day Four of the second trial, there really was a sense that the D.A. had Steel on the ropes.

Plus, just as a good football coach makes adjustments during halftime of a game in which his team is trailing, our lead prosecutor, Assistant D.A. Clinton Rucker, adjusted his game plan for the second trial, recognizing the areas where his opponent showed him to be vulnerable, and taking steps to minimize them. In our case, our most glaring vulnerability coming out of the first trial was Anand's testimony. "We were not expecting her to be substantially impeached with inconsistent statements," Rucker said in an article published in the *Fulton County Daily Report* on November 8, 2005. "It was not until Brian impeached her for a day and a half that we started looking for previous consistent statements."

Toward that end, in late October 2005, shortly before the start of the second trial, Rucker contacted Gary Guichard and requested permission to review the public defender's files on Rehka Anand. These files, as it happens, had been sealed by Judge Russell in July 2003, after Brian Steel had attempted to obtain these files himself from Guichard via subpoena. (Steel issued the subpoena earlier in 2003, after Anand agreed to testify against LeJeune as part of her plea bargain. Both Guichard and the prosecution filed motions to quash the subpoena on the basis that Anand had not waived attorney/client privilege, and that the public defender's files contained information that was shielded from discovery under the attorney work-product privilege.) A hearing was scheduled on July 11, 2003; Guichard testified at that hearing. According to a court transcript, when asked by Steel whether his files contained anything that could corroborate the account Anand gave in her videotaped confession of February 2003, Guichard said, "No." (Later, when asked by a reporter whether he had reviewed the contents of his files prior to testifying on July 11, 2003, Guichard also answered no. "I'm sure I felt no need to," he explained. "As far as I was concerned, the case was over. My client had pled [five months earlier].")

Upon completion of Guichard's testimony, Judge Russell reviewed the files *in camera*-that is to say, privately, in her chambers. She then announced that she would comply with Steel's request, but only in part. Russell provided Steel with a total of two pages, concluding that these pages contained potentially exculpatory material that fell within the realm of attorney/client privilege. The rest of the files, however, were ordered sealed because they contained documents that, in Russell's judgment, were protected under the attorney work-product privilege. That distinction, as we're about to see, would play a huge role in shifting the balance of power in this case.

The files remained with the court until sometime in 2005, when they were returned to Guichard's office. The seal on the files remained in effect. Apparently, that did not discourage Brian Steel from attempting to obtain them.

In March 2005, near the end of the first trial, Steel told Guichard that he would file a motion to release his files on Anand. (Guichard had been scheduled to testify for the prosecution, but that never materialized on account of the mistrial.) Steel explained that he needed to see Guichard's files in case they contained something exculpatory-that is, something that could prove his client's innocence. At that point, Guichard said, "Brian, you can pick up those files whenever you want-they're in my office. They're just too heavy for me carry over myself. All you need to do is get Kelly [Anand] to sign a waiver of her attorney/client privilege."

Brooks and I were in the courtroom at the time, so we witnessed the entire conversation. In the ensuing months, we had no idea whether Steel followed through on that invitation and obtained a waiver from Anand. Once the second trial started, however, it wasn't long before the answer to that question became abundantly clear.

In the meantime, at the urging of Brett Pinion, Rucker contacted

Guichard in October 2005 about obtaining a copy of his files. At the time he spoke with Rucker, Guichard apparently believed "that Steel already had the files," according to an article published in *The Fulton County Daily Report* on December 5, 2005. (Presumably, Guichard recalled the motion Steel had discussed filing more than six months before.) Guichard then asked Rucker whether the matter of work-product privilege invoked by Judge Russell had ever been settled. Rucker replied that to the best of his knowledge, the answer to that question was yes. "I said to [Gary] that I thought that the defense counsel already had a copy of his file," Rucker recalled in the December 5 article. "And since I had never seen it, I would like for him to bring it in."

"As far as I'm concerned," said Guichard in the same article, "if a copy was released to the defense, that resolved the privilege issue."

Guichard did not contact the court to verify whether Steel had obtained the files. In his opinion, there was no need to. "Clint has always been straightforward with me," Guichard also said in the December 5 article. "I had no reason to disbelieve his word... He certainly never played games with me before. When he said the judge had made a copy for the defense, I saw no reason to question that."

At some point, however, there was concern among the prosecutors that Steel might think they had something to hide, so the decision was made to have Rekha Anand sign a waiver of her attorney/client privilege with respect to Guichard's files. With that, Guichard agreed to deliver the files to the District Attorney's Office, provided that Rucker issue a subpoena requesting the files. The subpoena was issued, and Anand agreed to sign the waiver. State investigator G.G. Carawan picked up a large cart from Guichard containing several boxes of the files and delivered it to Rucker's office on October 27, 2006, four days before opening statements. However, because the signed waiver from Anand was not secured until November 3, 2005, that means, by law, the prosecution was barred from examining the contents of the files until November 3, four days into the trial.

This brings us back to Assistant D.A. Brett Pinion, whose job it was to review Guichard's files before the trial resumed on Saturday, November 5. Brooks and I remember seeing all those boxes. Surely, it would have taken anyone a long time to sort through them; after all, we're talking about five years worth of material. Fortunately, with no court session scheduled on Friday, that gave Brett a little bit of time to examine everything carefully. He worked well past midnight Thursday night, going over each document with a fine tooth comb, when suddenly he came across an item he had never seen before. It was about 50 pages of handwritten notes, taken by Guichard, of a conversation between he and Anand that occurred sometime in September 1998-nine months after the murder, eight months after Anand and LeJeune were arrested. The conversation took place at the Fulton County Jail., and was witnessed by Anand's social workers and three other public defenders assigned to her case.

The more Brett Pinion went through those pages, the more engrossed he became. Throughout those pages, Anand provided Guichard with graphic details of the events that led LeJeune to murder Ron on the afternoon of December 27, 1997, and the role she played in helping LeJeune dispose of Ron's body later that night. These notes, Brett quickly realized, were not the record of a routine conversation, but that of a bona fide confession-one that would forever tip the scales of justice against Michael LeJeune.

Remember, Brian Steel had pinned his entire defense on the premise that Kenneth Vaughn tried to frame LeJeune for Ron's murder so as to collect the $10,000 reward. To sell that story to the jury, Steel had to discredit Anand's testimony-which he certainly appeared to do in the first trial, by pointing out what appeared to be inconsistencies between the statements Anand made in her video-taped confession of February 2003, the letters she wrote LeJeune subsequent to that confession, and the testimony she gave in court in March 2005.

But with the written confession from September 1998, the prosecution suddenly had proof beyond any doubt that Anand had actually confided *to her own attorney* that she had participated in Ron's murder-and named LeJeune as Ron's murderer-*more than seven years before*. (As we understand, Anand's confession was never made public because she had been waiting for LeJeune to plead guilty-something, of course, that did not happen up to that point. Anand, as mentioned, remained in jail for nearly five years after her jailhouse confession before accepting a plea bargain in July 2003.) Not only that, the details of Anand's confession to Guichard in September 1998 were identical to the account she gave in her confession of February 2003, her testimony in the first trial in March 2005, her testimony in the second trial on November 3, 2005, the physical evidence as detailed by G.B.I. investigator Tim Brooks, and the testimony of Kenneth Vaughn, Tracy Ehman, and other witnesses for the prosecution. That took Steel's notion of "inconsistent statements" and blew it completely out of the water.

It was a startling discovery. Indeed, when Brooks and I arrived in court Saturday morning, the first thing Brett said after telling us he had found these handwritten notes was, "I truly felt as though it were divine intervention."

What is even more startling is that Brian Steel, whose meticulous attention to detail had been the bane of our existence from the very beginning of this case, knew absolutely nothing about it.

* * *

The trial continued with the resumption of Anand's testimony on Saturday, November 5. By this time, Steel was becoming more and more frustrated. Not only had he failed to rattle Kenneth Vaughn, the man on whom he had hoped to pin Ron's murder, but he found himself overruled on nearly every objection-even on issues in which he appeared to be on solid legal ground.

At one point on Saturday, Clinton Rucker posed a question to Anand concerning information she had seen on a TV news report about Ron's murder shortly after her arrest in January 1998. That report mentioned that the G.B.I. had gathered garbage bags and other forensic evidence from LeJeune's apartment-evidence, of course, that Judge Russell had long since thrown out, based on technicalities Steel had raised during the pre-trial phase of the case. Steel objected to Rucker's question and requested that the jury be removed from the courtroom. Judge Russell complied with Steel's request, and then asked Rucker why he had questioned Anand about a report concerning suppressed evidence. In response, Rucker assured Judge Russell that he had already briefed Anand "not to talk about these things," and that there was no bad faith attempt "to elicit a response which... went outside the scope of what I expected the witness to answer."

Brian Steel, of course, cried foul. "Why don't I say what I know about the case that I can't prove in evidence," he protested to Judge Russell. "This is a pattern and practice of this district attorney's office with their witnesses... I'm not looking to avoid a trial, but I am looking to play by the rules and have a fair one."

Brooks and I could not believe our ears. This man used every trick up his sleeve to delay this case for nearly eight years, and he has the temerity to say "I'm not looking to avoid a trial?" Talk about the pot calling the kettle black.

Steel appeared to have made his point, however. Judge Russell chastised Rucker for "a minimum gross negligence," adding that the mere mention of the garbage bags was the kind of detail the jury was not likely to forget. "It is your obligation, not [Anand's]," she said, "to ensure that when she answers a question, it doesn't address issues which raise these kinds of problems." She then allowed Steel to inform the jury that the evidence found in the apartment search had been ruled inadmissible.

But when the jury returned, and Anand's testimony continued, Steel was in for the shock of his life. Anand proceeded to tell the jury about the jailhouse confession she made in September 1998 before Guichard, her social workers, and the other public defenders working with Guichard, and that the account she gave in 1998 was identical to the one she gave in court just two days before. She also testified that one of her lawyers (not Guichard) advised her "not to tell Michael that they know what I told them."

Of course, Steel objected, and once again Judge Russell ordered the jury to leave the courtroom. Steel then demanded to see the contents of Guichard's files, arguing that, by mentioning to the jury the advice of her attorneys, Anand had waived attorney/client privilege.

Brooks and I clutched hands and held our breath. Was it possible that Steel would once again prevail on yet another technicality?

The answer this time was no. Judge Russell overruled Steel's objection, saying that in her opinion no discovery violation was committed. She did, however, order Rucker to limit any further questions to Anand to conversations she had only with Guichard.

As it happened, Rucker was just about finished with Anand. Judge Russell then called a brief recess to allow the defense to prepare for cross-examination. This was the time when the prosecution lowered the boom on Steel.

Judge Russell had just left the courtroom when Brett Pinion approached Steel. "Tell me, Brian," he said. "How are you going to cross our witness in the face of these notes? You realize she's cross-proof."

Steel, as you might imagine, was puzzled by that remark. "What are you talking about?"

"*You don't have the notes?*" said Brett. "How are you going to cross her when she's been saying this since 1998?"

At this point, Clinton Rucker chimed in. "You don't have the notes, Brian?"

"Have what?" sniped Steel.

Rucker and Pinion handed Steel a copy of Guichard's notes. Steel read about two pages before he went ballistic. As soon as court reconvened, he immediately moved for another mistrial. Once again, the jury was removed from the courtroom.

"I have never been told that Mr. Guichard waived any type of work-product privilege," Steel said to Judge Russell. "Trial strategy was developed based upon information we had at the beginning of trial... I cannot go forward with the cross-examination of Ms. Anand. We'll look like I'm crazy."

"Would the prosecution care to explain themselves?" Russell asked Rucker.

Rucker replied that when he asked Guichard for a copy of his files, it was his understanding that Steel had already a complete set himself. He added that he and Brett Pinion were completely shocked upon realizing during the just-concluded recess that this was not the case.

Steel argued vehemently for a discovery violation, but Judge Russell overruled him. It was here that she discussed the distinction she had made between attorney/client privilege and attorney work-product privilege after Steel subpoenaed to see Guichard's files in

2003. The two pages she released to Steel were documents "which the court deemed to be responsive to a waiver of the attorney/client privilege," she explained. "[Defense counsel] was not given documents which appeared to be subject to the work-product privilege, either because they appeared to have been prepared by counsel, or would have been prepared at counsel's direction.

"Based on what I've heard about the documents that have been turned over today," Judge Russell continued, "they appear to be documents that in the court's judgment would have fallen under [attorney work-product privilege], which is why they would not have been turned over to Mr. Steel by the court.

Russell then reminded both parties that the seal she had placed on Guichard's files on July 11, 2003 had never been lifted. "It appears that the state's representation to Mr. Guichard about the court rulings, in turn, caused Mr. Guichard to consent to turning over his file," she said. "And so, as a consequence, the state has Mr. Guichard's entire file, and the defense does not."

Brooks and I could not believe what was happening. We always tried to hold our emotions in check, as the prosecution had advised, but at that moment it was all we could do to stay in our seats. As a matter of fact, Brooks clenched the bench in front of him so hard, I was afraid I would have to sit on him. But through the grace of God, he kept his composure. He sat there quietly, looking straight at Judge Russell before staring coldly at Brian Steel. Steel, meanwhile, began preening like a rooster in a hen house. Once again, he moved for a mistrial-for a moment, it seemed certain that his motion would indeed be granted. But to Steel's surprise, and to our relief, Judge Russell denied the motion and allowed the prosecution to continue questioning Anand.

Clinton Rucker proceeded to ask Anand to waive her attorney/client privilege with regard to Gary Guichard.

"I don't understand your question," said Anand.

"I'm sorry, let me rephrase," said Rucker. "Do you have a problem if Mr. Guichard gives us his notes in this case?"

Before Anand had a chance to respond, Brian Steel once again moved for a mistrial. Once again, the poor jurors were asked to leave the courtroom.

"Tell me, Mr. Rucker," said Judge Russell. "Why was that necessary in front of the jury?"

"Your honor, I fully had the expectation through her testimony, the existence of [Guichard's] notes will come out in cross examination," Rucker replied.

"Your honor," retorted Steel, "I am not waiving that these notes are ever coming in-so now what do I do?" Then he turned and complained to Clinton Rucker about how the prosecution wasn't playing fair. This, coming from the same man who had no problem surprising the prosecution eight months before, when he sprung all those letters into court to impeach Anand's testimony. Clearly, Steel could dish it out better than he could take it. "You didn't have to ask her if she waives her privilege," he said to Rucker. "She [already] waived to her lawyer. You didn't have to ask her about notes. The only relevance is now the jurors know that there are notes."

The louder Steel protested, the more he revealed his true colors.

From the very beginning, Brooks and I had a sneaking suspicion about Steel. He was young, smart, and ambitious, and Michael LeJeune was his first death penalty case. Granted, he is a defense lawyer, and it is his job and obligation to vigorously defend his client, no matter how heinous his crimes have been. I understand that. But with every motion Steel filed, and every technicality he raised, I also got the impression that he was using our case as a springboard for his career.

Never mind that all the evidence pointed to LeJeune as Ron's killer, or the number of times LeJeune himself ran his mouth off about the crime. Forget the fact that his girlfriend and accomplice testified against him, and that her attorney had warned what would happen to LeJeune if she ever took the stand. (According to Clinton Rucker, Gary Guichard told Steel after Rehka Anand's confession and plea bargain in 2003 that if Anand "ever gets on the stand and testifies against you, she is going to kill [your case]."

None of that mattered, because LeJeune's lawyer was Brian Steel. Brian Steel was not only going to get his client off the hook, but show the world just how clever a lawyer he was in the process.

Yet at the end of the day, for all his cleverness, Brian Steel found himself hoisted on his own petard. "This turn of events will ruin my reputation," he bellowed to Judge Russell. "This will follow me the rest of my life."

I don't mean to sound boastful, but as I sat there watching him that Saturday, arguing desperately as the last remnants of his brilliant defense crumbled before his eyes, I couldn't help but feel a small measure of satisfaction. I believe at that point God was saying, *"Enough is enough."*

CHAPTER THIRTY

Bombshell

Saturday was clearly a victorious day, but the case was far from over. Brian Steel, to no one's surprise, refused to go down quietly. When Judge Russell denied his motion for a mistrial, he immediately challenged the authenticity of Gary Guichard's notes, saying that he would call in a writing expert from Washington, D.C. to determine their veracity.

From where we sat, he appeared to be grasping at straws. Yet at the same time, Brooks and I were all too familiar with Steel's ability to manipulate facts. As confident as we were that God was answering us, and that Ron's killer was about to be brought to justice, we also knew it was wise not to take anything for granted.

After court was adjourned, we couldn't help but notice the defense lawyers meeting with LeJeune and his family. We learned later from the prosecution that they were discussing a plea bargain. As I mentioned before, the state to this point had never accepted an offer from Steel, because he had always asked for a limited number of years with the possibility of parole. That way, given that LeJeune had already served nearly eight years in prison, he figured his client could be freed from jail in only a few years time.

Of course, until the start of the second trial, Steel had always believed he was negotiating from a position of strength. The last few days-and especially, the last few hours-had changed the landscape dramatically. Even though he continued to posture, one had the feeling that even Steel was realizing his options were down to this: either press on (which, at the rate the case was going, would almost assuredly mean sentencing his client to death), or cut his losses and accept the state's offer of life without parole.

Then again, even if the jury were to render a guilty verdict, that wouldn't be the end of things. Not with Steel as LeJeune's lawyer. This is a man who took an evidentiary motion all the way up to the U.S. Supreme Court. He would relish the opportunity to appeal a death penalty conviction. Knowing how long the appeal process can take, that would mean that Brooks and I could be reliving Ron's death for many years to come.

That's why I've described this entire case as an emotional roller coaster ride. There's no other way to explain it.

That is also why, when I sent an email to friends and family with an update on Saturday's events, I asked them to continue praying for us. Even though we felt that God was close to bringing us victory, we also knew we needed the strength that comes from prayer in order to keep going. Until we could close the book on this case, every trip to the courtroom was like another ride through the horror of Ron's murder, and the grief and stress that accompanies every twist and turn.

We certainly needed that strength when the trial resumed. Most of our family members had to return home on Sunday, so Diane was the only one with us in court on Monday, November 7. That also proved to be a most volatile day.

Court began with a hearing in which Steel moved for sanctions against Guichard for conspiring with the prosecution, and against Clinton Rucker for acting in bad faith with regard to the acquisition of Guichard's notes from September 1998. From where we sat, I can tell you it was certainly very stressful.

At one point, for example, Guichard was asked about a comment he'd made under oath on July 11, 2003, during the hearing in which Steel first tried to obtain Guichard's files. On that day, after Steel asked whether the files had anything that could corroborate the account, Rekha Anand gave in her February 2003 confession, Guichard replied, "No." But when Steel asked him the same question on November 7, 2005, Guichard had a different answer. "The more precise thing I should have said was, 'Not as far as I remember,'" he told the court. "I didn't remember writing all those notes.... Based on my practice, I generally don't take a lot of extensive notes on clients' statements."

I'll admit, that gave us pause, and for a while I feared the worst. But my fears were allayed moments later, when Judge Russell denied Steel's motion, ruling that while the prosecution clearly obtained Guichard's files "in error and in violation of the court's seal," in her opinion they acted negligently-but not in bad faith.

In explaining her ruling, Russell reminded Steel that while an attorney's work product is privileged, a client can in fact waive that privilege "absent an affirmative showing by the attorney that there is some reason for them not to obtain it." In light of that fact, the judge said that although Anand had waived her attorney/client privilege, she retained the right "to obtain the records from Mr. Guichard and turn them over to the state." Therefore, the notes from Guichard's office "were properly in the state's custody." While it was true that the records were technically obtained in violation of the July 2003 seal, because Anand had on Saturday, and in open court, waived any objection to turning over these files to the prosecution, "under those circumstances," Judge Russell concluded, "it appears that the violation of the court's order was the result of negligence, or a failure to prepare [that is to say, a failure on the prosecution to read the record], it is not bad faith or misconduct."

Brooks and I sighed in relief, but as it happens, we'd exhaled too soon. Judge Russell had barely finished speaking when Steel asked for permission to confer with LeJeune. After a brief recess, Steel took the podium and hit us with another bombshell: *he was resigning from the case, effective immediately.* He told the court that he and Bud Siemon, Steel's partner on the case, had visited LeJeune in prison on Sunday, and that "because of something" LeJeune said to him, he "could no longer serve" on the case.

Brooks and I were completely stunned. We never saw that coming. And from the silence that blanketed the courtroom at that moment, neither did anyone else.

"Mr. Steel," said Judge Russell. "Are you resigning from this case, even if I hold you in contempt of court?"

"Yes, your honor," said Steel. "Based on what Mr. LeJeune has just told me, he would rather have different counsel."

Russell called LeJeune to the microphone. "Your honor," he said, "I am no longer comfortable with Mr. Steel as my attorney."

Then Russell addressed Steel again. "Mr. Steel," she asked, "is your withdrawal permanent?"

"Your honor, I'll help in every way I can," he said. "But without instructions from Mr. LeJeune, I will not be cross-examining any witnesses, nor offering any further arguments on his behalf. Mr. Siemon will be handling the case from this point on."

"Mr. Siemon" was Bud Siemon, Steel's partner on the case. When asked by Judge Russell to comment on what LeJeune had said to Steel, Siemon explained that the window in the visiting cell was not large enough for more than one person to talk through. Therefore, from where he stood at the time LeJeune spoke to Steel, he was not able to hear exactly what was said.

Siemon then immediately moved for a suspension of the trial to allow him time to find another lawyer to replace Brian Steel. It broke my heart to hear this, but Judge Russell had no choice but to grant the motion. State law in Georgia requires that a defendant in a death penalty case is to be represented by two attorneys. So Russell announced that the trial would be suspended for 14 days. Once again, our lives were about to be put on hold.

That was the moment I lost it.

Up until then, through eight years of depositions, preliminary hearings, appeals, two court trials, and countless legal delays, I'd always kept my composure. No matter what a bundle of nerves I was on the inside, through the grace of God and with the love of my husband, I always looked strong on the outside. I felt I owed it to Ron to be that way, and also to my family.

But at that moment, with Steel dropping out of the picture, and yet another delay at hand, I couldn't help but think, *Please, Lord, not again.* Then a horrible thought came over me: *Can it be we're looking at another mistrial?* Suddenly, it was just too much.

I broke down and cried, right there in the courtroom. I didn't sob out loud... just sat there shaking, with tears in my eyes, wondering what on earth could possibly happen next.

CHAPTER THIRTY-ONE

"Justice Will Wait..."

B rooks and I met briefly with the prosecutors after court was adjourned Monday afternoon. Clinton Rucker and Brett Pinion kept apologizing for the torment we had just been put through. They kept assuring us how unusual this case was, and how lawyers "just don't drop out of a murder trial right in the middle of the court-room." They didn't need to do that-as far as we were concerned, they had nothing to apologize for-but we certainly appreciated it, as well as their honesty and mannerisms over the years.

Then we tried to regroup and think about our next step. Prior to adjourning, Judge Russell announced that the jury would remain sequestered throughout the entire two weeks the trial would be suspended, and that her deputy would arrange for outings or trips to keep the jurors occupied. Not to be critical, but it made no sense for us at all to keep the jury sequestered. When the trial resumed two weeks later, the first thing the jury was bound to notice once they walked back into the courtroom is that Brian Steel, the man who argued passionately for LeJeune's innocence from Day One, is no longer at his side. People being people, what other conclusion could they possibly draw?

We also speculated as to what LeJeune said that prompted Brian Steel to resign. Steel said in court that he had been "told some infor-mation" by LeJeune in prison the previous day. Apparently LeJeune's family was also present at that time. Could it be that LeJeune had finally confessed?

285

We also realized that with the case being suspended, we would have to go back to Charlotte. The hotel was nice, and also conveniently located within walking distance of the courthouse. But it wasn't the safest place to walk around at night, so we tended to stay in our quarters. (Besides, as I mentioned before, most evenings we were too exhausted after court to go anywhere in the first place.) We did have our car, though, so sometimes we'd drive somewhere for dinner. We also drove places on weekends. But with the case suspended for two weeks, there was nothing we could do but go home. Each time we returned home, we left our clothes at the hotel and paid for the weekend out of our own pocket. (Fulton County provided our lodging, parking, and a daily food allowance, but not our families.)

In the meantime, Bud Siemon was meeting with Fulton County D.A. Paul Howard to try and work out a plea: life plus parole in 15 years. Once again, Howard said that the only plea bargain the state would consider was the same one it had offered from the very beginning: life without parole.

"But, Paul," said Siemon, "don't you realize it's still entirely possible that the jury might give my client parole, even with a guilty verdict?"

"Why, yes, they may very well do that," Howard replied. "Then again, Bud, it is also entirely possible that when they look at your table, and see that your friend Brian Steel is long gone, they may just decide to give your client death."

I would have loved to have been a fly on the wall, just to see the look on Siemon's face.

* * *

When we left the courthouse on Monday, we were told to return for a hearing Tuesday morning. Brooks and I were still numb from the events of the previous day, so I don't recall the purpose of the hearing. Though the defense did make another motion for a mistrial on Monday, Judge Russell did not grant it. So that couldn't be it. For a while we wondered whether LeJeune might plea, but again that was speculation. We hadn't spoken to the prosecution since court adjourned on Monday-if something significant happened, and they were at liberty to tell us, they most certainly would have done so. So we just went to court Tuesday with many questions on our mind. We arrived to see Brian Steel at LeJeune's table. Despite his dramatic pronouncement that he was no longer attorney of record, his presence was no doubt required until he was officially replaced, given the state's law regarding representation on death penalty cases. Considering what was about to transpire, however, I suppose it no longer mattered. Court was called to order at 10:00 a.m. I don't remember much that happened, except that the defense was in and out the courtroom, and so was the jury. About 11:00 a.m., Judge Russell called a recess and informed us to be back at 12 noon. Brooks, Diane, and I decided to go to the cafeteria and have a cup of coffee. The cafeteria was located in another building that was joined by a covered walkway, so it was several minutes away from the courtroom. Once we got to the cafeteria, it occurred to us that with court scheduled to resume at noon, it might be a while before lunch. So we decided to order something light before we returned to court.

As it happened, we no sooner sat down with our food when suddenly my cell phone rang. I had just turned it on check messages at home. It always stayed off in the courtroom, and sometimes I'd forget to turn in back on.

On the line was Theresa Strozier from the Fulton County Victim Witness Assistance Program, who stayed with us continually during the trial. With panic in her voice, she said, *"Jean, hurry back to the courtroom."* Apparently, they had been looking everywhere for us, even outside the building.

We had no idea what was going on, but there was no time for questions. We simply got up from our chairs and raced back there as quickly as we could. We hurried our way across the walkway, into the courthouse, and finally through security before catching an elevator up to the fifth floor, where Judge Russell's courtroom was located.

I will never forget the sight of G.G. Carawan in the hallway, running frantically toward us with a strange look on her face. As she ushered us into the courtroom, Michael Benjamin LeJeune was already on his feet, facing Judge Russell. *This was the moment we had waited nearly eight years for-and would you believe we almost missed it.*

With Bud Siemon at his side, LeJeune pled guilty to the murder of our son Ronnie Allen Davis on charges of malice murder, felony murder, aggravated assault with a deadly weapon, concealing the death of another, and possession of a firearm during the commission of a felony. Clinton Rucker stood at the podium, asking a series of questions to confirm that LeJeune was entering this plea willfully and on his own volition. LeJeune replied yes to them all.

Later on, Rucker told Brooks and me that he looked long and hard at LeJeune throughout the entire plea. There was no emotion on LeJeune's face, nor any shred of remorse. "Frankly," Rucker said to us, "that comes as no surprise."

Judge Russell then announced that she was sentencing LeJeune to life imprisonment without the possibility of parole. It was approximately 11:30 a.m. on Tuesday, November 8. Just like that, after eight long years, justice was finally served.

We were told that LeJeune's family-his father and his two sisters-played a significant role in finally persuading him to confess. LeJeune's father was scheduled to testify for the defense. Had the trial continued, he would have been put in the unenviable position of possibly lying under oath in order to protect his son. (During the first trial, Rekha Anand testified that, before she and LeJeune had rowed out to the middle of Lake Lanier to dispose of Ron's head, LeJeune had asked his father where the deepest part of the lake was. Surely, the prosecution would have brought that up during cross examination. I can't imagine Mr. LeJeune would ever want to admit that.)

I've said this before, but I feel nothing but compassion for LeJeune's family. Brooks and I have always said that we would rather be in our shoes than theirs. Yet at the same time, as much as that family continued to grieve over what LeJeune did to our son, it was also clear that they were ready for him to go to prison and move on with their lives. We were told that LeJeune had already bankrupted his father, morally as well as financially. His mother had died several years earlier of congestive heart failure. We expressed our sympathy to Mr. LeJeune and his two daughters one day at a recess. I can only imagine just how badly LeJeune had broken his poor mother's heart by the time she died.

I'll never forget the sight of LeJeune's father and sisters outside the courthouse later that day. We were speaking to reporters when I noticed the LeJeune's walking past us. They were carrying Michael's suits and shirts, along with a boat paddle from Mr. LeJeune's house that Brian Steel had planned on using when he questioned Mr. LeJeune. My heart went out to them.

When the trial ended so abruptly, we had not realized that we were also supposed to give our impact statements that day. I spoke first:

> There are no winners today in our families. We can't take our son home, and the LeJeune's can't take theirs.
>
> Ron and I were very close-a bond that grew stronger over the years. Even though he suffered with addiction at times, we had a strong relationship. Time after time, since his death, when we talked with others (here in Atlanta and at home), they would say to us, "Ronnie really loved his parents and his family."
>
> I'll never again have the opportunity to see his handsome face, listen to his sense of humor and laughter, have those long conversations together and times when he called on the phone to talk over his plans and dreams for the future-39 years old and his life brutally taken-those dreams destroyed forever. In Ron's sobriety, he was a man of strong conviction and faith and he loved to discuss a morning devotion or ask my advice on various things.

The next part of my statement was directed at Michael LeJeune.

> *YOU deprived me of even seeing my son's dead body. It was as though he disappeared._*I will never be able to get the horror out of my mind of seeing his smoldering body parts, laying near that cemetery in the snow and seeing in my mind his head being carried around in a bucket. I'll never get over the day we walked into the Forsyth County Sheriff's office and the chill that went all over me, when the first thing I

saw was a manikin dressed in clothes they had gone out and bought like what Ron was wearing-clothes that I recognized. Some nights, I can't sleep, tossing and turning with horrible visions in my mind. There is no pain like the pain of losing a child. It's like a deep hole inside and your heart is about to burst. There's a horrible wound which will always leave a huge ugly scar.

What YOU did to our son has changed our lives and our family's forever.

Then Brooks gave his statement:

Your Honor, the impact of the brutal murder of our son, being dismembered, decapitated and his body set on fire with gasoline was something so unreal and something you thought no one could ever do. It was like the terrorists hit the World Trade Center on September 11, 2001, in that no one could ever believe those unreal things could happen. All of us will never forget that people walked into airplanes with bombs and bodies were torn apart and burned. We will never forget what happened to our son on December 27 and 28, 1997. I loved my son very much. No one deserves to die this way and have such evil things done to his body.

He always said that I was his best friend, a friend he could enjoy talking with about many subjects. Also, he was a business partner in a second fabrication shop we were growing together. I will never have the opportunity to see his smiling face, his happiness of running and owning the business. Now, I have the responsibility of dealing with it in my retirement years. It's enough to lose him, but all the added stress of the past eight years has taken its toll on our bodies, emotionally as well as physically. Who knows, a trauma like this could take years away from our lives. I will never forget the opportunity to watch him enjoy working with his quarter horses.

Ron was seeking help here in Atlanta, because of a relapse. He was a dedicated Christian and knew the Bible.

He spent a lot of time helping others at the expense of leaving himself behind. I will never forget the sadness in Ron's voice as he told me it had been the worst Christmas of his entire life, because the man he was rooming with was of the Jewish faith and did not celebrate Christmas. The guy, Mike, from where he was calling did not believe in God and professed to be an atheist. His car was being kept from him and all this made a sad Christmas. It broke our hearts. We reminded him that we would be there later that day and he was to phone us as to where to meet him.

I will never be able to go to sleep at night, without thinking about his smoldering body. I will wake every morning grieving our loss. I'm angry that his head was put in a bucket and carried around as a trophy. It reminds me of how similar it was to John the Baptist, who was beheaded and his head placed on a platter. This heinous crime not only ruined our lives forever, but also hurt many other people's lives, who loved Ron.

Brooks then had a few remarks for Brian Steel. He said that no matter what Steel put us through, or said about our son, he always tried to be civil with him. (Considering how Steel always smiled and smirked like a used-car salesman whenever he spoke to us, that certainly wasn't easy.) But with the trial now over, the gloves came off. Brooks called Steel a "wannabe Johnnie Cochran," while he compared Clinton Rucker to Atticus Finch, the attorney played by Gregory Peck in the movie *To Kill a Mockingbird*.

Then it was Diane's turn. Remember, of all our family members, Diane was the only one who was able to be with us practically every day throughout our eight-year legal ordeal. She was there for all the ups and downs, and everything in between. She was also very close to Ron.

Diane was our rock, a wonderful source of strength-but with the case ending as quickly as it did, even she got overwhelmed. Though she had prepared a beautiful statement, she was so choked up with tears that she never used it. Instead, she turned to Brian Steel and said:

I have to express my disgust with you, Brian Steel-you knew he was guilty. *You did.* You *had* to know he was guilty, and yet you put this family through this for eight years... this emotional roller coaster that we've been up and down, because of this animal sitting right here!

At this point, Bud Siemon stood up and said, "Your Honor, I object. She should be talking to you."

Judge Russell sustained the objection. "Mrs. Grooms," she said to Diane, "look at me when you talk." But by this point, Diane was sobbing so uncontrollably, she was no longer able to continue.

Diane may have lost her composure, but she became our hero. The words she levied against Brian Steel left an imprint throughout the courtroom. As soon as court adjourned, the court reporter immediately walked up and gave Diane a warm embrace. Soon others came up to congratulate her, saying things like "You said what some of us could not say." Even D.A. Paul Howard gave Diane a great big hug. He began to refer to her as "the famous Diane Grooms," and at another time, "the infamous Diane Grooms"-though I like to think Mr. Howard meant to say that Steel was "infamous" and that my sister was merely "famous." Be that as it may, their feelings for each other were mutual.

We were then asked to give comments to the media. As the cameras and recorders were being readied, Brooks asked if he could say a few words to Judge Russell. We were escorted back to her conference room, while she gave final instructions to the jury before officially dismissing them from the case.

When she was finished with the jury, Judge Russell entered the conference room. Diane was near the door. Russell walked promptly to her and also gave her a big bear hug.

Diane was taken aback. "Judge Russell," she said, "I was afraid you might put me in jail!"

Judge Russell smiled and said, "Mrs. Grooms, you said what you needed to say." At that point, we all laughed. Then she turned to Brooks and me and gave us each a hug.

Then Brooks had a chance to say his piece. "Judge Russell, I just want to say-and I mean this as a compliment-that I have seen a lot of maturity in you over these past eight years."

Brooks needn't have worried. Russell understood exactly what he meant. As I mentioned before, she had only been a judge for about a year when she was assigned our case in 1998. It was her first death penalty trial, and she really did grow in the job. She was very cordial to the both of us and had big tears running down her cheeks. What a change from the early phase of the case. Later on, when we told the prosecutors, they could not believe she was shedding tears. "Wow," they said. "That is a first for Judge Russell."

I remember one day Judge Russell called a break, and I was the first one to come back into the courtroom. As she emerged from her chambers, looked at me, and mouthed "Hello." I really appreciated that.

Brian Steel had controlled the courtroom all those years, but apparently he went too far. He really made Russell look bad in March 2004, when the Georgia Supreme Court unanimously overturned her August 2003 ruling that threw out the physical evidence obtained in February 2003 because the search warrants were invalid-a ruling she had made on the basis of yet another technicality raised by Steel. (We have been told that she has a friend that is a Supreme Court Justice.) From the judge's chambers, Brooks and I were whisked outside for a news conference. As I mentioned before, the Atlanta press corps has always treated us with kindness and respect. One of them asked a question about closure. I'll never forget Brooks' response. "We will never have closure," he said. "I don't like the word closure, because we will think of Ron every day. Let's just say that we will start a new chapter in our lives."

Then we headed off to a nearby steakhouse for a celebration luncheon. (Brooks had promised G.G. Carawan, a senior investigator with the D.A.'s office, that he would buy her a steak when this was all over.) There were about nine of us all together, including Diane, Clinton Rucker, Brett Pinion, G.G. Carawan, investigator Fred Hall, Theresa Strozier, and Niki Burger, director of the Fulton County Victim Witness Assistance Program. It was a nice opportunity for all of us to talk, vent, laugh, and finally unwind after a long, stressful journey.

The last we saw of Brian Steel, he was standing outside the

courthouse, on the corner below where our news conference was held, loading large garbage cans that he was going to use in court to prove that Ron's body could not possibly fit inside them. (Like I said, he saw himself as the second coming of Johnnie Cochran.) We understand that for the longest time, Steel was none too popular around the Fulton County Courthouse, after the trial. They say the uproar he caused took quite a while to die down.

I always said I would write him a letter when this was all over. About a month later, I did just that. It was not at all a slanderous letter; just one that I hoped might offer some food for thought. And who knows...perhaps something in that letter might cause him to think twice about putting another family through the pain that he put us through.

Several weeks later it was returned to me marked, "Undeliverable." At that point, I just tossed it aside. At the very least, I got a few things off my chest.

Watching Steel in the courtroom could be infuriating, but Brooks and I have never been bitter towards him. Again, it was God's strength and our faith in God that carried us. Through it all, we were always reminded that "He never puts more on us than we can bear," and that "He will never leave us or forsake us."

* * *

The morning after the trial ended, Paul Howard invited us over as guests to his staff meeting. This was a meeting to hear follow-ups on cases his staff were handling. It was a large conference room, and there must have been about 75-100 people there. He had us seated facing the group, along with the prosecution team. Mr. Howard gave Clinton Rucker a copy of *To Kill a Mockingbird* by Harper Lee, which all of us gladly signed. (Mr. Howard, as I mentioned, was in the courtroom when Brooks compared Rucker to Atticus Finch in *To Kill a Mockingbird* during our Impact Statements. There were also clips of the movie playing on the screen up front.) Mr. Howard then congratulated his team of prosecutors, investigators, and Agent Jeff Branyon from the Georgia Bureau of Investigation, and gave them all an opportunity to speak. Then he turned to Brooks and me and asked if we could make some comments.

Brooks told a story about how he'd always wanted Ron to go dove hunting with him, but Ron never wanted to go. One day, Brooks asked him why.

"Dad," said Ron, "who would want to kill a little bird?"

Remember, Brian Steel once made a motion (which Judge Russell promptly overruled) to have Ron declared a violent person. Now you tell me, is that the kind of thing you'd expect to hear from a so-called violent person?

Mr. Howard then presented everyone on the team with a small trophy: a small clear box, with a number 8 billiard ball inside. He had one for Brooks and me, too. The inscription on the trophy read:

"Justice will wait, even if it takes eight."
State of Ga. vs. Michael LeJeune, 1997-2005.

When it came time for me to speak, after I had seen the trophy, I just had to share the list of "8s" I'd kept that chronicled dates in Ron's life that were turning points. How shocking it was, I said, for the trial to end on *November 8* after *eight* years of litigation.

I looked at everyone in the room. They were all truly amazed.

CHAPTER THIRTY-TWO

The Legacy of Ronnie Davis

O n a Saturday morning in June 1997, during a weekend visit home to help celebrate his Dad's 65th birthday, Ron was quietly sitting on our patio when he asked me to join him for his morning devotional. When we finished praying, he looked up to me and said, "Mom, what I'm about to say to you, I've only shared with one other person. But I truly feel in my spirit that someday God is going to give me a word for my home church, Mount Harmony, and this community where I grew up. It won't be from Ron, but from God. For now, I'll just walk the walk."

Little did we know that six months later Ron would be dead, and that the word from God that he felt in his spirit that day would be the many ways in which God has used Ron's life and brutal death to help the lives of others.

God doesn't tell us "some things work for good," but rather that "all things work together for good to those who love Him." When something devastating happens in our lives, it's difficult to realize how God is going to use it for good.

Brooks and I walked many miles with Ron along his journey through addiction. Sure, there were disappointments along the way. But there were also a lot of triumphs-both for Ron, as well as for the two of us. With each triumph, our trust in God continued to grow.

As hard as these past eight years have been, Brooks and I continue to take comfort in the good God has brought forth from the seeds that Ron once sowed. For that reason, we can never be defeated.

I've mentioned before how each time Ron recovered from a relapse, we would grow closer to each other than we'd ever been before. He would hug us and tell us how grateful he was for never giving up on him. He'd talk about the many people he knew in recovery houses who had no one to turn to, or care about them, or encourage them not to lose hope.

Ron stumbled many times as he walked this earth. But when he was sober he often went the extra mile to help those in need, even at the expense of his own recovery. "Whatsoever a man sows, that he shall also reap." *Galatians 6:7. (KJ)*

Ron understood that as well as anyone. Even the smallest kindness can yield a hundredfold, especially when we least expect it.

Remember Linda, the nurse Ron befriended after completing his rehabilitation at Caring Services over in High Point, North Carolina? She was a recovering alcoholic who was trying desperately to pick up the pieces of her life. Her parents had custody of her children until she could prove she had turned her life around.

At the time neither Ron nor Linda was strong enough for a serious relationship, but they liked each other's company. They'd read together at the library, see a movie, grab a cup of coffee, or just hang out together in the way that friends do. He had a car and she didn't, so he drove her to work every day. She had her own apartment but could not afford to furnish it, so he gave her some of the furniture that was locked away in storage from the Christian Unity Men's Home: a sofa, some kitchenware, a bed and other essentials which he divided from his own apartment. Ron always encouraged Linda while she was putting her life back together, missing her children and working to reinstate her nursing license.

Linda has kept in touch with me in the years since Ron's death, and has especially asked that we keep her updated on the trial. In a recent note, she spoke of how often she thinks "of Ron's goodness and how he touched my heart." She also said that she recently accepted the role of Clinical Facilitator in the Emergency Department at the hospital where she works. In addition, she remarked that she still has the book that I once gave her by acclaimed Christian writer Max Lacado. She said, "I will never forget your kindness that you showed me." (There were so many people that Brooks and I had the opportunity to minister to wherever Ron was rehabbing or living at the time.)

Nine years later, Linda remains sober and continues to lead a productive life and successful career. She not only won back custody of her children, I'm happy to report that she has since bought a house and that one of her daughters recently had a child of her own. Besides her job, she went to back to school and is currently working on her master's degree.

* * *

Occasionally someone will ask us whether Ron was aware of the impact he had on other people. While that is not an easy question to answer, I believe he was to some degree. When he was a boy, he wanted so badly to be like his grandfather Barney: the kind of man that people naturally gravitate toward, in other words, a leader.

In his own way, that's exactly what he became. Ron may have been denied the victory that comes with lasting sobriety, but he never stopped trying to attain it. Nor did he ever stop encouraging other addicts to try to attain it. He knew that victory was possible because he had tasted it before.

That's why I know he'd be proud of the work that continues to be done through the relapse prevention program established in his name by Becky Yates, the executive director of Caring Services. A strong leader and administrator, Becky is also one of the most selfless persons I have ever met and continues to do remarkable work in the field of addiction. After originally starting off with one halfway house, she now has six facilities throughout High Point, North Carolina.

Several years ago, Becky had a dream of converting an old funeral home into a facility for veterans. Bureaucracy and red tape being what they are, the odds of this seemed long at first. But Becky can be a very persuasive person, and she was determined to make this happen. With the help of a government grant and the generous donations of private individuals, she was able to secure the finances needed to fund the project. With the help of her family and friends, she put in many long hours restoring the home, overcoming each obstacle with optimism.

I am happy to say this new veteran's facility was completed over three years ago. This building also provides a nice meeting room for the weekly Relapse Prevention Group that began as a result of the Ronnie A. Davis Memorial Scholarship-the fruits of yet another seed Ron had once sown that would yield an abundance of good.

Founded in 1998, the Ronnie A. Davis Memorial Scholarship for chronic relapsers of chemical addictions continues to be a great success. The counselors, Gordon and Jo Rayle, have been with the program from the beginning and the reports that come in on each individual who participates in it is a reflection of Gordon and Jo's good work, as well as the sincerity of each client about their sobriety. It is truly a blessing to hear the success stories about those who have had their lives restored because of the help they received through this program.

The scholarship is funded entirely by individual donations and regular fund raisers. Here's what Becky Yates has to say about why a program such as this is so vital:

> During the time that Ron was with Caring Services in 1996, he donated items and furnishings from the Christian Unity Men's Home in Lenoir, which he had established, did volunteer work in our offices, and reached out to anyone in need. Unfortunately, Ron's post-acute withdrawal syndrome lured him back into the dark and destructive world of substance abuse.
>
> Ron was not alone in his struggle. The recidivism (relapse) rate for substance abusers is 75-90%. It is often difficult for lay people to understand that sobriety-based symptoms, especially post acute withdrawal, make sobriety so difficult. The presence of brain dysfunction has been documented in 75-95% of recovering alcoholics studied. Post acute withdrawal is a bio-psycho-social syndrome which results from the combination of damage to the nervous system caused by alcohol and drugs and the psycho-social stress of coping with life without drugs and alcohol. Recovery from the nervous

system damage usually requires six to twenty-four months with the assistance of a healthy recovery system.

Last year at Caring Services, our recidivism rate was 45%. 106 of the 195 clients we served last year are still clean and sober today. While we are exceedingly grateful for the success of our program, we will not be satisfied until we are 100% successful, until young men and women stop dying at the hands of the greedy and evil.

I mentioned earlier that Ron was the first client at Caring Services to lose his life. Each April, Brooks and I attend a ceremony in which a tree is planted to mark the lives of those who have died as a result of their addiction. Sad to say, that number has increased by a staggering rate over the past ten years.

Becky Yates is an extraordinary person who continues to do tremendous work in the field of addiction. She and her husband Jim has been another steady encourager to us over the years. Brooks and I are fortunate to count them among our special friends.

CHAPTER THIRTY-THREE

Keep On Keeping On

Any parent who knows the pain of burying a son or daughter also knows that life can never be the same. There will always be that void in your heart that will never quite be filled. There are times when you feel so despondent, you'd just as soon give up and make no effort to go on living.

And yet life does go on. Our faith reminds us that this earth is just a stepping stone for the day when God reunites us with our friends and loved ones in Heaven. Despite our grief we must keep on living, for it is our faith that gives us hope.

I'll admit, there were times over those eight years when it wasn't easy to do that. You sit helplessly in the courtroom, enduring all the delays while the case against the man who murdered your son crumbles before your eyes, and you can't help but wonder, "How much longer will this be? How much more do we have to take?" You desperately want some sort of closure, some way to complete the natural grieving process that everyone needs to go through. And yet with each trip to Atlanta, and each delay in the judicial process, you have to relive the horror of what happened to your son again and again. Sometimes it just seemed so unfair.

One thing that has always helped us cope has been the words of the famous Serenity Prayer:

God, grant me the Serenity
to accept the things I cannot change,
the Courage to change the things I can,
and the Wisdom to know the difference

So much in this life is out of our control. It's easy for us to become bitter and angry when things don't go our way.

We have tried not to do that. Instead, Brooks and I have tried to focus on the many things that we are grateful for and the ways that God has blessed us.

One thing for which we're grateful is the ability to travel periodically. Over the past ten years Brooks and I have gone on cruises to places such as Alaska, Caribbean, New England and Canada, plus two trips to Europe and one to the Holy Land. In the past four years, we have also purchased a motor home, which enables us to travel leisurely, rather than to fly. Last year, we made a nine week trip out west. We feel very fortunate to have the finances to do this, as well as our health holding up to travel.

We've talked before about the stress of a legal trial and what it can do to your mental well being. Getting away from our everyday routine and experiencing a new environment has been a simple yet effective way of dealing with the ups and downs of this emotional roller coaster. It doesn't make your troubles go away ... but it does "distance" you from them, so to speak, at least for a while.

Getting away on occasion has certainly helped strengthen our emotions. By the time we come home, we feel rested, healed and ready to tackle the roller coaster once again.

Of course, you don't have to pack a suitcase or buy an airline ticket in order to take yourself away. Even hopping in the car and going on a long drive can do the trick. There are many places close to us where we can recharge our mental batteries. The ocean, or the mountains, or even a local park are all tranquil places where we can go and feel the presence of God. The grass, or the trees, or the sight of a young child playing all remind us of God's power and creation.

* * *

All of us both bounce back and forth with our emotions. Sometimes a little quality time with our spouse, friends or loved ones is what we need to get us right.

In February 2001, more than three years after Ron's death, Brooks and I celebrated a very special occasion: our 50th wedding anniversary. About a year before this, it occurred to me how wonderful it would be to do something special for the many family members, friends and loved ones whose love, prayers and encouragement have kept us going, especially in the years since the tragedy. Rather than celebrate our life together, I asked Brooks what he thought about using the occasion to celebrate the many people who helped shape our lives over the past 50 years.

Brooks totally agreed. I would spend the next several months finding the right venue for it, planning the guest list, sending out invitations, meeting with the caterers, going over the menu, and all the other various preparations that come with arranging a special occasion.

Next to writing this book, planning that event was the best therapy I've ever had. Besides the sheer satisfaction that comes with doing something special for your friends, it provided another kind of outlet that would help me "get away" from the strain of the legal case. Sometimes it just helps to have a project that you can lose yourself in.

One part of the evening that was unplanned was when Diane, Carolyn and Rick each went up to the dais to share a few memories. I can't tell you how special that was. Sometimes, whenever I've had a particularly bad day with depression and stress, I'll go back and play the video that was made from that evening. That always picks up my spirits.

That video, by the way, contains another surprise for which Diane was also the catalyst. Unbeknownst to me, in the months leading up to the event Diane would sneak into our home while Brooks and I were away and "borrow" snapshots from all our photo albums. She then scanned them onto her computer and put them all together into a wonderful, heartwarming video montage of our entire married life, from raising the boys when they were babies to the many fun times with friends and family. All of this was accompanied by very special music, which Diane spent much time selecting.

Brooks and I have not only been husband and wife for over 57 years, we're also each other's best friend. At the time we were married on Friday, February 16, 1951, we could not afford a fancy wedding with all the accoutrements-we had a simple ceremony in the church parsonage with just two guests other than family: Forrest and Shirley Putnam, my longtime friends from the fifth grade. (Shirley has been a constant encourager who has never failed to pray for us.)

Not only that, because Brooks had to be at work first thing Monday morning, our honeymoon was just a short weekend trip into the mountains of North Carolina. So in a way, this big party was like the wedding celebration we had always wanted, but could not have.

Our memories of this special evening will never fade. Nor will we ever forget the many special people who helped shape our lives with their love and support.

* * *

I mentioned before how God blessed me with new friends in the years since Ron's death. But He also put me back in touch with some people from Ron's past.

I had not seen Ron's ex-wife Melissa but twice over the past ten years: once at his funeral, followed by a brief visit from her on the first Mother's Day after his death. But one day, as I was writing this book, she called me out of the blue, and I cannot tell you how good it was to hear from her. This was just after Brooks and I returned from Atlanta after hearing the oral arguments before the Georgia Supreme Court in January 2004. With so much riding on how the Court decides, you can imagine how worn out and emotionally spent we both were. So to come home to that phone call was a real shot in the arm. I suppose you might even call it yet another nugget of gold.

That day, Melissa told me how much our relationship meant to her. She talked about the ways I helped her change her life, and that the memories of that time still guide her today.

Once again, God's timing is always perfect.

During the conversation, I told Melissa I was writing a book about Ron, and that I hoped our story might offer hope to other families who were hurting and struggling with addiction. She was not only excited to hear this; she wrote me a beautiful letter a few weeks later. I was so touched by her letter that I asked her if I could share it in the book. Happily, she said yes.

Dear Jean,

I just wanted to write you a note to tell you what an impact you and Brooks have had in my life. This has been something I feel has been laid on my heart by God to help you both in the incredible journey that you have traveled over the past years.

I have often thought of both you and Brooks since our separation. As I reminisce back over time of all the ladies in my life who have had an impact on and in my life, I would have to say that you are the one who stands out most in my mind and heart.

Even today as I rummaged through some of the gift cards that I have cherished over the years, I ran across one that you had given me on Mother's Day. The card read, "Bless you for being all a daughter could be … for the friendship, help and support," and you went on to write that even though I physically was not a mother that God had given me a special quality to share with others.

You are the one who has those special qualities I feel that God would have you share with others. Oh how your card even now has touched my life again even though we are apart. I also remember back to the time we first met, I saw something in you that I had not seen in any other lady before at that time and at that time I didn't know what it was. I just knew I wanted whatever you had.

Over the next four years, you did just that, not only in telling me that Jesus loved me but also showing me by your walk that he is an awesome God and that you are an awesome lady for submitting unto him and allowing him to work through you to be a great witness to me and to others as well. Even today ten years later you continue to be a witness that you could have never known through one little powerful book that you gave me called Streams in the Desert. Jean, just know that every day God has ministered to me through your giving me that devotional.

Our time together was just way too short. It is difficult even now to find a Godly woman, the "Titus woman," who is willing to mentor to those who are to follow behind her. You are a rare and precious gem to me even today as I think back on all the wonderful times we had together.

Thank you for being there, for keeping focused on him, for the light that you shine to be seen among all women and men. What a great and positive influence you have been in my life. Oh, how at times I wish to travel back just so I would be able to treasure and savor the short moments we shared together.

Jean, you know it is difficult to really put into words all that you have meant to me. These words that I have written have just flowed straight from my heart just to tell you how much you have meant. I do hope that God will continue to bless both of you in a mighty way, that he gives you comfort and guidance to press onward toward the mark that has been set before you.

With all my love,
Melissa

I can't express how humbled and touched I was when I read that letter. Even when things don't exactly turn out the way we'd like them to, life moves on ... and as it does, God continues to shed His light upon us.

Brooks and I have walked through some wonderful times in our journey together, as well as some exceptionally rough ones. Through it all, God has shown us that even in the bad times, he continues to watch over us and help us grow, teaching us lessons about life and strengthening us for whatever the future may bring.

Sure, life would be much easier if it were all mountain top experiences. But it's through the valleys that we grow stronger and really learn to put our trust in God.

> *Those who hope in the Lord will renew their strength.*
> *They will soar on wings like eagles;*
> *They will run and not grow weary,*
> *They will walk, and not be faint.*
>
> *Isaiah 40:31 (NIV)*

* * *

As horrible and as inexplicable as it was, Ron's death brought forth a torrent of goodness that continues to fortify us.

Ron's life may have ended in tragedy, but his legacy is filled with hope. No matter how despondent he became in his struggle to overcome his addiction, he never once gave up the fight. To anyone who reads his story, he'd be the first to say *"Keep on keeping on."* Focus on the strength that God has given you, the strength that enables us to rise above the circumstances if we are willing to let go and to trust in Him.

That's what kept Ron going.

That's what keeps us going.

Printed in the United States
119112LV00002B/400-447/P